G000109959

MODELS OF THE UK ECONOMY

Models of the UK Economy

A Third Review by the ESRC Macroeconomic
Modelling Bureau

K. F. WALLIS (editor), M. J. ANDREWS, P. G. FISHER,
J. A. LONGBOTTOM and J. D. WHITLEY

OXFORD UNIVERSITY PRESS
1986

Oxford University Press, Walton Street, Oxford OX2 6DP
Oxford New York Toronto
Delhi Bombay Calcutta Madras Karachi
Petaling Jaya Singapore Hong Kong Tokyo
Nairobi Dar es Salaam Cape Town Melbourne Auckland
and associated companies in
Beirut Berlin Ibadan Nicosia

Oxford is a trade mark of Oxford University Press

Published in the United States
by Oxford University Press, New York

British Library Cataloguing in Publication Data
Models of the UK economy: a third review
by the ESRC macroeconomic modelling bureau.
I. Great Britain—Economic conditions—
1945- —Econometric models
I. Wallis, Kenneth F.
330.941'0858'0724   HC256.6
ISBN 0-19-828585-X
ISBN 0-19-828584-1 Pbk

Library of Congress Cataloging in Publication Data
Data available

Set by Katerprint Typesetting Services, Oxford

Printed and bound in
Great Britain by Biddles Ltd,
Guildford and Kings Lynn

Preface

The Macroeconomic Modelling Bureau was established at the University of Warwick by the Economic and Social Research Council in September 1983. The main purpose of the Bureau is to improve the accessibility of macroeconomic models, to promote general understanding of the properties of models of the UK economy, and to allow comparison between models to be made more easily. The Bureau's comparative research programme comprises continuing analysis of overall model properties and forecast performance, and a sequence of studies of specific economic and statistical features. The main output of this programme is an annual series of review volumes, of which this book is the third. Although reference is made from time to time to our previous reviews (Wallis *et al.*, 1984, 1985), this book is self-contained.

Seven current models of the UK economy are appraised in this book. Five of these receive support from the ESRC, namely, the models of the Cambridge Growth Project (CGP), the City University Business School (CUBS), Liverpool University (LPL), the London Business School (LBS), and the National Institute of Economic and Social Research (NIESR). Added to these are the models of Her Majesty's Treasury (HMT) and the Bank of England (BE), the latter making its first appearance in these studies. All the models are installed at the University of Warwick Computer Unit, and are thence available to other academic researchers via the Joint Academic Network (JANET) and a specially written interface program. This system also underpins the analysis in this book, which is based on the results of computer exercises designed and executed by the authors. Such exercises produce a large volume of material, of which that selected for presentation and discussion represents only a small part. Full results of any exercise reported in the book are available to readers on request.

Responsibility for the content, opinions, and conclusions of the book rests with the authors, and not with the Economic and Social Research Council. The authors gratefully acknowledge the continuing assistance of the modelling teams, the help and advice of the staff of the University of Warwick Computer Unit, and the secretarial services and research support of Kerrie Beale and Frances Barnes. Thanks also to our former colleague, David Bell, for continued assistance in computing matters, to Ron Smith (Birkbeck College) and Grayham Mizon (University of Southampton) for comments and suggestions on Chapters 4 and 5 respectively, and to Rob Marshall of Scicon Ltd.

Contents

List of Tables

List of Figures

Chapter 1

Introduction

1.1 Overview

Macroeconometric models of the UK economy continue to develop and continue to support both professional research and public discussion of economic policy analysis and forecasts. They are constructed for many purposes, and the nature of economics as a discipline and the nature of the statistical evidence are such that a number of different models may legitimately coexist. Often the reasons for these differences, and their relative importance for the conclusions drawn from the models, are not well understood. To remedy this deficiency is the objective of our research programme, and this book represents the third instalment. Through systematic analysis of models and forecasts, and detailed scrutiny of their economic and statistical foundations, we hope to contribute to improved understanding of the UK economy and the models thereof, and to improved modelling procedures.

A macroeconometric model is a mathematical representation of the quantitative relationships among macroeconomic variables. Its equations comprise technical relations and accounting identities that reflect the national income accounting framework, and behavioural equations that describe the aggregate actions of consumers, producers, investors, financial institutions, and so forth. Its specification rests on both economic theory and the analysis of historical data, and different modellers place different weights on these two contributions. In the present volume we continue appraisals of the models as a whole and their policy prescriptions, while placing greater emphasis than hitherto on statistical and econometric questions. Models are constructed piece-by-piece and their overall properties are apparent only when the construction is complete. The two statistical studies included in this book reflect a distinction between complete-model and component analyses. The statistical performance of the model as a forecasting system is studied by comparing a previous set of forecasts with the actual outcomes, after the fact. A part of the models, and of the economy, of especial interest — namely, the labour market — is studied through an econometric evaluation of the different models' descriptions of labour market behaviour.

The seven models analysed are those of the London Business School (LBS), the National Institute of Economic and Social Research (NIESR), Her Majesty's Treasury (HMT), the Bank of England (BE), the Cambridge Growth Project (CGP), the City University Business School

(CUBS), and the Liverpool University Research Group in Macro-economics (LPL). The first four are quarterly models, the last three annual. The basic frame of reference for our work is as follows. Each year, usually in the autumn, the modelling teams deposit the current version of their models together with associated software and databases at the Macro-economic Modelling Bureau. In the case of the ESRC-supported groups, the deposit coincides with the publication of a forecast or projection, and the information supplied enables us to replicate the published material, as a first check on our implementation of the model. The corresponding publications by the model proprietors and the respective forecast horizons are as follows:

LBS   *Economic Outlook*, vol. 10, no. 1 October 1985   1990(4)
NIESR *National Institute Economic Review*, no. 114,
         November 1985   1991(1)
CUBS *Economic Review*, vol. 3, no. 2, Autumn 1985   2000
LPL   *Quarterly Economic Bulletin*, vol. 6, no. 3, September
         1985   1998

Forecasts with the CGP model are prepared privately by Cambridge Econometrics (1985) Ltd, and the forecast made in September 1985 for the period 1985–90 has been supplied to the Bureau. The Treasury model is in the public domain by virtue of the Bray amendment to the 1975 Industry Act, and new versions are released each January. The assumptions on which Treasury forecasts are based are not published. The model is used for forecasting by the Independent Treasury Economic Modelling (ITEM) Club, however, who have been kind enough to make available to the Bureau a forecast database for the January 1986 public release. The ITEM Club consists of economists from UK industry and finance who utilize the Treasury model; the model is maintained and operated, under licence, by Scicon Ltd, who also administer the Club. Finally, the Bank of England model (summer 1985 version), appearing in our collection for the first time, is run over a constructed database supplied by the Bank. This comprises smooth trajectories for the future values of exogenous variables, and does not correspond to any Bank forecast. These versions of the seven models are the ones used in our subsequent analysis.

After this introductory chapter, the following two chapters update and extend our systematic analysis of overall model properties and the published forecasts. In Chapter 2 we study the properties of the models as revealed by dynamic multiplier analysis for a set of six simulations. Five of these assess the responses of the models to changes in various domestic economic policy variables, and the sixth assesses the models' responses to a change in the international economic environment. For changes in fiscal policy, attention is given to the treatment of the public sector budget constraint and the framework of monetary policy into which the change is

introduced, in particular to ensure that the results are genuinely comparable across models. Moving away from the emphasis on broad macroeconomic responses, we also consider in this chapter the information provided
by the models at a more disaggregate level. After a description of the extent
of disaggregation of output and employment and a survey of the methodology used in disaggregation, we analyse the responses of output and
employment in the manufacturing and non-manufacturing sectors to the
same shocks used to illustrate the macro properties of the models. The
relevance of these results to the de-industrialization debate is also covered.

Three of the models (LBS, NIESR, and LPL) make use of the rational
expectations hypothesis. Expectations of future values of endogenous
variables, such as expected inflation or expected exchange rates, often
appear among the explanatory variables in the behavioural equations of a
model. Sometimes the unobserved expectations are assumed to be functions of the current and lagged values of a few observed variables, and so
are substituted out. If, instead, the expectations are assumed to be rational, in the sense of being the conditional expectations of the variables
based on the model itself, and on information up to the current period,
then a number of complications arise, as discussed by Minford and Peel
(1983) and Holden *et al.* (1985), for example. First, it is necessary to solve
the model over a forecast period in an internally consistent manner, so that
the future expectations variables appearing in the model coincide with the
model's forecasts. At the last point in the solution an expectation of a value
outside the solution period is required, and in order for a unique solution
to exist, this value must be determined in some manner. This usually
requires the imposition of terminal conditions which specify that the
expectations of these variables at the end of the forecast horizon must be
consistent with the likely stable solution. In this chapter we examine the
sensitivity of both the base solution and the simulation responses to the
terminal conditions actually employed. This analysis shows that both the
LPL and LBS models appear to achieve stable solutions, but that the
NIESR model, by design, does not have a unique stable solution for the
real exchange rate. We find little sensitivity to the terminal date in the LPL
model, but find some sensitivity in the two quarterly models due to
seasonality. Second, in conducting economic policy analysis with models
containing forward–consistent expectations, it is necessary to specify
whether the policy intervention is temporary or permanent, and whether it
is anticipated or unanticipated. In each case the response of forward-
looking firms or households may differ. We analyse the sensitivity of the
macro responses of these models to these different types of shock. Usually
this consists of altering the dates at which shocks are entered or removed.
In general, we find that experiments comparing temporary and permanent
shocks or anticipated and unanticipated shocks change the dynamic
response path, rather than altering the long-run solution. In one of the

models (LPL) there are also alternative ways of simulating temporary and anticipated shocks, and this has more marked effects than merely altering the dates of the shock.

In Chapter 3 we analyse the model-based forecasts published in late 1985, addressing the question of whether forecasts differ and, if so, how and why. By recomputing the forecasts under different assumptions about the future course of events, the impact of a particular team's assumptions can be assessed. Likewise, by recomputing the forecast, having removed all residual adjustments, the impact of the forecaster's judgement, as reflected in these adjustments, can be assessed. Such 'mechanical' or 'hands-off' forecasts show considerable divergence, and the residual adjustments are seen to bring the forecasts closer to a consensus, although not to complete unanimity. There are some indications that the NIESR forecast is more judgementally based than the other forecasts. In particular, the treatment of the exchange rate in the NIESR model means that it is, in effect, exogenous, and the inflation forecast relies heavily on the value attached to the exchange rate. In the case of the LBS forecast, it is the calibration of the financial sector that is critical to the inflation forecast.

In the remaining two chapters we consider two distinct aspects of the general question of the statistical performance of the models. First, in Chapter 4 we study the statistical performance of the system as a whole by analysing the errors made in the first forecast deposited with the Bureau in autumn 1983. Comparisons of those forecasts with the actual outcomes in 1984 and 1985 are presented, and the forecast errors are then examined, analysing the contribution of the exogenous variables and the residual adjustments using a similar framework to that adopted in Chapter 3. In most cases it is found that using the actual values of the exogenous variables does not reduce forecast error very much, and that the use of residual adjustments has improved the accuracy of the forecasts, thus suggesting some value-added by the forecaster. The model-based forecasts are compared with mechanical forecasts generated by a vector autoregressive model, which are seen to perform less well. We also assess the effect of data revisions on forecast error. Finally, we consider how far it is possible to combine the forecast errors on the main macroeconomic variables for each of the models in order to provide an overall measure of forecast performance. In this example, we conclude that the LBS forecast performed better than that of LPL, which in turn performed better than that of CUBS. In general, the VAR forecasts are inferior to model-based forecasts, whether these include residual adjustments or not.

In Chapter 5 we present an econometric evaluation of the labour market sector of each of the models. The first step is to recompute the individual econometric equations. These correspond to the equations in the models where these have been freely estimated. Each is then subjected to a comprehensive battery of diagnostic tests which reveals a variety of inadequacies in the specifications: these relate to parameter instability and predictive failure, simultaneous equation bias, instrument validity, covariance information, residual autocorrelation, incorrect functional form, heteroscedasticity and non-normality of residuals. The frequency with which each model is rejected on these tests suggests a degree of misspecification in all the models. Although the various diagnostic tests may not be independent, the models are most frequently rejected by the tests of parameter stability and predictive failure and the RESET test for misspecification of the functional forms. However, rejection on the basis of one or more of these tests does not necessarily indicate the direction in which respecification might proceed.

Since the econometric structures are quite different, in terms of lag length, functional form, and choice of regressors, it is natural to regard these specifications as competing models, and to apply non-nested testing procedures. These address the question of whether a given model accounts for all the information contained in an alternative explanation of the same phenomena. Such a model is said to encompass its rivals. We present a variety of non-nested tests between the various wage equations and manufacturing employment equations. The results suggest that in both cases no single equation is dominant.

In the remainder of this Introduction we provide some background material on the models. First, an outline description is given of each model. Then we present some comparative notes, in which similarities and differences of the models are briefly highlighted.

1.2 The UK models in outline

This section gives a brief summary of the structure of the models. The emphasis is on the relations among economic variables represented by the structural form, and no attention is paid at this point to dynamic aspects of those relations. We discuss first the four quarterly models, then the three annual models.

London Business School (LBS)

The LBS model is an aggregate quarterly model covering 770 variables (of which 70 are exogenous), with a little over 100 behavioural equations: the model has a separate financial sector containing one-third of the total number of variables in the model. It is based around the income–expenditure framework but is often referred to as an 'international monetarist' model.

The determination of expenditures is based on the GDP accounting framework, as in the other quarterly models. Consumer demand, fixed investment, stockbuilding, exports, and imports are determined endogenously, with government current expenditure predicted by a set of forecasting rules. Inflation is generated via the interaction of wages, prices, and the exchange rate.

Total consumer spending is explained by real incomes, the rate of inflation, and real financial wealth, plus the real value of the housing stock and nominal interest rates. The latter captures the substitution effect between current and future consumption, and the income effect of changing interest rates is included in real disposable income. The long-run marginal propensity to consume is unity, the long-run elasticity of consumption is −0.1 with respect to interest rates and 0.1 with respect to wealth. There is a separate relationship for durables expenditure. Private non-oil fixed investment is determined endogenously and is split into two sectors: housing and non-housing. Housing investment is derived from housing starts, which are explained by real incomes, relative housing prices, and nominal interest rates, whereas output and the share of non-oil profits in GDP determine non-housing investment.

Stockbuilding is separated into manufacturing and distribution, with demand and nominal interest rates the explanatory variables. Imports and exports are disaggregated, with the key difference that total exports are derived from the sum of the disaggregated components, whereas disaggregation is from the top down for imports. The main determinants are world demand for exports and domestic demand for imports, with relative cost competitiveness terms appearing in both cases. World trade affects exports of manufactures with a long-run elasticity of 0.6, and the competitiveness elasticity is −0.35. The comparable elasticity of total imports with respect to domestic demand is 1.8, with a competitiveness elasticity of −0.18.

The labour market consists of a set of equations determining employment, the size of the working population, and wages. Employment is split between manufacturing and non-manufacturing and the principal determinants are the level of output and real wages. The real price of raw materials and fuel appears additionally in the manufacturing equation, where long-run increasing returns to scale are present, and where the long-run real-wage elasticity is −0.7. In the case of non-manufacturing there are constant returns to scale and a larger long-run real-wage elasticity of −1.1. The model distinguishes between male and female labour force participation with the latter depending on relative earnings, unemployment, aggregate real wages, and the female population of working age. There are three wage equations: manufacturing, non-manufacturing, and public administration. In the first of these wages are determined by expected prices, indirect taxes, real unemployment benefits, and the level of unemployment. Earnings in manufacturing enter the non-manufacturing equation and wholly determine earnings in public administration.

The LBS model derives indices of producer output and input prices in the manufacturing sector, in addition to the customary final expenditure deflators, which are necessary to produce current price estimates of final expenditure items. The producer output index is explained by a cost mark-up equation, and producer prices then enter into the consumer price equation along with unit labour costs and indirect taxes.

The model contains a full financial sector. This determines asset demands by a general portfolio approach, in which each sector's asset demand is a function of the own return, the return on other assets, and the sector budget constraint. Given asset supplies, market-clearing prices for government gilt-edged stock, equities, and foreign currency are derived, and thus the exchange rate is determined within this system in a way that makes it dependent on the supplies of assets in both domestic and foreign markets rather than merely on money. The stock of money is also determined by this portfolio approach. If the monetary authorities pursue an interest rate target, then it is assumed that they are residual suppliers of commercial and Treasury bills. If there is a monetary target, this is achieved by funding of public sector debt and by movements in short-term interest rates. Forward consistent expectations are assumed in financial markets, and the operation of the financial sector implies that there are no single relationships which can be referred to as either the exchange rate or the money demand/supply equation.

There is a small model of the world economy in the LBS model. However, this is essentially recursive and is causally prior to the domestic economy. North Sea oil expenditures and incomes are distinguished, with the main effect of these variables on the remainder of the model being through the determination of government tax revenues.

The major difference from the previous version of the LBS model is the inclusion of rational expectations in the financial sector. Most of the equations have been re-estimated since the previous version so that there are numerous minor changes. There are now disaggregated equations for labour force participation; the earnings equations now include unemployment benefits; and company sector interest, dividend, and rent flows are now derived from the financial sector.

National Institute of Economic and Social Research (NIESR)

The NIESR model is an aggregate quarterly model. There are almost 320 variables distinguished by the model, of which just under 100 are treated as exogenous; about 45 expectational variables, and some 90 stochastic equations. The model follows the Keynesian income–expenditure tradition. It can be viewed largely as a quantity adjustment model, being driven more by expenditures than by relative prices.

The part of the model that can be considered as the *IS* curve consists of relationships for consumer demand, fixed investment, stockbuilding, exports, and imports, with government expenditure exogenous. These items are largely demand-driven, although cyclical influences enter into the determination of investment and relative prices influence exports and imports. The generation of inflation comes from the interaction of the wage, price, and exchange rate relationships, and inflation itself adversely affects consumer demand. Monetary factors have a minor role, with some effects from interest rates on expenditure. Forward-looking behaviour enters into the equations for employment, stockbuilding, investment, wages, the exchange rate, and the demand for narrow money (M_1).

Consumer demand is disaggregated into durables and non-durables, the main determinants being real income and the inflation loss on personal sector liquid assets. Fixed investment is split into nine categories with four determined endogenously: (1) housing, (2) manufacturing, (3) distribution, financial and business services, and (4) the rest of industrial private investment. Housing investment is related to interest rates, relative costs, and the availability of finance, the latter determined in a building society sub-sector. The net manufacturing (inclusive of leasing) investment equation is driven by expected output, past levels of the capital stock and retirements from the stock, the latter varying during the cycle. Investment in distribution, etc., has the same explanatory factors as the manufacturing equation, and other private investment is determined by current output and a time trend. Stockbuilding is derived from equations determining the levels of stocks in manufacturing, distributive trades, and the rest of industry; expected output is the principal explanatory variable. The treatment of imports and exports is fairly standard in that domestic activity and relative prices explain imports, with world demand and relative prices explaining exports; each variable is disaggregated into three or four groups. In the imports of manufactures equation, the long-run propensity to import is unity.

The labour sector comprises a set of employment demand equations (for manufacturing and other private industries), an aggregate wage equation, an hours equation, and a relationship to determine the level of unemployment from the labour force and employment. Employment is determined by expected output and, in the case of manufacturing, by the real wage with a long-run elasticity of -1.3. Wages depend on the target real wage, unemployment, and (rationally) expected prices. The unemployment relationship distinguishes changes in employment by sector, with manufacturing employment having a much larger propensity to register than non-manufacturing employment.

Prices depend on unit import prices and unit labour costs with an allowance for indirect tax effects. The real exchange rate is determined by real interest rate differentials (exogenous), its own expectation, and changes in the trade balance. In practice, the exchange rate is highly dependent on the terminal condition for the expected exchange rate.

The measure of the broad money supply is explained by definitions relating the PSBR to the money stock, with bank-lending, debt sales, and currency transactions explained by behavioural equations. Real interest rates are exogenous.

The NIESR model distinguishes a North Sea oil sector whose main role is to determine the government tax take through North Sea revenues, although the value of North Sea oil reserves also affects the exchange rate. Key variables in this sector are world oil prices, domestic oil output, and the exchange rate, with the first two being treated as predetermined.

The main development in the present version of the model is the inclusion of forward expectations in equations for employment, investment, stocks, the exchange rate, wages, and narrow money demand. The exchange rate equation has been radically changed, and significant changes have been made to the employment–unemployment relationship. Real wages now enter the manufacturing employment equation, and the stock equations are now in levels rather than first differences, as previously. However, roughly one-half of the behavioural equations are exactly the same as in the previous version of the model.

Her Majesty's Treasury (HMT)

The Treasury model is the largest of the quarterly models. However, its size (over 700 equations and 1275 variables) reflects a detailed treatment of the public sector, rather than theoretical complexity or empirical disaggregation. Our description relates to the public version of the HMT model made available in January 1986.

The Treasury model follows the income–expenditure tradition. Consumption is separated into durables and non-durables. The former depend on real income, net financial wealth, and real interest rates. The income variable in the non-durables equation includes an adjustment for the effects of the inflation tax on real liquid assets. It also includes a net liquidity variable and terms in the nominal short-term interest rate and the rate of inflation.

Private non-residential fixed investment is disaggregated into manufacturing and non-manufacturing. Manufacturing investment is determined by the level of output and the real cost of labour and the cost of capital. The long-run solution of the equation is consistent with constant returns and has an elasticity with respect to relative factor prices of -0.2. Output and capital stock are the main driving variables in the non-manufacturing equation. Housing investment is related to relative prices and interest rates. Stockbuilding is principally determined by demand and the cost of inventories. Both exports and imports are disaggregated. Exports of manufactures are determined by relative total costs (long-run elasticity, -0.14), world trade (unit long-run elasticity), and the absolute profitability of exporting (long-run elasticity, 0.5). Exports of non-manufactures depend on world industrial production (long-run elasticity, 0.7) and relative normalized unit labour costs (long-run elasticity, -0.2). Imports of manufactures are influenced by relative unit costs (long-run elasticity, -0.8), trend world specialization (measured by the ratio of world trade to world production), domestic demand (long-run elasticity, 1.2), and capacity utilization.

The Treasury model includes a set of company sector adjustments whose rationale is to impose omitted liquidity effects in various company sector equations. Thus, liquidity effects are not part of the estimated structure of the model, but in simulation analysis any deviation of the ratio of net liquidity to private sector total fixed expenditure from its base-run value is assumed to affect fixed and working capital, dividends and employment, whereas equivalent variations in the gross liquidity ratio affect bank lending.

The labour market consists of a set of employment and wage equations and a relationship to determine the level of registered unemployment from the exogenous labour force and employment. Employment in manufacturing depends on planned output and relative factor costs. Planned output is generated by a vector autoregressive model, using stock–output ratios, the CBI measure of business confidence, and measures of aggregate demand (although in practical operations actual output is substituted for this variable). In the long run there are constant returns to scale, and the elasticity with respect to relative factor costs is -0.3. In the relationship for non-manufacturing employment, planned output is proxied by a distributed lag of current and past output levels, and the long-run factor cost elasticity is imposed at a value of -0.1. Wages in the private sector depend on a variety of influences including output, prices, taxes, and public sector employment. Prices are based on costs, with additional influences from capacity utilization, the level of activity, and competitors' prices. The exchange rate is determined by the expected future rate and the uncovered interest differential. The expected rate adjusts towards a long-run equilibrium which depends on relative money supply, the real value of North Sea oil production, and the level of the short-term uncovered interest differential.

The monetary sector of the model calculates financial surpluses for the four institutional sectors in order to produce net financial wealth. Total financial wealth is then allocated between sterling and foreign currency assets and finally between money, gilts, and other sterling assets. Thus, sterling M_3 is demand-determined and is dependent on gross domestic wealth, total final expenditure, and interest rates. Short-term interest rates are all related to each other by simple mark-up relationships, with long rates related to short rates and inflation expectations. The general level of interest rates can be either exogenous or endogenous if some aggregate measure of the money supply is fixed.

As in the LBS and NIESR models, the North Sea oil sector is modelled separately.

The main revisions to the Treasury model, compared with the previous version, are some changes to the employment and investment equations, changes to the calculation of the cost of capital, re-specification of the stocks equations, new equations for private sector liquid assets, and changes to the equation for manufactured export volumes.

Bank of England (BE)

The Bank of England is the latest of the models to be deposited with the Bureau. It was originally based on the London Business School model and, although the two models have since developed in quite different ways, the BE model shares the same income–expenditure framework as the LBS model (and the other quarterly models).

It is of a similar order of magnitude to the LBS model, having 800 variables, of which just over 300 are exogenous. Consumption is divided into durables and non-durables. Durables expenditure is determined by real income (adjusted for the inflation loss on net liquid assets), real interest rates, the liquidity ratio, and mortgage lending. Non-durables expenditure is determined by real income (adjusted as for durables) and the ratio of real net liquidity to income. Private residential investment is explained by real incomes, real interest rates, the real value of house loans, relative prices, and net liquid assets. Industrial investment is broken down into manufacturing, and distribution and services. Both depend on output in the sector and the lagged value of the capital stock. Stockbuilding in manufacturing distinguishes between materials and fuel, and finished goods and work in progress. Both are influenced by manufacturing output, liquid assets, real interest rates, and the corporation tax rate. Distributors' stocks depend on demand and liquid assets. Both exports and imports are disaggregated on similar lines to the other quarterly models. Exports of manufactures depend on world industrial production (long-run elasticity of unity), the ratio of world trade to world production, and the relative export price (long-run elasticity, -0.45). Imports of finished manufactures depend on domestic demand and relative prices.

The labour market consists of a set of disaggregate employment and wage relationships and an unemployment–employment relationship. Employment in manufacturing industry is modelled in terms of person-hours and has a long-run output elasticity of unity, with a small real-wage elasticity of -0.1. Similar elasticities are present in the equation for non-manufacturing, but here only numbers of employed, and not person-hours, are modelled. Average earnings in manufacturing are influenced by unemployment, prices, earnings in the public sector, incomes policy, and the retention ratio. Earnings in the non-trading public sector are also influenced by prices, unemployment, and incomes policy, but also by earnings in manufacturing. Earnings in the residual (non-public) sector are driven in the long run by earnings in manufacturing. Wholesale prices are related to wage costs and import costs, with a fixed mark-up in the long run. Changes in taxes have no long-run effects on wholesale prices. Consumer prices have a similar mark-up framework with an additional element from taxes bearing on consumption.

There is a fairly full treatment of stocks and flows associated with the financial sector, including transactions with the overseas sector. Implications for the stock of sterling M_3 therefore emerge from the standard accounting identities. The exchange rate is related to its equilibrium level and to the expected and actual change in the pressure on the dollar exchange rate.

Cambridge Growth Project (CGP)

The CGP model is a structural Leontief input–output model embedded within a conventional macroeconomic model. The model is basically of the Keynesian type, emphasizing real flows rather than monetary or financial ones. Owing to the high degree of disaggregation (39 industries and commodities), the model is very detailed, with over 5000 endogenous variables, 500 exogenous variables, and around 16,000 behavioural parameters and coefficients. The model is annual, and the version described here corresponds to model MDM6.

Like the quarterly models, the CGP model determines expenditure and output using the framework of the GDP identity, but relationships are disaggregated into 39 commodities. Like the NIESR model, the CGP model is driven primarily by quantity factors rather than relative prices, with monetary factors having a minor influence. Whereas other models occasionally disaggregate, they usually do so only as a matter of convenience or necessity. In contrast, disaggregation in the CGP model is a methodological issue. This is not to say, however, that there are no aggregate relationships. Thus, there is an aggregate consumption equation, in which aggregate consumption is explained by current real income (marginal propensity to consume, 0.6), real wealth, and a term representing the revaluation of financial assets due to capital gains/losses. There then follow disaggregated consumption relationships, whose role is to allocate total consumption between individual commodities.

Private fixed investment is disaggregated by asset and industry. The main explanatory variable is gross output (aggregate long-run elasticity of 0.5). Stockbuilding is also disaggregated by asset and commodity, and explained by output, real interest rates, and the real liquidity of companies.

The share of imports in the total supply of each commodity is determined by aggregate final demand and the relative price for each commodity. In addition, there is a capacity utilization effect. Exports are driven by relative prices and world demand. Long-term relative price elasticities are similar in aggregate for imports and exports, both having a value of around −1. The long-run demand elasticity is around 2 for imports, but below unity for exports.

The final demands for commodities obtained in this way are augmented by intermediate demands from the input–output matrix. These real demands are met by domestic output or imports.

The labour market consists of a set of employment and hours functions where industry output, the aggregate unemployment rate, and real wages are the main explanatory factors for employment. The implied aggregate long-run elasticity of employment with respect to output is unity, and is −0.3 with respect to real wages. Wages are determined by a real-wage target, a term reflecting the application of incomes policies, and a (weak) unemployment effect.

Domestic prices are determined largely by a mark-up on costs, although for some industries the price of competing imports plays a role. There is also an allowance for capacity utilization.

As in the quarterly models, sectoral surpluses and deficits can be derived. The main difference is in the degree of disaggregation of the institutional sectors and the use of these surpluses/deficits to form a matrix of financial assets and liabilities which then determine the supply of money and external capital flows. Interest rates are assumed to be predetermined, and these explain financial returns. The exchange rate is determined by relative interest rates, relative prices, the real value of oil reserves, and official intervention in the foreign exchange market.

Along with most of the other models, the CGP model separately distinguishes the North Sea sector, but in this case, the sector is treated as an industry with a full accounting framework. The CGP model also has an energy sub-model; relations connected with energy demand are otherwise only found in the CUBS model. The main contrast between this version of the CGP model and the previous version is in the inclusion of endogenous exchange rate behaviour.

City University Business School (CUBS)

The CUBS model is the newest of the UK macroeconomic models. It is a small annual model with just under 130 variables (of which 70 are exogenous) and 10 behavioural equations.

The CUBS model differs from most of the other models in the absence of an income–expenditure framework and in the emphasis on supply-side factors in the determination of output. The model distinguishes four factors of production: capital, labour, energy, and raw materials. Demands for these factors are based on profit maximization within a perfectly competitive framework, and therefore labour demand depends upon the real wage to employers (with a long-run elasticity of just below unity), capital stock, and energy and materials prices (with long-run elasticities of −0.16 and 0.47 for these last two, respectively). The labour market includes a labour supply schedule which depends on the real employee wage and population. In the long run, the natural rate of unemployment is determined by the level of unemployment benefits. However, there is a very sluggish process of adjustment by the real wage to this long-run market-clearing position so that in practice the labour market is not market-clearing.

The factor demand equations and the assumed production function determine the supply of total private sector output for given factor prices and output price. A higher output price raises profits and factor demands, thus increasing production. In the long run the level of private sector output depends on the labour input, the change in the real money stock, energy demand, real material prices, and the capital stock. Constant returns to scale are present with an elasticity of −0.16 on real material prices. The overall price level is influenced positively by aggregate supply and negatively by output. The supply curve is assumed to be vertical in the long run, but aggregate demand can have a short-run influence on the level of output. The exchange rate is influenced by relative prices and the difference between the UK oil balance and that of other industrialized countries. The real exchange rate balances the current account of the balance of payments.

There is no explicit modelling of the monetary sector. Official foreign exchange reserves are assumed to be exogenous and a given PSBR is assumed to be financed by money (M0) or government debt.

The present version of the CUBS model is similar in broad outline to the previous version. There is now an equation for nominal interest rates, but this is post-recursive to the rest of the model.

Liverpool University Research Group in Macroeconomics (LPL)

The Liverpool model is a small annual model with less than 20 behavioural equations and with just over 50 variables in total (of which 20 are exogenous). It is 'new classical' in nature and is solved using a rational expectations algorithm which forces consistent expectations on the model. It is a monetarist model in the sense that higher monetary growth directly increases inflation with no role for cost factors.

One of the main distinctions between the LPL model and other models is that private expenditure decisions are related to wealth and not income. Substitution between goods and financial assets is influenced by real interest rates. The budget surplus and balance of trade affect private financial holdings, with inflation reducing the real value of private money holdings and nominal interest rate changes altering the capital values of government debt and hence financial wealth.

Another distinctive feature of the LPL model is that government spending is determined within the model, given a target PSBR/GDP ratio and an assumption about the average tax rate. Permanent changes in government spending therefore can arise in the LPL model only as a consequence of a different PSBR target or a change in the average tax rate.

The labour market is market-clearing by construction, with a demand/ unemployment function which contains real-wage and output variables and a labour supply/real-wage equation which depends on population, unemployment benefits, trade union membership, and expected inflation. The real exchange rate responds immediately to relative price changes and to real wages, with an elasticity that reflects the labour share in total costs. The change in the nominal exchange rate is determined by uncovered interest differentials. Exports and imports are modelled jointly as a function of world trade, domestic income, and actual and expected real exchange rates. Inflation depends on the domestic money supply (which in turn is related to the long-run PSBR/GDP ratio) and the demand for real money balances.

As noted above, a key distinction on the LPL model is the use of consistent expectations; thus such variables as expected future inflation or expected future exchange rates coincide with the model's forecasts of inflation or exchange rates, respectively. North Sea oil does not appear within the LPL model.

This version of the LPL model is very little different from the previous version. It contains a new terminal condition for the exchange rate, but otherwise only the values of the constant terms have been changed.

1.3 Similarities and differences of the models

The UK models under discussion cover a wide range of methodological and macroeconomic approach. In this section we identify several different aspects of these approaches, and classify the models according to our interpretation of their structure and overall properties. In some instances, this interpretation does not coincide with that of the model proprietors. Fuller details are provided in subsequent chapters of this volume and in our previous reviews, and no attempt is made here to quantify model differences.

Methodological approach

In principle, it might be possible to contrast the models in terms of the relative weights placed on data and theory in their construction. Economic theory may influence the model in two particular ways. First, it may influence the model by defining fairly precisely its overall structure so that the individual relationships, even if statistically based, are consistent with the overall aim. Second, economic theory may influence the specification of individual relationships (or sub-blocks of the model) without necessarily constraining these to conform to an overall economic structure. In this sense the properties of the model as a whole emerge only after the model is built and simulated. In contrast, where the overall structure is carefully predefined, many of the properties of the model are known *a priori*. The LPL model is an example of this type of model.

The CUBS model also places a relatively high weight on the overall economic structure but allows estimation to play a greater role than the LPL so that the final overall properties of the model may in some respects differ from the original theoretical design. The other models do not possess an overall theoretical ideal and as such fall into the second classification.

Temporal and sectoral aggregation

Three of the models (CGP, CUBS, and LPL) are based on annual data and are usually regarded as medium-term models, although the phrase 'medium term' is used loosely. They are typically used to solve over a period of 10–15 years. In contrast the LBS, NIESR, HMT, and BE models, which are quarterly, are used over a time horizon of up to five years, although many of the NIESR forecasts typically have a shorter range, of between 18 months and two years. The presence of forward-consistent expectations in the LBS and NIESR models usually requires them to be solved over a longer period than is required for analysis. This aspect is discussed in Section 2.5 below.

With the exception of the CGP model, the models are highly aggregate in nature. There is no sectoral disaggregation in the LPL model. CUBS, HMT, LBS, NIESR, and BE separate the public and private sectors, and the latter three also distinguish between manufacturing and other private sector activity. Often, however, the disaggregation is based on a top-down sharing approach rather than one that builds up aggregate activity as the sum of its components. The CGP model uses a 39-fold industrial breakdown with each sector satisfying accounting identities and with total activity determined as the sum of the individual sectors. Sectoral disaggregation is described more fully in Section 2.4 below.

Broad classification of models

The models can be classified into those that imply rapid price adjustment to any internal or external shock, those that contain sluggish price adjustment, and those that emphasize the role of quantity adjustment. The first class of model is typically an equilibrium model which assumes market-clearing in all sectors of the economy and corresponds to the new classical paradigm. The LPL model is clearly an example of this class. Models that are contained in the second class are often regarded as being Keynesian, if the cause of the sluggishness is nominal wage/price rigidity, while those in the third class are neo-Keynesian in spirit. Both the sluggish price adjustment and quantity adjustment cases imply disequilibrium models in the short run. The CUBS model can be regarded as a sluggish price adjustment model but with the adjustment processes so protracted that the existence of long-run equilibrium in the labour market might be regarded as of little practical importance. The CGP and NIESR models fall into the quantity adjustment class of model where there is no mechanism that guarantees a return to equilibrium. Much the same can be said about the LBS and HMT models except that their slightly greater emphasis on price adjustment places them on the borderline of the sluggish price adjustment and quantity adjustment classes. However, the rapid adjustment of the exchange rate in the LBS model owing to the incorporation of forward-consistent expectations in the financial sector, together with the sluggish reaction of domestic wages and prices, leads to an overshooting of the exchange rate, and the quantity adjustment is therefore sluggish relative to that of HMT. The BE model is quite hard to classify as it has a relatively limited simulation base; however, the results obtained from this model suggest that it occupies a position somewhere between NIESR and LBS.

Treatment of the supply side

The CUBS model treats the supply of output explicitly through a production function which distinguishes capital, labour, energy, and raw material inputs. There is also a model of labour supply. The natural rate of unemployment is sensitive to the rate of unemployment benefit through the real-wage adjustment mechanism. Labour supply is also modelled by LPL but there is no explicit modelling of supply-side influences in other markets. The supply decision in both CUBS and LPL is in terms of heads rather than hours of work. The 'natural' rate of output and unemployment in LPL is influenced by unemployment benefits and trade union power and taxes. The other models are essentially demand-driven, although there is usually an implicit supply side through the impact of utilization, the generation of inflation, and open economy effects. LBS, in common with LPL and CUBS, contains a supply-side instrument (unemployment benefits), but there are no influential supply-side policy instruments in CGP, BE, and NIESR (if one discounts incomes policy variables in the first two of these). The HMT model contains a set of company sector adjustments which reflect liquidity pressures; however, these are not based on empirical estimation.

Treatment of expectations

The most comprehensive treatment of expectations is in the LPL model, where rational expectations are assumed throughout so that all future policy changes are anticipated by economic agents and assumed to influence their current behaviour. However, the model can also be used to simulate a policy where the initial effect of policy is unanticipated. Forward-consistent expectations enter the LBS model through the financial market. These determine the prices of gilt-edged stock, equities, and the exchange rate. Price expectations (generated by a backward-looking adaptive rule) influence wage behaviour. The NIESR model also contains forward-consistent expectations, and these appear in equations for employment, investment, stockbuilding, the exchange rate, wages, and narrow money (M_1). The terminal condition for the expected exchange rate in the NIESR model essentially makes it exogenous. Expectations appear in the CGP model in the determination of the exchange rate. In the CGP model the expected exchange rate determines the actual rate along with other variables; however, this is programmed as a reduced form with similar properties to the structural equation. Although expectations mechanisms may be implicit in the CUBS and BE models, they are not separately distinguished. Expectations enter the HMT model through two main routes. First, expected exchange rate movements influence the actual exchange rate, and second, planned output, determined by a vector auto-regression, affects employment. In practical use, however, actual output is substituted for the planned level. The expected exchange rate moves to adjust to the equilibrium value of the exchange rate.

Role of money

The importance of money in the models largely corresponds to the degree of monetarism of the model. Money is very important in the LPL and CUBS models where it determines the rate of inflation. In the case of LBS and HMT the main influence of money is on the behaviour of the exchange rate, whereas in the CGP and NIESR models money plays a very minor role. In the LBS model money is only one of the assets influencing the exchange rate, and in the BE model it is the relative velocity of money that is the appropriate variable.

Role of the exchange rate

The exchange rate has an important role in most of the models as a transmission for policy changes, and some of the different policy responses can be attributed to differences in exchange rate behaviour. It is formally endogenous in all the models. In the LPL model the real exchange rate depends only on real factors (output and real wage) and responds quickly to exogenous influences, whereas the change in the nominal exchange rate is directly related to the level of interest rates. In the NIESR model the real exchange rate is determined by its expected value, real interest rate differentials, relative prices, and the change in the trade balance. The exchange rate is a random walk, and the terminal condition required for forward-consistent expectations basically determines its value. In the CUBS model the real rate depends on relative prices and the relative trade balance in oil. In the LBS model the exchange rate is one of a number of variables jointly determined within the financial sector under rational expectations, and this results in its rapid adjustment to shocks to the economy. In the CGP model the exchange rate is determined by relative interest rates, relative prices, the real value of oil reserves, and official intervention in the foreign exchange market.

Price and wage formation

In keeping with their monetarist leanings, the LPL and CUBS models determine prices by the level of the money supply, whereas the other models set prices as a mark-up on costs with some influence from the level of demand. In the LPL and CUBS models money wages respond immediately (i.e., within a year) to a change in prices, whereas this is a longer-run property in the HMT, LBS, and NIESR models. Policy variables that can be used to influence real pre-tax wages directly are unemployment benefits in the LPL, CUBS, and LBS models, and tax rates and employees' national insurance contributions in LPL, CUBS, and HMT and BE. There are no policy instruments that operate directly on the level of real or money earnings in the NIESR model. The CGP and BE models contain variables that can be used as incomes policy instruments. Both real and money wages are determined within the models.

The labour market

The labour market is clearing by construction in the case of LPL. In the CUBS model it is market-clearing in the long run, but the very sluggish adjustment process means that in practice it is not market-clearing. The other models cannot be classified in this way, but their properties would suggest that they too are not market-clearing. All the models give relative factor prices a role in the determination of employment (but not for non-manufacturing in the case of NIESR).

North Sea oil

Only CGP has a complete set of accounts for this sector. North Sea oil is not distinguished in the LPL model, and its role in the other models is primarily to set the level of oil output. This, together with the oil price, determines the dollar value of revenues. These are then disaggregated into sterling company profits and government taxation by applying the appropriate exchange rate and tax parameters.

Role of technology

Only the CUBS model contains an explicit production function with a capital stock variable, although the capital stock enters investment equations in the NIESR and BE models. There is no role for technology in the LPL model. In the CGP model the input–output part of the model incorporates assumptions about the pace of technical change, but in all of the other models (including CUBS) changes in the pace of technological progress can be made only by modifying time trends in the models.

Policy assumptions

With the exception of LPL, the models contain no formal policy reaction by the authorities to past, present, or future outcomes. Policy considerations in this sense therefore are outside the formal scope of the models. However, there are certain policy rules that are built into the models, and these generally relate to the method of financing a given public sector deficit. In the LPL model the authorities are assumed to select a target value for the ratio of the PSBR to GDP. Given assumptions about tax rates, this determines the level of government expenditure that is permissible, and the target PSBR/GDP ratio itself determines the rate of monetary expansion. In the other models both government expenditure and tax rates are policy instruments, and the level of the public sector deficit merely emerges as a result of these assumptions and the conjunctural state of the economy. Finance of the deficit is at constant interest rates in the CGP, BE, HMT, LBS, and NIESR models (constant *real* rates in the last of these). This roughly corresponds to a money-financed deficit. In contrast, the LPL model assumes balanced finance, which is also the long-run assumption in CUBS. However, in the short run monetary growth is fixed in the CUBS model and interest rates appear only in a post-recursive relationship. In some of the models it is possible to vary the financing policy so that various measures of money stock are held constant. This area is discussed further in Section 2.2 below.

Where the models adopt tax rates as policy instruments, there is usually some distinction between income tax rates and allowances (often disaggregated), specific duties, VAT, and employers' and employees' national insurance contributions. For government spending LBS, CUBS, and HMT distinguish between procurement and employment-related current expenditure on goods and services, HMT and CGP between local and central government current expenditure, and CGP between different functional areas. All except LPL identify capital formation by general government, but in varying degrees of detail. Current grants by central government are usually treated as endogenous, although some models do incorporate a policy influence through the rate of unemployment benefit. Monetary policy variables are usually either interest rates or the money stock, together with minimum deposit rates on credit purchases. Some models (BE and CGP) contain incomes policy variables, but in general there are very few policy variables other than those concerned with monetary and fiscal policy.

Chapter 2
Comparative Model Properties

2.1 Introduction

This is our third review of the overall properties of the models using simulation exercises and dynamic multiplier analysis. On this occasion we have an additional model to consider (BE), and we now have three models (LBS, NIESR, and LPL) where there are elements of rational expectations. We therefore consider some of the issues involved in conducting simulations with rational expectations models, as well as considering the impact that the introduction of rational expectations has had on the properties of the LBS and NIESR models. The models contain different degrees of disaggregation, and in this review we consider the extent of sectoral disaggregation, the methodology adopted, and the implications of the simulation exercises for sectoral output and employment.

Our approach is to examine the sensitivity of the endogenous variables to changes in particular exogenous variables, allowing for all feedbacks, contemporaneous and lagged. A base run of the model is first computed, usually the published forecast. A new solution run is then computed by perturbing an appropriate exogenous variable by a given amount. The effects of this shock are derived by comparing the results of this simulation with the base run. Both solutions include all the residual adjustments and exogeneity assumptions in the published forecast (or base run).

Dynamic multipliers are usually distinguished from partial elasticities calculated from single equations, since they allow other endogenous variables to vary. They characterize the full model response to individual interventions, with no additional effects, and represent the numerical equivalent, in nonlinear models, to the reduced-form coefficients of a linear model. These coefficients embody either an implicit or an explicit assumption regarding the stance of policy. Our general approach is to maintain a consistent policy assumption across the simulation experiments for variables other than those actually perturbed, but we consider different possibilities. Policy assumptions correspond to those incorporated in the base run of the model as deposited with the Bureau, and they are detailed below. In the analysis of practical policy questions it may not appear plausible to maintain the policy assumptions used in the base run when shocks of a different nature occur. Adjusting the policy stance in the light of different shocks would confuse the process of intra-model comparison, but inter-model comparisons, in contrast, would still be possible if the policy stance were standard across the models. However, the appropriate policy for one model might be deemed inappropriate for another. Although the design of the appropriate policy stance in the face of alternative shocks to the economy is of obvious interest to those engaged in policy-making, it is not our present aim. Nevertheless, we examine the sensitivity of some of the results to different assumptions regarding the finance of the budget deficit.

The choice of simulations reported follows that used in previous reviews and is intended to enable us to monitor changes in the models over time, although it is hoped at the same time that they are of interest in their own right and allow some of the different distinguishing features of the models to emerge. In exploring a range of shocks, less attention can be given to the details of each simulation and the elaboration of the various mechanisms at work in the model, although we attempt to report on the interesting features of each simulation. Attention is focused on the major macroeconomic indicators, particularly output, unemployment, and inflation; full results are available on request.

The input shocks have been selected to represent magnitudes observed in the actual data, at least in annual terms. To the extent that the models can be regarded as approximately linear, the results can be interpreted as ready reckoners. Thus, the effects of a decrease of £386 million in the level of government expenditure can be calculated by changing the sign of the simulation results describing the impact of an identical *increase*; or the results of a 10 per cent reduction in the standard rate of tax can be estimated by doubling the effects shown in the 5 per cent case. Earlier tests on one of the models (NIESR) suggest that the results can be used in this ready-reckoner sense. However, this is legitimate only in the neighbourhood in which the linear approximation holds. More generally, the model itself might be regarded as a valid approximation only over the range of its sample experience, and hence we emphasize the use of shocks equivalent to observed changes in the data. For example, it would be inappropriate to generalize the results from a 5 per cent reduction in the tax rate to a complete removal of income tax. Moreover, the simulations might then be regarded as introducing a new policy regime and thus might become more susceptible to the Lucas critique.

In nonlinear models the simulation results also depend on the values of the exogenous variables in the base run. Tests on a slightly earlier version of the NIESR model using an historical database reveal little difference in the multipliers, but this result is not necessarily of general applicability.

Differences in model size often reflect the policy objective of the model. Thus, the somewhat large size of the Treasury model reflects the need to model in a detailed way the accounts of the public sector. Other models, such as CUBS and LPL, are concerned more with broad aggregates and a smaller, more compact model is sufficient. In focusing on broad aggregates, we neglect the fact that a larger model may provide more information on matters about which a smaller model has nothing to say. Our discussion of sectoral output and employment responses redresses the balance a little.

Similar considerations apply in respect to the time dimension. Models aimed more specifically at explaining short-term fluctuations in output and employment may say very little of interest about medium-term developments, while models designed to focus on the latter may abstract from short-run changes. However, we make no major distinction between the quarterly and annual models. An input shock is imposed as a step change in the first period of the simulation, whether this refers to a quarterly or an annual observation, and in some of the simulations this may imply that the size of the impact shock is quite large for the quarterly models. In general, the input shocks are assumed to be unanticipated and permanent; other possibilities are considered in a later section.

In Section 2.2 we report the broad macroeconomic responses observed in the simulation experiments. In Section 2.3 we then focus on two further aspects of these results which appear in the policy debate, namely, their balance of payments implications and the relative costs per job of the policy measures. Next, in section 2.4 we consider the extent of disaggregation of output and employment in the models, and the effects on sectoral output and employment observed in the simulations. The results are related to the debate on de-industrialization (or the 'Dutch disease'), where the role of the manufacturing sector is highlighted. In Sections 2.5 and 2.6 we discuss some of the issues associated with rational expectations models. In Section 2.5 we examine the sensitivity of the models with forward expectations (LBS, NIESR, and LPL) to the terminal date and the type of terminal condition. In the following section we contrast results derived from temporary shocks in these models with those of a permanent nature, and similarly compare anticipated with unanticipated shocks. Finally, we summarize our findings in Section 2.7.

2.2 The simulation experiments

Six standard simulations are conducted and compared across the models. Five cover areas of domestic policy, and the final simulation examines the responses of the models to a change in the external environment. The five policy simulations are:

(i) a permanent increase of £386 million (1980 prices) per quarter in government current expenditure on goods and services (or some $3\frac{1}{4}$ per cent of current expenditure): the magnitude of this shock has been chosen to be comparable with that used in the previous set of simulations;

(ii) a permanent reduction in the standard rate of income tax of 5 per

cent from its value in the base solution (corresponding approximately to a reduction of the rate from 30 to $28\frac{1}{2}$ per cent);

(iii)   a permanent 10 per cent reduction in the rate of VAT from base
values (corresponding to a reduction of the rate from 15 to $13\frac{1}{2}$ per
cent);

(iv)   a permanent reduction of 2 percentage points in nominal short-term
interest rates;

 (v)   a 10 per cent reduction in the rate of unemployment benefit.

The external shock is:

(vi)   a permanent 10 per cent reduction in world oil prices in dollars (with
no other impact on world economy variables).

Several variants are computed around the first simulation, reflecting
different assumptions about the mix of procurement and employment-
related expenditure and about the financing rule in operation. The financing rules used in simulations (ii)–(v) correspond to those that are standard
in the models. These are, respectively: constant nominal short interest
rates in LBS, HMT, and BE, constant real short interest rate in NIESR,
balanced finance in CUBS, and constant PSBR/GDP ratio in LPL.

In general, simulations were conducted over the following periods: LBS,
1986(1)–1994(4); NIESR, 1985(3)–1991(1); HMT, 1986(1)–1992(1); BE,
1985(3)–1988(4); CGP, 1983–1990; CUBS, 1985–1999; LPL, 1985–1988.
The periods over which the simulations are conducted thus range from 3
years (BE) to 14 years (CUBS). In our presentation of results we restrict
attention to the first five years. As discussed in our second review, simulation results with the LPL model may be sensitive to the length of the
simulation period, that is, to the date at which the terminal condition is
imposed. We find that the results for the first five years are insensitive to
small variations in the terminal date from its present 1998 setting. However, the analysis of Section 2.5 implies there is some sensitivity in the two
quarterly models with rational expectations (LBS and NIESR).

Increase in government expenditure

In the first simulation we are concerned with the response of the models to
a permanent shock in government current expenditure under various
monetary policy regimes. The increase in current expenditure is assumed
to be the equivalent of £1600 million per annum at 1980 prices (approximately $£2\frac{1}{4}$ billion at 1986 prices). The standard assumption adopted in
models that distinguish between procurement and employment expenditures is that the increase in expenditure is divided proportionally between
the two categories. The results shown in Table 2.1 are obtained under a
'money finance' assumption; thus, short-term interest rates are fixed in the
LBS, NIESR, HMT, BE, and CGP models. (In the case of NIESR, it is the

Table 2.1 *Government expenditure simulation: money finance (fixed interest rates)*

Year	LBS		NIESR	HMT		BE	CGP	CUBS	LPL
	(a)				(a)				
GDP (% difference from base run)									
1	0.7	0.7	0.7	0.7	0.5	0.6	0.5	1.8	—
2	0.9	1.0	0.7	0.7	0.5	0.7	0.6	1.3	0.3
3	1.0	1.0	0.7	0.7	0.6	0.7	0.6	−0.9	0.2
4	1.0	1.0	0.6	0.6	0.5		0.6	0.1	0.2
5	1.0	0.9	0.6	0.5	0.4		0.5	—	0.3
Prices (% difference from base run)									
1	0.2	0.3	0.1	0.2	0.2	0.2	—	7.4	1.9
2	0.9	1.0	0.6	0.7	0.7	0.4	—	6.3	3.6
3	1.7	1.9	1.1	1.5	1.4	0.8	—	17.1	5.3
4	2.6	2.9	1.8	2.4	2.2		—	21.9	7.0
5	3.5	4.0	2.5	3.2	2.9		−0.1	25.8	8.3
Unemployment (difference from base run, '000)									
1	−135	−45	−52	−119	−34	−72	−156	−173	−76
2	−159	−100	−52	−135	−77	−126	−167	−184	−130
3	−177	−140	−47	−138	−91	−127	−174	−200	−124
4	−189	−157	−39	−121	−81		−180	−396	−102
5	−191	−156	−27	−96	−61		−184	−526	−86
Nominal exchange rate (% difference from base run)									
1	−3.7	−4.4	−0.3	−0.4	−0.6	−0.1	—	−5.4	−4.3
2	−4.2	−4.6	−0.6	−1.2	−1.4	−0.5	−0.1	−9.6	−5.3
3	−4.9	−5.0	−1.0	−1.9	−2.1	−1.1	−0.1	−16.1	−6.4
4	−5.7	−5.6	−1.5	−2.6	−2.6		−0.1	−22.1	−7.6
5	−6.6	−6.2	−2.0	−3.3	−3.2 ·		−1.0	−25.2	−8.6

(a) procurement only

real interest rate that is held constant.) For the CUBS and LPL models, the increase in spending is directly money-financed, which is accomplished by exogenously augmenting monetary growth by an amount equivalent to the increase in PSBR arising from the additional spending. In the CUBS model only the impact effect is added to monetary growth, as this model otherwise becomes unstable. For the LPL model, equilibrium government spending is determined by the exogenous PSBR/GDP ratio. Hence any change is required to occur as a temporary residual effect, in this case financed by a temporary addition to money: the temporary increase covers a five-year period. The distinction between temporary and permanent effects is discussed further below.

Implied expenditure multipliers are shown in the upper panel of Table 2.2. The multipliers for HMT, NIESR, and BE are close to unity, and all gradually decline over time. The CGP multiplier is a little lower than unity,

Table 2.2   *Government expenditure multipliers*
(i) Fixed interest rates

Year	LBS		NIESR	HMT		BE	CGP
	(a)				(a)		
1	0.97	1.03	0.98	0.95	0.74	0.90	0.82
2	1.36	1.47	0.97	0.99	0.81	0.95	0.86
3	1.52	1.57	0.96	1.10	0.85	0.86	0.86
4	1.52	1.48	0.93	0.91	0.75		0.87
5	1.51	1.36	0.87	0.81	0.66		0.87
6	1.46	1.23		0.75	0.61		0.87
7	1.36	1.09					0.87
8	1.26	0.93					0.87
9	1.20	0.77					0.87

(ii) Fixed money target

Year	LBS	HMT		BE
	(b)	(b)	(c)	(c)
1	0.88	0.74	0.74	0.90
2	1.01	0.36	0.27	0.95
3	1.11	0.10	−0.14	0.83
4	1.18	−0.12	−0.49	
5	1.25	−0.38	−0.86	
6	1.26	−0.62	−1.31	
7	1.35			
8	1.50			
9	1.81			

(a) procurement only
(b) fixed weighted average of monetary aggregates
(c) fixed $£M_3$

but remains fairly constant. In contrast, the LBS multiplier rises from around unity in the first year of the simulation to around 1.5. This result arises as a product of the financial sector of this model together with the assumption of forward-consistent expectations. Here, the expectation of rising inflation and hence of a future loss in international cost competitiveness induces a contemporaneous reduction in the nominal exchange rate in order to maintain an unchanged real exchange rate. However, since domestic wages and prices are sluggish, there is a reduction in the real exchange rate in the interim, providing a boost to output. Although this is only a temporary adjustment effect, the results reveal that in practice the lags are quite long, so that the output increase is sustained for several years.

The fall in the exchange rate in the LBS model is far greater than in the HMT model, but both produce roughly similar estimates for the impact on the price level. In the NIESR model the exchange rate also depreciates, but by less than in LBS and HMT. Owing to the presence of forward expectations of output in the NIESR model, the effects on the current levels of output and unemployment are accentuated. Although the output response in the NIESR model is of a comparable magnitude to that in the other quarterly models and to that of CGP, the impact on the level of unemployment is much less. This reflects the treatment of the employment–unemployment relationship in this model, where there is a different propensity to register as unemployed according to the sector of employment. As most of the extra employment occurs in the non-manufacturing area of the economy, where there is assumed to be a low propensity to register, the unemployment effect is reduced in size compared with the other models, despite approximately comparable total employment effects. Effects on the price level in the BE and CGP models are relatively small. This is a consequence of a negligible impact on the exchange rate and the absence of any marked pressure of demand effect on wages. In contrast, the increase in government employment itself exerts upward pressure on wages in the HMT model, in addition to inflationary pressure as a result of higher private sector output.

The results from the two remaining models (CUBS and LPL) are quite different from the others. In the CUBS model there is a very large increase in GDP in the first two years of the simulation, but the rapid inflation generated by the initial money finance of this increase later reduces output. Inflation accelerates and the price level rises continuously, reflecting the unstable nature of this model. Despite the short-lived increase in output, the level of unemployment falls continuously, as the labour market adjusts extremely slowly. In the LPL model very little additional output is generated, although the unemployment effects are not a great deal smaller than some of the other models (and greater than those of NIESR, where there is a much larger output increase). The price level effects are much greater for LPL, however, reflecting the nature of finance of the extra spending. The analysis of Section 2.5 reveals that the results for the LPL model depend on the exact way in which money finance is accomplished. In particular, more expansionary output effects emerge when the long-run PSBR/GDP ratio is adjusted.

Sectoral implications of the simulations are discussed in detail in Section 2.4; in the meantime we note that a major part of the additional employment arises in the government sector itself. Further results with the LBS and HMT models are shown in Table 2.1, where the increases in expenditure are concentrated solely on procurement, thus eliminating this direct employment effect. The LBS model delivers a very similar increase in output to the balanced expenditure increase, with the price level slightly higher. The level of unemployment is not much lower than in the balanced case after five years, but the initial impact is considerably reduced. This reflects the substitution of a lagged employment adjustment in the private sector for an immediate adjustment in government employment. In the HMT model output is a little weaker under the pure procurement case, but so too is the effect on the price level. The latter result probably reflects the removal of the effect of higher direct public employment on wages. As with LBS, the unemployment impact is lower, but there is not the same narrowing of the gap between the level under the balanced case that can be seen for LBS.

The contribution of the various components of demand differs between the LBS model and those of NIESR, HMT, BE, and CGP. For the latter the main effects, in addition to public expenditure itself, arise from higher consumer spending, higher investment and stockbuilding (but with weaker effects here for CGP), and an offsetting influence from a deterioration in net trade. For LBS the exchange rate depreciation ensures a positive net trade influence together with a strong rise in fixed investment and stock-building. However, consumer demand remains largely unchanged.

There have been some major changes to the structure of some of the models since out previous review. The LBS model now includes forward expectations in the financial sector, and this form of expectation also enters the employment, investment, stockbuilding, wage, and exchange rate equations of the NIESR model. In addition, the latter now includes a new employment–unemployment relationship where the propensity to register depends on the sector in which the change in employment takes place. The CGP model now includes an endogenous exchange rate. There is greater interest rate sensitivity in the HMT model. The CUBS and LPL models, however, remain virtually the same as the previous vintage, and so the CUBS and LPL results are almost identical to those reported in our previous review. The introduction of an endogenous exchange rate into CGP has little impact on this simulation, but the reduction in the level of unemployment is a little larger than in the previous version of this model. The HMT results are very similar to those reported from earlier versions of the model, but there are more significant changes to the results for LBS and NIESR. In the former, there is now a stronger depreciation of the exchange rate in the short run, leading to faster growth and a greater reduction in the level of unemployment than in the previous version, and price level effects are increased. Although eventually the real exchange rate returns to its base level and the increase in output disappears, this is not evident in the time span shown here. Nor is it in an examination of this simulation over a longer (nine-year) horizon — although the output effects are now reduced marginally. For NIESR the output effects are also reduced marginally, but greater revision occurs in the effects on the price level and on the level of unemployment. The latter effect occurs as a result

Table 2.3   *Government expenditure simulation: fixed money target*

Year	LBS	HMT		BE	CUBS	LPL
	(*b*)	(*a*)	(*b*)	(*b*)		
GDP (% difference from base run)						
1	0.6	0.5	0.5	0.6	0.5	0.4
2	0.7	0.2	0.2	0.7	0.5	0.3
3	0.7	0.1	−0.1	0.6	0.4	0.3
4	0.8	−0.1	−0.3		0.4	0.3
5	0.8	−0.2	−0.5		0.3	0.3
Prices (% difference from base run)						
1	—	0.1	0.1	0.1	0.3	−0.2
2	0.1	0.3	0.3	0.3	0.1	−0.3
3	0.4	0.6	0.5	0.5	−0.1	−0.4
4	0.7	0.8	0.5		−0.2	−0.4
5	1.1	0.9	0.3		−0.3	−0.3
Unemployment (difference from base run, '000)						
1	−124	−114	−114	−73	−154	−41
2	−128	−104	−102	−126	−93	−52
3	−128	−79	−68	−122	−45	−54
4	−131	−54	−33		−28	−52
5	−132	−33	−7		−25	−45
Nominal exchange rate (% difference from base run)						
1	−0.5	0.4	0.5	—	−0.3	0.6
2	−1.4	0.7	1.0	—	−0.4	0.7
3	−2.0	0.6	1.3	—	−0.1	0.7
4	−2.6	0.7	1.7		0.4	0.7
5	−3.1	1.0	2.5		0.7	0.7

(*a*) fixed weighted average of monetary aggregates
(*b*) fixed £M$_3$

of the introduction of the new employment–unemployment relationship. The NIESR model now predicts the smallest unemployment effects of all the models, by a factor of about 3 by the end of the simulation period.

In Table 2.3 we show some results from the government expenditure simulation where the increased spending is assumed to be wholly financed by bonds (CUBS, LPL) or where interest rates adjust to maintain a fixed monetary target (LBS, HMT, and BE). Two alternative money targets are shown for the HMT model: a weighted average of the various measures including private sector liquidity, and £M$_3$, the latter alone being used in the other quarterly models. Crowding-out is more marked than in the previous version of the model. It is also greater when the money target is £M$_3$ than when the weighted average is used, as interest rates have to rise more in this case to reduce money demand. Complete crowding-out occurs after about three years. Despite the lower level of output after this period, there is still a fall in the level of unemployment by the end of the simulation, although this is negligible in the case of £M$_3$. Whereas the exchange rate depreciates under money finance, there is now a small appreciation, and this is responsible for the weaker price effects observed under bond finance. The CUBS and LPL results are virtually identical to those described in our previous review. In the case of CUBS, on the one hand the increase in output is sustained under bond finance and there is not the large price response observed under money finance (owing to the price level being determined primarily by money); on the other hand, the unemployment effects are much weaker. In the case of LPL, the shock in spending is once again assumed to be temporary (five years). The increase in output is similar to that under money finance, but price effects disappear for the same reason as CUBS. Again, like CUBS, the unemployment effects are considerably lower than under money finance. In the BE model there is very little difference in the multipliers under bond finance, especially in the first year of the simulation. Since the rise in the money stock is quite small under money finance ($2\frac{1}{2}$ per cent after three years) the rise in interest rates required to maintain a constant money stock is similarly modest, and consequently no significant additional effects take place.

Bond-financed government expenditure multipliers for the LBS model are greater than unity except in the first year. Thus they continue to exceed those from the other models, whether money- or bond-financed. The bond finance multipliers rise steadily over time, but, as the money finance multipliers rise and then fall, the implied degree of crowding-out (the difference between the two sets of multipliers) also rises at first before falling. The average degree of crowding-out is weaker than in the previous version of this model. The exchange rate declines in the fixed-money target simulation for LBS, and this explains the lower degree of crowding-out relative to HMT, where the exchange rate appreciates. The depreciation is, however, less than in the fixed interest rate case, and this results in a weaker price response.

There are problems in establishing a control rule for real interest rates which maintain a constant money stock in the NIESR model. In general, there appears to be an unstable link between real interest rates and the money stock in the dynamic setting. The closest approximation to a constant money stock is via a once-and-for-all adjustment to the real interest rate in the first period of the simulation. This permits variations in the money stock (which has an oscillatory pattern) of around 1 per cent. However, since the exchange rate depends on the change in real interest rates at the terminal date, the real exchange rate then remains unaltered. Given the implications of this effect, compared with those derived from a permanent shift in real interest rates, we do not report results from this simulation, our conclusion being that bond finance is not possible with this model.

Table 2.4 *Government expenditure simulation: balanced finance*

Year	CUBS	LPL
GDP (% difference from base run)		
1	0.5	—
2	0.6	0.2
3	0.6	0.2
4	0.5	0.1
5	0.4	—
Prices (% difference from base run)		
1	0.4	2.2
2	0.6	4.1
3	0.8	5.9
4	1.7	7.8
5	3.1	9.6
Unemployment (difference from base run, '000)		
1	−154	−93
2	−94	−132
3	−52	−111
4	−44	−71
5	−65	−41

In Table 2.4 we illustrate the features of the CUBS and LPL models under the assumption of balanced finance between money and bonds. Both unemployment and price level effects are larger than under pure bond finance, given that there is now a change in the money stock, but the impact on these variables is far larger for LPL than for CUBS. Output effects are more transitory for LPL.

Finally, we consider an alternative method of finance. In this case the expenditure increase is financed by additional taxes so as to maintain a constant PSBR/GDP ratio. This is the familiar balanced budget case, noting that the results relate to an *ex post* balanced budget. The LPL model already adopts a constant PSBR/GDP ratio and the simulation is carried out by raising taxes, which results in the required rise in government spending. In the other models type 2 fixes, or similar methods, are applied to produce the balanced budget requirement. Residual finance is via money (constant interest rates in the quarterly models). The results are shown in Table 2.5.

The lack of any monetary stimulus in the CUBS and LPL models leads to a lack of any marked price response. The (pre-tax) real wage rises in the CUBS model, reducing labour demand in the traded goods sector, but this effect is more than compensated for by higher employment in the non-traded goods sectors. The results of the tax-financed increase in public expenditure reveal the impact of tax cuts relative to increases in public expenditure. The NIESR, HMT, LPL, and CUBS simulations show weak

Table 2.5   *Government expenditure simulation: tax finance*

Year	LBS	NIESR	HMT	BE	CUBS	LPL
GDP (% difference from base run)						
1	0.5	0.5	0.5	0.5	0.5	0.1
2	0.5	0.4	0.4	0.4	0.5	0.1
3	0.5	0.3	0.4	0.3	0.4	0.1
4	0.5	0.2	0.2		0.4	0.1
5	0.6	0.2	0.1		0.3	—
Prices (% difference from base run)						
1	—	0.1	0.1	0.3	0.4	0.4
2	0.2	0.5	0.5	0.5	0.2	0.7
3	0.4	0.8	1.1	0.7	—	0.9
4	0.6	1.0	1.7		—	1.1
5	0.9	0.9	2.1		—	1.2
Unemployment (difference from base run, '000)						
1	−129	−44	−109	−62	−182	−27
2	−131	−30	−106	−99	−109	−37
3	−127	−14	−91	−90	−67	−35
4	−127	—	−61		−65	−26
5	−126	9	−26		−77	−15

medium-term effects on output and unemployment. Since tax cuts work through private sector behaviour, the response of output and employment tends to be more sluggish than for increases in public expenditure, where a direct effect is engineered. In consequence, the short-run balanced budget multipliers are somewhat greater than those calculated after an interval of three to four years. The LBS model, however, gives a steady response in output, with the implied increase in tax rates declining from 4 per cent at the beginning of the simulation to $1\frac{1}{2}$ per cent at the end. This result arises largely as a consequence of the weak PSBR effect of higher government expenditure in the medium term, so that only a modest tax increase is required.

Thus there are some important differences in the present set of models under this simulation. Much weaker responses are observed for NIESR, but a stronger impact on output and employment arises for the LBS model. The maximum size of the balanced budget effects is an increase in GDP of around $\frac{1}{2}$ per cent.

Reduction in the income tax rate

In the second simulation, which is shown in Table 2.6, we assume a permanent 5 per cent reduction in the rate of income tax. For all the models except CUBS, this occurs under the assumption of constant short-term interest rates (and real interest rates for NIESR). For CUBS, the deficit is assumed to be financed by a balanced increase in money and

Table 2.6 *Tax rate simulation*
(5 per cent reduction in the standard rate of tax)

Year	LBS	NIESR	HMT	BE	CGP	CUBS
GDP (% difference from base run)						
1	0.2	0.2	0.2	0.1	0.2	—
2	0.6	0.3	0.3	0.3	—	0.1
3	0.7	0.4	0.3	0.3	0.1	0.2
4	0.8	0.4	0.3		0.2	0.1
5	0.7	0.4	0.3		0.2	0.1
Prices (% difference from base run)						
1	0.3	—	0.1	−0.1	−0.4	—
2	1.1	—	0.4	−0.1	−1.2	0.5
3	2.0	0.2	0.8	−0.1	−1.5	0.8
4	3.0	0.7	1.3		−1.8	1.8
5	4.1	1.4	1.7		−2.1	3.1
Unemployment (difference from base run, '000)						
1	−10	−7	−9	−8	−56	30
2	−41	−21	−33	−27	−72	−1
3	−75	−32	−54	−42	−88	−1
4	−99	−35	−65		−109	4
5	−110	−31	−68		−122	−15
Nominal exchange rate (% difference from base run)						
1	−3.9	−0.3	−0.4	—	1.6	—
2	−4.6	−0.4	−1.0	−0.1	1.0	−0.3
3	−5.4	−0.5	−1.4	−0.3	1.3	−0.9
4	−6.4	−0.7	−1.8		1.6	−2.0
5	−7.3	−1.2	−2.2		1.9	−3.5

bonds. Although the LPL model contains tax variables, its structure is slightly different from the other models. The PSBR/GDP ratio is given exogenously, and government spending is then determined endogenously given assumptions about the tax rate. Thus the PSBR is assumed to be adjusted for any change in taxes by variations in government spending, whereas the other models allow the level of the PSBR to change. Consequently, the LPL results are not comparable and are not shown here, but appear earlier in the reporting of the balanced budget simulation.

The LBS model shows the greatest impact of lower taxes on the level of output, but the CGP model reveals similar estimates of the change in unemployment. In the case of LBS, the unemployment reduction is moderated by an increase in the number of women seeking work, although this effect is not quantitatively large. The relatively large increase in GDP for the LBS model is again due to the operation of the financial sector of the model, with forward expectations resulting in an immediate depreciation of the exchange rate, but with sluggish wage and price response. All the other models reveal output effects of similar order of magnitude. Given the degree of decline in the nominal exchange rate, it is not surprising that the LBS model generates the greatest increase in the price level for this simulation; although it should be noted that the CUBS model also generates higher prices, in this case as a response to faster monetary growth. A retention ratio effect in the wage equations of both BE and CGP results in a lower price level, although the decline is negligible for BE. In the first year of the simulation the CUBS model produces a rise in the level of unemployment as the labour supply increases in response to the tax cut, but over the longer term the effects become negative (not shown in the table). Lower unemployment is observed throughout for the other models, with relatively small effects for NIESR and CUBS. In the case of NIESR, this reflects the bias in the increase in employment towards non-manufacturing (see Section 2.4) as this sector has a lower propensity to register. For CGP, consumers' expenditure alone is the main expenditure effect, but for the other models the principal expenditure contributions to higher output are from consumption, investment, and stockbuilding. In the case of LBS there is also an expansionary influence from net trade.

Despite significant changes to the NIESR model, the results from this simulation are broadly unchanged from those described in our previous review. With little change to the CUBS model there is no difference in results here, either. Both the LBS and CGP results differ, however, and reflect differences in the behaviour of the exchange rate. The more immediate depreciation of the exchange rate in LBS produces a greater output and unemployment response. In the CGP model the appreciation of the exchange rate lowers the output response, although the unemployment effect is increased. This occurs as a consequence of the switch of expenditure towards more labour-intensive areas of demand.

Reduction in the rate of VAT

Turning now to indirect taxation, we present the results of reducing the standard rate of VAT by 10 per cent, roughly equivalent to $1\frac{1}{2}$ percentage points. (For LPL it is also necessary to adjust the aggregate tax variable to ensure that the revenue effects of the new rate of VAT are calculated appropriately.) As shown in Table 2.7, the simulation has the expected result of reducing prices in all the models except CUBS and LBS. In the latter model the direct effects of a lower VAT rate are offset by the induced rise in prices consequent on a fall in the exchange rate. Output falls in the CGP model where the exchange rate appreciates. The impact of this on inflation increases real wages and leads to a secondary reduction in wages via the real-wage resistance formulation. Elsewhere output rises by around $\frac{1}{4}$–$\frac{1}{2}$ per cent, with a somewhat larger effect for HMT where the consumer demand reaction is greater. Unemployment effects are less marked for CUBS, NIESR, and BE than for the remaining models. Both

Table 2.7 *VAT simulation*
(10 per cent reduction in the VAT rate)

Year	LBS	NIESR	HMT	BE	CGP	CUBS	LPL
GDP (% difference from base run)							
1	0.2	0.2	0.3	0.1	0.2	—	0.5
2	0.4	0.2	0.5	0.2	−0.5	0.1	0.2
3	0.4	0.3	0.6	0.2	−0.3	0.1	0.2
4	0.3	0.3	0.7		−0.2	—	0.3
5	0.2	0.3	0.7		−0.2	—	0.4
Prices (% difference from base run)							
1	−0.4	−0.7	−0.9	−0.4	−1.5	−0.1	−2.0
2	0.1	−0.7	−1.0	−0.8	−3.2	0.1	−2.8
3	0.8	−0.8	−0.9	−0.9	−3.9	0.4	−3.2
4	1.5	−0.7	−0.5		−4.3	0.9	−3.6
5	2.3	−0.4	—		−4.5	1.5	−3.8
Unemployment (difference from base run, '000)							
1	−17	−9	−9	−8	−45	3	−65
2	−59	−29	−54	−25	−18	−3	−71
3	−89	−48	−93	−35	−3	−7	−87
4	−98	−61	−118		−7	−14	−107
5	−94	−66	−124		−9	−26	−119
Nominal exchange rate (% difference from base run)							
1	−2.9	−0.3	—	—	5.1	−0.2	0.7
2	−2.7	−0.4	−0.3	−0.1	3.5	−0.5	1.1
3	−2.6	−0.3	−0.7	−0.4	3.9	−0.8	1.2
4	−2.9	−0.3	−1.1		4.3	−1.4	1.4
5	−3.4	−0.4	−1.5		4.5	−2.1	1.5

CUBS and BE have weak output effects, whereas the NIESR response reflects the nature of the employment–unemployment relationship rather than a smaller estimate of the employment response.

Compared with out last review, the LBS model now has a stronger, and NIESR a weaker, price response. However, the unemployment and output differences are greater for NIESR. The CGP model now generates falling output. The results from the other models are little changed.

Reduction in the rate of unemployment benefit

The impact of a 10 per cent cut in the rate of unemployment benefit is shown in Table 2.8. Only in the LBS, CUBS, and LPL models does the variable appear in the labour market specification. Its absence from labour market behaviour in the other models often reflects a lack of supporting evidence (e.g. NIESR), although the variable does appear as part of the public sector accounts. In all three models considered, lower benefits result in lower levels of unemployment and prices and higher output, but the

Table 2.8   *Unemployment benefit simulation*
(10 per cent reduction in the rate of benefit)

Year	LBS	CUBS	LPL
GDP (% difference from base run)			
1	−0.1	0.2	1.6
2	−0.3	—	2.0
3	−0.4	−0.1	2.1
4	−0.4	0.3	2.2
5	−0.5	0.4	2.2
Prices (% difference from base run)			
1	−0.3	−0.7	−0.8
2	−1.2	−2.2	−1.6
3	−2.0	−3.2	−2.2
4	−2.8	−6.2	−2.6
5	−3.4	−9.9	−3.0
Unemployment (difference from base run, '000)			
1	−2	−30	−213
2	−34	−57	−387
3	−62	−75	−490
4	−72	−76	−533
5	−70	−32	−526
Nominal exchange rate (% difference from base run)			
1	1.5	0.5	0.3
2	2.6	2.2	−0.1
3	3.8	4.3	−0.3
4	4.8	7.7	−0.4
5	5.7	12.9	−0.4

estimates of CUBS and LBS differ substantially from those of LPL. This is a direct result of a higher coefficient on benefits in the wage/supply equation in the LPL model than in comparable equations in the other models. In the LPL model the fall in benefits is implicitly offset by a lump-sum transfer to consumers. These results are very similar to those derived from the previous vintage of these models.

A reduction of 2 percentage points in short-term nominal interest rates

In this simulation we investigate the effect of reducing short-term nominal interest rates by 2 per cent. Nominal interest rates are endogenous in the LPL and CUBS models, and this experiment is therefore conducted only on the remaining models. In the standard version of the NIESR model it is real interest rates that are exogenous, rather than nominal interest rates. For the purpose of this simulation, we have made real interest rates depend on a given nominal rate. The effects on GDP, prices, and unemployment are shown in Table 2.9. Model responses vary from negligible (NIESR,

Table 2.9 *Interest rate simulation*
(reduction of 2 percentage points in short-term nominal rates)

Year	LBS	NIESR	HMT	BE	CGP
GDP (% difference from base run)					
1	0.7	0.1	0.6	0.1	—
2	1.4	0.1	1.2	0.1	−0.1
3	1.3	0.1	1.5	—	−0.2
4	1.0	0.1	1.4		−0.2
5	0.8	—	1.3		−0.1
Prices (% difference from base run)					
1	0.6	0.2	0.3	—	−0.4
2	2.0	0.1	1.3	−0.1	−1.0
3	3.5	—	2.7	0.2	−1.0
4	5.2	0.1	4.3		−1.0
5	7.0	0.2	5.8		−1.0
Unemployment (difference from base run, '000)					
1	−52	−6	−20	−4	−4
2	−147	−15	−102	−20	1
3	−216	−15	−154	−24	16
4	−234	−13	−146		25
5	−218	−7	−102		26
Nominal exchange rate (% difference from base run)					
1	−7.6	−0.6	−3.4	−0.1	1.4
2	−7.6	—	−5.0	−0.3	1.6
3	−7.7	−0.2	−6.2	−0.6	1.2
4	−8.4	—	−7.2		1.0
5	−9.3	−0.1	−8.1		0.8

BE, and CGP) to substantial (LBS and HMT). In the LBS model output rises sharply in the short run as the exchange rate depreciates in order to maintain uncovered interest parity. The primary expenditure contributions to higher growth are from consumption, and particularly from fixed investment and stockbuilding. The stockbuilding and consumption effects are in part a direct response to lower interest rates, but the impact on non-housing investment arises from induced changes in output and company profits. The price level is some 7 per cent higher after five years, with the level of unemployment 200,000 lower. The HMT model generates a fall in the exchange rate and an increase in output of a similar order of magnitude to that of LBS. Interest rates operate directly on consumption, fixed investment, and stockbuilding. In the LBS model nominal short-term rates determine total consumption, residential investment, and stock levels. In the HMT model, however, it is the nominal long-term interest rate that enters the manufacturing investment equation, while the short-term interest rate influences consumer durables and stockbuilding. Interest rates appear in only one of the NIESR expenditure equations, namely, private housing investment. They affect residential investment, stockbuilding, and durable consumption in the BE model.

For CGP a fall in output occurs as the exchange rate appreciates modestly and investment and exports fall. The rise in the exchange rate is difficult to explain. The stock of money (£M₃) is increased in this simulation, with the exception of LBS, where there is a marginal decline. The rise in the money stock is particularly marked for NIESR: after five years it is 23 per cent higher than in the base run, compared with 1 per cent for BE (after three years) and 4 per cent for HMT.

In the LBS model long-term interest rates rise throughout the simulation, but the long rate adjusted for capital gains *falls* in the first year of the simulation before returning gradually to its base level. In the NIESR model the nominal long-term rate falls by just under half of the fall in the short-term rate, whereas the decline in the long rate is even smaller for HMT and BE.

A reduction of 10 per cent in world oil prices

We consider the results of reducing the world price of oil (in dollars) by 10 per cent while leaving all other indicators of world activity and prices unchanged. Oil prices do not enter the LPL model and so no results are presented in Table 2.10 for this model.

In general, output is increased and unemployment lowered as a consequence of lower oil prices. However, the magnitude of the relative effects across models differ, as does the direction of the price response, according to the reaction of the exchange rate. In the CGP model there is a very sharp decline (owing to the fall in the value of oil reserves), and this generates a relatively high output response together with a higher domestic price level. The exchange rate also falls in the LBS and HMT models, but not so dramatically. Even so, the decline in the rate is sufficient to lead to higher prices, at least by the end of the simulation period. In contrast, there is little exchange rate reaction in the NIESR and BE models and hence little impact on output. A small decline in the price level then reflects the lower cost of imported oil. Despite higher output in the LBS model, the unemployment response is relatively weak as the fall in raw material prices lowers employment requirements per unit of output. The relative oil trade balance term in the CUBS model induces an appreciation in the exchange rate; this lowers inflation, increases growth, and leads to a considerable short-term reduction in unemployment.

2.3 Policy aspects of the simulations

In this section we briefly assemble results from the simulation experiments to illuminate two economic policy questions.

Table 2.10 *Oil price simulation*
(10 per cent reduction in the world price)

Year	LBS	NIESR	HMT	BE	CGP	CUBS
GDP (% difference from base run)						
1	0.2	—	0.1	—	—	0.6
2	0.5	0.1	0.1	—	1.9	1.4
3	0.5	0.1	0.2	0.1	1.3	1.3
4	0.4	0.1	0.1	0.1	0.6	0.9
5	0.3	0.1	0.1		0.4	0.9
Prices (% difference from base run)						
1	−0.3	−0.1	0.1	−0.1	−0.2	−1.1
2	−0.1	−0.2	0.5	−0.4	3.7	−1.7
3	0.3	−0.2	0.8	−0.7	4.0	−2.2
4	0.7	−0.1	1.0	−0.8	3.5	−3.0
5	1.1	—	1.1		2.7	−4.4
Unemployment (difference from base run, '000)						
1	−1	−2	—	—	−5	−248
2	−31	−8	−16	—	−134	−279
3	−59	−14	−20	−2	−223	−189
4	−68	−18	−4	−7	−193	−64
5	−64	−20	12		−166	35
Nominal exchange rate (% difference from base run)						
1	−3.5	−0.4	−1.4	—	—	0.3
2	−2.9	−0.3	−1.8	—	−11.0	1.2
3	−2.6	−0.3	−1.9	−0.1	−6.3	2.4
4	−2.6	−0.3	−1.9	−0.2	−4.7	3.6
5	−2.6	−0.4	−1.9		−3.6	5.1

Balance of payments effects

The balance of payments is an area of economic policy which continues to receive attention, partly in relation to fears of a deteriorating position as domestic oil production declines. It is also related to the de-industrialization debate discussed in Section 2.5. The current account of the balance of payments is not distinguished in the CUBS model, nor in the LPL model in a comparable form to the other models, and hence comparison is limited to the quarterly models and CGP.

Despite the large differences in the exchange rate reaction between the models in the government expenditure simulation, the estimates of the effects on the balance of payments are perhaps surprisingly close. All the models predict a worsening of the current account of between £0.8 and £1.2 billion after three years. There is also unanimity over the direction of current balance effect in the income tax simulation where all the models show a deterioration, with the initial worsening most marked in the LBS model. After three years, the impact is estimated to lie between £0.6 and £0.9 billion. There is some divergence after this point, as LBS predicts a substantial increase in the deficit, whereas CGP suggest a modest improvement. VAT-induced effects are again in the same direction for all the models but with a greater range, from −£1.6 billion (CGP) to −£0.4 billion (LBS) after three years, although in the first year of the simulation the largest impact is given by the LBS, with the weakest effect occurring for CGP. The interest rate simulation generates the most marked difference between the models. A large deterioration (£2$\frac{1}{2}$ billion) occurs for LBS throughout the simulation; the NIESR model predicts a small first-year effect and then an increase in the deficit of £1.1 billion in the second year, climbing to £1.8 billion after five years. The BE model has a slightly smaller effect, but the HMT model produces an initial worsening followed by an improvement, and the CGP model an improvement succeeded by a worsening of the balance.

Lower oil prices induce a fall in the balance of payments in the models of between £0.6 billion (BE) and £1.2 billion (LBS) in the first year of the simulation. But after three years there has been an improvement in the CGP model of a £3.6 billion as a result of the sharp depreciation of the exchange rate, and there is a weaker adverse effect for both LBS and HMT. After five years the HMT and LBS models show a return to base run values, but there is still a net improvement for CGP of £1.3 billion. However, the degree of deterioration in the balance remains constant for BE and NIESR throughout.

In sum, there does seem to be some consensus among the models concerning the balance of payments implications of expansionary fiscal policy, but also some divergence between the models in respect of interest rate and world oil price shocks.

Relative costs per job

In considering the relative merits of alternative methods of generating additional employment, a criterion that often receives attention is the cost per job. In Figure 2.1 we show the costs per job derived from the expenditure and tax simulations. These are defined as the change in the PSBR per 1000 jobs created. Actual costs per job vary quite considerably over the simulation period, and the figures presented are based on an average of the first three years of the simulation in order to provide a more useful comparative guide. The government expenditure simulations reported are those using fixed interest rates or money finance. The lowest cost emerges from the LBS model, where the additional cost to the PSBR is very low. This arises as a result of a large gain in petroleum revenue tax as the pound depreciates against the dollar. The average cost per job is then approximately half that of HMT, which is in turn a little less than NIESR, BE, and CUBS. The CGP model also gives an estimate of the

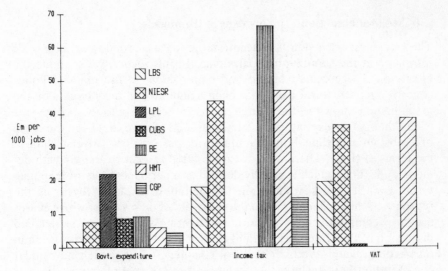

Fig. 2.1   Relative costs per job — average of first three years.

PSBR cost of similar magnitude to that of LBS, whereas LPL shows the highest cost.

Relative costs per job appear to be considerably higher for the income tax reduction. The CUBS model generates the largest cost per job effects, particularly in the first year. Over three years, the average cost is £450,000 per job. The first year cost is also particularly large for NIESR, HMT, and BE (between £80,000 and £125,000 per job), although by the third year of the simulation the range from the models is £16,000–£30,000 per job. Both LBS and CGP give greater cost effects than the equivalent costs for higher government spending, but produce the lowest estimates of cost per job of all the models in the income tax simulation. Costs for the VAT simulation are very small for the BE and LPL models. The estimates from the NIESR and HMT models are smaller than for the income tax simulation but are still larger than the other models, with the exception of CUBS. Estimates of the cost per job for the CUBS model in both the direct and indirect tax simulations are not shown in Figure 2.1 on account of their very high relative size. In contrast, costs per job in the LBS model for this simulation are lower than for the case of an income tax reduction.

In conclusion, there is considerable diversity between the models in the implied cost per job effects of the various fiscal measures, and also substantial variation in these effects over time. In general, however, it appears that average costs per job are lower for increases in government current expenditure than for reductions in income taxes. The implied cost per job for lower VAT appear to lie somewhere between those from the other two simulations.

2.4   Sectoral output and employment in the models

The foregoing discussion is concentrated upon the broad macroeconomic responses in the simulation experiments. In this section we examine the effects on disaggregated output and employment in the models. Policy concern over structural issues has been heightened in recent years by the phenomenon known as the 'Dutch disease'. According to the proponents of this theory, the exploitation of new major oil reserves has been the cause of a substantial decline in the manufacturing base owing to adverse shifts in the terms of trade. The Dutch disease is often associated loosely with de-industrialization, which is usually defined as a permanent loss of manufacturing capacity. A key factor in the de-industrialization theory is the response of the exchange rate to the discovery of oil reserves, which causes a loss in competitiveness in the manufacturing sector. A more detailed discussion of the Dutch disease and the impact of North Sea oil is given in our second review (Wallis *et al.* 1985: Chapter 5). The models now under consideration here include the decline in the UK manufacturing base as part of their sample experience. It is therefore of interest to see how far the incorporation of this information influences the standard responses of the models. We begin by describing the extent of disaggregation. We then outline the methods used to derive sectoral output and employment and proceed to analyse the actual effects derived from the simulations reported in Section 2.2.

Extent of disaggregation

In general, disaggregation is very limited in the UK models. The LPL model analyses the economy as a whole and there is no disaggregation at all. Thus for example, there is no special treatment even for the oil sector, since it is argued that efficient markets adjust for the development (and later the disappearance) of a domestic oil sector, with no overall impact on the level of activity and prices. The CUBS model is much more of a non-market-clearing model and adopts a separate treatment for the oil sector, the traded goods sector, public utilities, dwellings, and government. The price of oil is determined largely by world markets and the output of oil is exogenous. Output and employment in the government sector are derived from exogenous assumptions concerning the growth of public expenditure, and output and employment in public utilities are determined by total output in the economy. The prime relationships in the model are those of output and employment in the traded goods sector.

At the other extreme is the CGP model, where the economy is separated into 39 different industrial activities, each with its own accounting framework. In between we have the four quarterly models, LBS, NIESR, HMT, and BE, who adopt a similar level of disaggregation. All distinguish the oil sector, manufacturing, and general government. LBS, HMT, and BE then have a residual sector which is called 'non-manufacturing' and includes the service sector, agriculture, coal mining, construction, and public utilities. Agriculture and public utilities are defined separately in the NIESR model but output in these sectors is taken to be exogenous. Consequently the main sectors whose behaviour is described by the model are manufacturing and non-manufacturing. This appears to be the lowest common denominator in the models and is the disaggregation we use in the following analysis.

Not all analysis is conducted at this level within the models. For example, the LBS model does not treat separately manufacturing and non-manufacturing investment, nor is the principal behavioural equation for imports broken down in this way. Only aggregate earnings are distinguished in the NIESR model, and in general price disaggregation relates only to manufactured goods. A distinctive feature of the latest vintage of the NIESR model is the disaggregation of the employment–unemployment relationship, where labour in the manufacturing sector is assumed to have a lower propensity to register as unemployed than that in non-manufacturing.

Approaches to disaggregation

In most of the models, where disaggregation occurs it is usually as a matter of convenience or necessity. Thus we observe that not all components of the manufacturing/non-manufacturing sectors are modelled consistently. However, in the CGP model disaggregation is a methodological issue. Although there are some aggregate relationships, such as consumption and wages, the essence of the approach is to derive both sectoral output and the level of GDP by summation over the individual industries. Each industry is modelled separately using behavioural relationships and accounting identities. Relationships between sectors through intermediate demand flows are derived by input–output analysis. In contrast, the other models ignore intermediate demand and determine net rather than gross output. Sectoral output is derived by breaking down GDP into constituent parts (the top-down approach), whereas the CGP model builds up GDP from its constituents (the bottom-up approach).

The LBS, NIESR, and HMT models use input–output weights and the expenditure components of GDP to calculate the level of output in the manufacturing sector. Fixed weights are used so that the assumption is that the marginal weight of manufacturing in total consumption, say, is equal to the average weight. Manufacturing output then typically drives employment, investment, and stockbuilding in the models so that the manufacturing output relationship plays a simultaneous rather than a purely recursive role. It should be noted that often very aggregate expenditure items enter into the manufacturing output relationship. Although the models separate out consumer durables from non-durables, for example, the information gain from allowing for a different contribution to manufacturing output is not always exploited in the output relationship (for example, LBS, NIESR). The particular weights chosen for the LBS equation (see Table 2.11), which are also typical of those for NIESR and HMT, imply that manufacturing output increases by only 0.4 per cent if all the expenditure elements (and hence GDP) each increase by 1 per cent. Thus there is a built-in tendency in the models for balanced expansion to be relatively detrimental to the manufacturing sector. The nature of the weights also implies that expenditure has to be biased towards stockbuilding or net trade (export less imports) in order for manufacturing output to sustain its share in GDP. The relatively low weight on fixed investment reflects the role of investment in buildings which determines construction sector output.

Table 2.11   *The determination of manufacturing output in the models (weights on expenditure variables)*

	LBS	NIESR	HMT	BE
Consumption	0.198	0.195	0.131 (total)	0.23 (non-durables)
			0.302 (clothing, durables)	0.9 (durables)
			0.143 (food, drink, tobacco)	
Government current expenditure	0.328*	0.170	0.347*	0.18
Fixed investment	0.386	0.390	0.31	0.6 (priv. non-housing)
			0.28 (plant, machinery)	0.3 (priv. housing)
				0.47 (govt. non-housing)
				0.44 (govt. housing)
Stockbuilding	0.600	0.660		0.6 (mats., fuel)
				0.9 (distributors)
				0.6 (other)
Exports	0.436	1.0 (manufactures)	0.65 (manufactures)	1.0 (manufactures)
				0.9 (other)
Imports	−0.296	−1.0 (manufactures)	−0.654 (manufactures)	
Factor cost adjustment	−0.230	—		

* procurement

Output in non-manufacturing is derived as a residual given GDP and manufacturing output.

The BE model allocates GDP to manufacturing and non-manufacturing through a two-stage approach. In the first stage the total demand for manufactures is calculated using a weighting method similar to that of the other models but ignoring the import contribution and exploiting some of the other disaggregated information in the model. In the second stage the share of imports in total demand is derived from an equation that has relative prices as one of its determinants.

The determination of employment at the sectoral level in the models is described in Chapter 5.

Simulation results

We now examine the responses of output and employment in manufacturing and non-manufacturing in the simulation experiments. For the CGP model these are computed by aggregating across the relevant 23 industrial sectors to give a manufacturing total, taking non-manufacturing as the

Table 2.12 *Sectoral output and employment effects: LBS model (differences from base run)*

Year	Output %			Employment %		'000	
	GDP	Mfg	Non-mfg	Mfg	Non-mfg	Mfg	Non-mfg
Government expenditure							
1	0.7	0.4	0.3	0.2	0.1	13	10
3	1.0	0.9	0.5	0.9	0.4	48	47
5	1.0	0.8	0.7	1.3	0.5	71	55
Income tax rate							
1	0.2	0.3	0.3	0.2	0.1	13	9
3	0.7	1.0	0.7	1.1	0.5	57	60
5	0.7	0.8	0.9	1.5	0.8	84	90
VAT							
1	0.2	0.3	0.3	0.2	0.1	13	12
3	0.4	0.6	0.3	0.7	0.7	38	84
5	0.2	0.2	0.3	0.5	0.9	29	106
Interest rates							
1	0.7	1.0	0.8	0.6	0.3	32	30
3	1.3	2.0	1.3	2.1	1.5	116	179
5	0.8	1.1	0.9	2.1	1.6	111	201
Oil prices							
1	0.3	0.3	0.3	−0.1	0.1	−5	8
3	0.5	0.8	0.3	0.6	0.4	35	43
5	0.3	0.4	0.4	0.8	0.4	42	48

aggregation of the remaining 15 non-oil sectors. We analyse the results in two ways: first, we consider the results from each model in order to see whether different exogenous shocks have different sectoral implications; second, we analyse the results across the models in order to observe whether sectoral effects differ between models for the same exogenous shock. The results are shown in Tables 2.12–2.16. Given that the non-manufacturing sector is somewhat larger than the manufacturing sector, we give employment responses in both absolute and percentage deviations from the base run.

We turn first to the results from the LBS model (Table 2.12). In the government expenditure simulation there is an implicit increase in output of the public sector; consequently, both manufacturing and non-manufacturing output increase less than GDP. The rise in manufacturing output is greater than that in non-manufacturing initially, as the sharp fall in the real exchange rate boosts net trade, which is favourable to manufacturing output. After five years, however, the initial impetus weakens and the differential output effect is considerably less. Employment in manufacturing is still adjusting to the peak effect on output after five years so that the balance of employment effects continues to favour manufacturing. In terms of absolute effects on employment the difference between sectors is negligible, however. The exchange rate adjustment in the income tax simulation also favours manufacturing output with a similar peaked reaction to that under the government expenditure simulation. Here the manufacturing employment response is somewhat greater relative to that of output by the end of the simulation, but although the percentage response of manufacturing employment is almost twice that of non-manufacturing after five years, there is yet again little difference between relative employment effects when measured as deviations in the numbers employed.

Even though the scale of GDP effects differs between the simulations, there is a pronounced tendency for the impact to favour manufacturing output relative to non-manufacturing. This is not surprising, given that the exchange rate falls in each case and thus gives a (temporary) boost to net trade. The relative impact is weakest for the VAT and oil price simulations, where the decline in the exchange rate is more modest than in the other simulations. The relative proportional employment responses largely follow from those of output with the exception of the VAT experiment. The fall in manufacturing employment in the oil price simulation occurs as a result of the change in the price of inputs relative to the price of manufactured output. In both the VAT and interest rate simulations the absolute deviations of employment are far greater for non-manufacturing than for manufacturing. The LBS sectoral results therefore reflect the macro responses, and in particular the exchange rate adjustment. Given that this has a primary effect on net trade, output in the manufacturing sector is affected to a greater extent than non-manufacturing output.

Table 2.13 *Sectoral output and employment effects: NIESR model (differences from base run)*

Year	Output %			Employment %		'000	
	GDP	Mfg	Non-mfg	Mfg	Non-mfg	Mfg	Non-mfg
Government expenditure							
1	0.7	0.6	0.1	0.1	—	6	3
3	0.7	0.6	—	0.2	0.1	10	7
5	0.6	0.5	−0.1	−0.1	—	−6	3
Income tax rate							
1	0.1	0.2	0.4	0.1	0.2	4	14
3	0.4	0.4	0.6	0.2	0.8	12	72
5	0.4	0.5	0.6	−0.1	1.4	−4	134
VAT							
1	0.2	0.2	0.3	0.1	0.1	7	11
3	0.3	0.3	0.5	0.7	0.6	36	55
5	0.3	0.4	0.5	0.7	1.2	39	109
Interest rates							
1	0.1	0.2	—	0.1	—	7	1
3	0.1	0.1	0.1	0.2	0.1	13	8
5	—	0.1	—	0.1	0.1	4	9
Oil prices							
1	—	0.1	—	—	—	2	1
3	0.1	0.2	0.1	0.2	0.1	11	11
5	0.1	0.3	0.1	0.2	0.3	13	25

The comparable NIESR results are given in Table 2.13. In the absence of such a strong exchange rate reaction in this model, the effects on output are not so biased towards manufacturing. Indeed, a marked bias of this kind appears only in the government expenditure simulation. In the income tax simulation, output effects are strongest in the service sector as consumers' expenditure is boosted. The other simulations produce a balanced effect on sectoral outputs. The response of non-manufacturing employment is greater than that of output in the income tax and VAT simulations. In the latter, for example, employment is $1\frac{1}{4}$ per cent higher after five years compared with an increase in output of $\frac{1}{2}$ per cent. This may reflect the dynamics in the equation since the long-run output elasticity is only 0.6 (compared with the equivalent elasticity of 1.5 for manufacturing).

Sectoral effects for the HMT model are shown in Table 2.14. Here the impact on manufacturing output is at best equal to that of non-manufacturing, but is often weaker. In particular, the VAT simulation is biased more towards non-manufacturing output. This is a consequence of increased

Table 2.14   *Sectoral output and employment effects: HMT model
(differences from base run)*

Year	Output %			Employment %		'000	
	GDP	Mfg	Non-mfg	Mfg	Non-mfg	Mfg	Non-mfg
Government expenditure							
1	0.7	0.2	0.3	0.1	0.1	6	15
3	0.7	0.3	0.4	0.3	0.2	15	35
5	0.5	0.1	0.2	—	−0.1	−2	−9
Income tax rate							
1	0.2	0.2	0.2	0.1	0.1	3	10
3	0.3	0.4	0.4	0.5	0.4	25	56
5	0.3	0.4	0.5	0.6	0.5	31	71
VAT							
1	0.3	0.2	0.4	—	0.1	2	12
3	0.6	0.5	0.8	0.7	0.7	37	101
5	0.7	0.5	1.0	1.0	0.9	48	135
Interest rates							
1	0.6	0.8	0.7	0.2	0.1	13	16
3	1.5	1.7	1.9	1.7	0.9	89	138
5	1.3	1.3	1.8	1.6	0.5	78	74
Oil prices							
1	0.1	0.1	0.1	—	—	—	1
3	0.2	0.2	0.2	0.1	0.2	6	23
5	0.1	0.1	0.1	−0.5	—	−26	7

expenditure on consumption and investment goods. There is greater variation in the output–employment response across sectors for this model, however. In several simulations the proportional response of non-manufacturing is weaker than that of manufacturing despite a stronger relative output effect. This is most apparent in the VAT and interest rate simulations. It does not seem possible to explain this feature in terms of real-wage movements, given that real wages rise in both simulations and that the real-wage elasticity is higher for manufacturing than for non-manufacturing. Nevertheless, the absolute increase in non-manufacturing employment consistently exceeds that of manufacturing in the simulations with this model.

Results for the BE model are shown in Table 2.15. It is more difficult to discern relative sectoral differences from this model since the scale of GDP effects is much smaller than for the other models. There does appear to be a tendency towards a higher manufacturing output response throughout the simulations, however, and this translates directly into employment. In some cases this implies a greater absolute increase in employment in

Table 2.15 *Sectoral output and employment effects: BE model (differences from base run)*

Year	Output %			Employment %		'000	
	GDP	Mfg	Non-mfg	Mfg	Non-mfg	Mfg	Non-mfg
Government expenditure							
1	0.6	0.3	0.2	0.1	0.1	7	10
3	0.7	0.6	0.2	0.4	0.1	23	24
5							
Income tax rate							
1	0.1	0.1	0.2	0.1	0.1	3	8
3	0.3	0.5	0.3	0.4	0.3	21	39
5							
VAT							
1	0.1	0.2	0.1	0.1	0.1	4	9
3	0.2	0.4	0.2	0.4	0.2	21	28
5							
Interest rates							
1	0.1	0.2	—	0.1	—	8	−3
3	—	—	—	0.5	—	29	1
5							
Oil prices							
1	—	—	—	—	—	1	−1
3	0.1	0.2	—	0.1	−0.1	7	−6
5							

manufacturing than for non-manufacturing, contrary to the experience of the other models.

Finally, we turn to the results for the CGP model (Table 2.16). Here we observe a fall in manufacturing output in several of the simulations. This occurs largely where the exchange rate appreciates in response to an exogenous shock (the reverse of the LBS case). Thus, trade performance is weakened and this adversely affects the manufacturing sector. Only in one case, the oil price simulation, does manufacturing output improve more (or deteriorate less) than that of non-manufacturing, and here the exchange rate declines sharply. In general, therefore, the proportionate employment responses are weaker for manufacturing relative to non-manufacturing in this model, and hence the absolute increase in manufacturing employment is considerably smaller than that for non-manufacturing.

We can summarize the sectoral results so far as follows. The LBS model tends to favour the manufacturing sector in terms of output across the simulations, mainly on account of the exchange rate depreciation in this model. This favours manufacturing through the trade response. In con-

Table 2.16   *Sectoral output and employment effects: CGP model (differences from base run)*

Year	Output %			Employment %		'000	
	GDP	Mfg	Non-mfg	Mfg	Non-mfg	Mfg	Non-mfg
Government expenditure							
1	0.6	−0.3	0.2	−0.1	0.1	−3	15
3	0.5	−0.2	0.3	—	0.2	—	34
5	0.6	−0.2	0.3	0.1	0.3	4	43
Income tax rate							
1	0.2	0.1	0.2	0.4	0.3	23	38
3	0.1	−0.1	0.2	0.6	0.5	31	68
5	0.2	—	0.1	0.8	0.6	44	92
VAT							
1	0.2	0.3	0.2	0.4	0.2	22	27
3	−0.3	−0.9	−0.3	−0.1	—	−8	6
5	−0.2	−0.6	−0.3	—	0.1	−2	14
Interest rates							
1	—	0.1	0.1	0.1	—	5	—
3	−0.2	−0.4	−0.2	−0.2	−0.1	−10	−7
5	−0.1	−0.2	−0.1	−0.3	−0.1	−14	−14
Oil prices							
1	—	0.2	—	—	—	2	3
3	1.3	2.9	1.3	2.1	0.9	120	119
5	0.4	0.9	0.5	1.7	0.6	90	89

trast, the CGP results favour non-manufacturing output in general since the exchange rate adjustment is the reverse of that for LBS. The NIESR and HMT simulations tend to produce a more balanced output effect across the sectors since expenditure changes are more balanced than for LBS or CGP. However, the relative employment responses differ, in that for NIESR the response is stronger for non-manufacturing employment than for output with the reverse occurring for HMT. In terms of absolute employment effects, the LBS model produces the largest differential in favour of non-manufacturing for the VAT and interest rate simulations and this is supported by the HMT results. The NIESR simulations reveal that the income tax and VAT simulations induce the greatest differential in favour of non-manufacturing employment, and the CGP model produces this effect for the income tax simulation. The differential employment effects are all small for BE, with the most pronounced effect once again occurring for the income tax simulation. The LBS model gives the largest impact on manufacturing sector employment in the income tax simulations and the NIESR model the smallest. The former arises from the exchange rate decline, whereas the weakness of the NIESR result is due to the employment response relative to that of output. In contrast, the CGP model has a weak output but stronger employment reaction. There is less discrepancy between the estimates of the impact on non-manufacturing employment in the income tax case. For the VAT simulation the main difference is between the responses of BE and CGP and the other models. The exchange rate rise leads to a fall in output in both sectors for CGP.

Concluding comment

In this section we have examined the extent of sectoral disaggregation of output and employment in the models and described the approaches used. There is a clear contrast between both the extent and the method of disaggregation in the CGP model and the other models. In aggregating over the 39 industries of the CGP model to obtain the sectoral estimates, we lose some of the richness of information given by the individual industrial responses. Some quite marked compositional effects are present within these aggregate sectors in the simulations. Taking the VAT simulation as an example, the aggregate fall in manufacturing output after five years is 0.6 per cent and for non-manufacturing is 0.3 per cent. Within manufacturing, the range lies between +0.7 and −4.0 per cent, however, and within non-manufacturing between +0.2 and −4.1 per cent. Similar effects are observed in the other simulations.

Although the methods of disaggregation adopted are similar for many of the other models, the simulation responses in terms of manufacturing and non-manufacturing output and employment differ quite substantially. A key element in these differences is the behaviour of the exchange rate and its effect on net trade. Where the simulations generate a depreciating exchange rate, this tends to favour manufacturing output relative to that of non-manufacturing. Where an exchange rate effect is absent, the models tend to produce a balanced change in output in both sectors with the exception of the income tax and VAT simulations, which tend to be more favourable to non-manufacturing on account of the bias in expenditure change towards consumption. Employment implications follow in general from those of output, although there are one or two major exceptions to this (e.g., HMT for interest rates, NIESR for income tax).

Despite the difficulties in using existing macro-models to test hypotheses concerning the Dutch disease (see Chapter 5 of our second review), it does appear at least that the impact of alternative shocks on the manufacturing sector is dependent on the response of the exchange rate. Some of the overshooting features associated with the literature on the Dutch disease are apparent. However, the exchange rate movements can be initiated by changes in monetary and fiscal policy, rather than by structural factors, such as the extraction of new oil reserves, implying that the development of the manufacturing sector is not entirely dependent on structural features of the economy.

2.5   Terminal conditions in rational expectations models

In our second review we discussed the role of terminal conditions in large-scale nonlinear macroeconomic models with rational or forward-consistent expectations, with reference to the LPL model, then the only model to contain such a feature. We now have three models in which rational expectations appear — the LPL, LBS, and NIESR models — and so it is necessary to update and extend this discussion to include the two quarterly models. First we consider the sensitivity of the base solution, and then we examine the impact on the simulation responses.

Terminal conditions and the base solution

In models that contain expectations of future values of endogenous variables, such as the expected exchange rate, a consistent solution is generated by setting the expected value equal to the actual outcome of the model solution in the future period. At the last point in the solution, an expectation of a value outside the solution period is required. In order for a unique solution for the model to exist, this value must be determined in some manner. In general, it is desirable that models should inherently possess only one stable solution path, and this terminal condition should therefore be chosen to be consistent with the likely stable solution trajectory. The two main methods of imposing terminal conditions are to use equilibrium conditions derived from prior knowledge of the model structure, or endogenous conditions which specify a constant rate of growth in order to approximate the stable solution path of the model. Both methods depend on sufficient time elapsing so that the model has settled to its appropriate state — approximate equilibrium or the stable path towards equilibrium, respectively. A longer solution period is generally required to reach level (equilibrium) conditions than is necessary for growth conditions. It is an empirical question whether the time horizon is sufficiently long for any given conditions. The use of equilibrium (or level) terminal conditions poses an additional problem in that an innapropriate choice may lead to distortions from the stable solution path as the solution approaches the terminal date. By varying the terminal date we can judge the sensitivity of the solution path, which in turn determines how much of the solution can be regarded as a genuine product of the model rather than a product of the assumptions regarding terminal conditions.

Changes in the type of terminal condition, together with evidence from the different solution periods, can also suggest whether or not a unique stable solution path exists, since the solution algorithm may select an unstable solution if no stable solution exists, or an arbitrary solution if there were to be multiple stable solution paths.

All three models are tested for sensitivity to the terminal date by progressively shortening the solution period, and for sensitivity to alternative level or growth conditions by substituting for the existing terminal conditions.

The LPL model

The LPL model uses a set of terminal conditions based on the properties of the underlying theoretical model. The expectational variables in the model and their terminal conditions are given in Table 2.17. In our previous review we found that the use of equilibrium terminal conditions caused a serious distortion of the stable solution path for up to six years prior to the terminal date, mainly owing to the requirement that the real exchange rate should reach its equilibrium value despite the fact that the model itself produced a wedge between the actual and equilibrium exchange rate. Consequently the actual exchange rate was required to jump towards the equilibrium level five periods before the terminal date. This distortion has now been removed (see Figure 2.2) by basing the terminal condition for the expected real exchange rate on the *growth rate* of the equilibrium exchange rate. The solution is now very insensitive to a change in the terminal date. A distinctive pattern in the last five years of the simulation remains, owing to the five-year-ahead expectations of the inflation rate and the real exchange rate. In addition, there is a small blip in the final period as real debt interest, which either falls or is constant for most of the solution, is required to grow in line with GDP. These effects are very small, however, and the entire solution period can be used for analysis of the model. Nor is the solution path very sensitive to a switch to constant growth terminal conditions. The main choice between equilibrium and

Table 2.17 *Expectational variables and terminal conditions in the LPL model*

Expectational variables	Terminal conditions (T denotes the last time period of the solution)
Capacity utilization	Measured as deviation from trend output and projected at zero
Real debt interest	Projected by its value in period T times the growth of equilibrium GDP at period T
Real exchange rate 1 year ahead 5 years ahead	Projected forward 5 periods by its value in period T plus the growth of the equilibrium level of the real exchange rate
Inflation 1 year ahead 5 years ahead	Projected forward 5 periods at constant value using the value of the exogenous PSBR/GDP ratio at period T

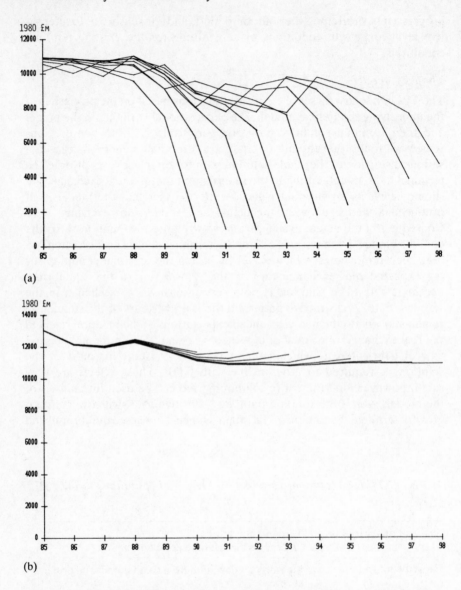

(a)

(b)

Fig. 2.2   Sensitivity of LPL model to terminal dates. (a) Real debt interest, 1984
forecast; (b) Real debt interest, 1985 forecast.

endogenous growth rate terminal conditions for this model rests on their
relative ease of use in situations where alternative simulations are undertaken which require changes to the equilibrium position of the model and
hence to the terminal conditions.

The LBS model

This model contains three rational expectations terms, each with a one quarter lead. These variables all appear in the financial sector and represent asset prices; namely, the price of gilts, the price of equities, and the price of overseas assets (the exchange rate) (see Table 2.18). The gilt price

Table 2.18   *Expectational variables and terminal conditions in the LBS model*

Expectational variables	Terminal conditions
Gilt price	Constant level, quarter-on-quarter
Equity price	Constant rate of growth, quarter-on-quarter
Overseas assets price	Constant rate of growth, quarter-on-quarter

is projected at a constant level and the other two variables at a constant rate of growth. The base solutions for two of these variables are shown in Figure 2.3, and the sensitivity of one of the major endogenous variables in the model (GDP) and one of the expectational variables (the price of gilts) to the terminal date are shown in Figure 2.4. The early part of the solution can be seen to be relatively insensitive to the terminal date, suggesting that a unique (stable) solution path has been selected. However, there is more variation towards the end of the solution path, the range of effects on GDP being around $1\frac{1}{2}$ per cent. Considerable variation can be observed in the

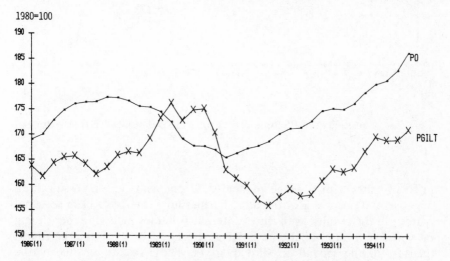

1980=100

Fig. 2.3   LBS forecast base: price of gilts (PGILT) and price of overseas assets (PO).

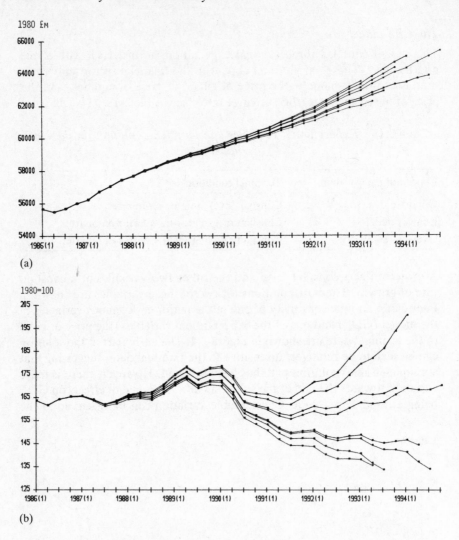

Fig. 2.4   Sensitivity of LBS forecast base to terminal dates. (a) GDP; (b) Price of gilts.

price of gilts, with a range of nearly 50 per cent, encompassing both negative and positive growth paths. Furthermore, there is a clear seasonal pattern in the results, with three different solutions emerging, depending on whether the terminal date is the first quarter of the year, the fourth quarter, or the second or third quarters. These results are due to the seasonal nature of the base solution itself in combination with the choice of terminal conditions.

The three variables of which expectations are formed all have seasonal patterns in the base solution. Such seasonality can be introduced into a model solution, even when the model is estimated and solved with seasonally adjusted data, via an exogenous seasonal input, such as regular annual uprating of tax allowances and duties. Seasonality in one part of a simultaneous equation model is in general transmitted to all jointly determined variables, and we observe a small degree of seasonality in all the endogenous variables in the LBS base solution. There may also be some effects from the use of seasonally unadjusted data in the financial sector. Where expectations variables use a terminal condition specifying a constant level or constant quarter-on-quarter growth (that is, $\hat{y}_t = \hat{y}_{t-1}$ or $\hat{y}_t/\hat{y}_{t-1} = \hat{y}_{t-1}/\hat{y}_{t-2}$, the time index denoting quarters) then the solution automatically becomes sensitive to the terminal date when these conditions do not match the seasonal pattern. In the case of the LBS model we can predict the resulting distortion. For example, the price of both equities and gilts fall in the second quarter of each year, rise modestly in the third quarter, and rise quite steeply in the first and fourth quarters (see Figure 2.3). With constant quarter-on-quarter growth terminal conditions, we expect an overshoot of the long-run solution path when the terminal date is based on the first quarter, an undershooting when the second or third quarter is chosen, and a fairly accurate estimate when the fourth quarter is used. Since the terminal date in the base solution uses the fourth quarter, this ought to be the most reliable guide to the long-run solution path.

An alternative method of dealing with quarterly models that exhibit seasonal variation is to express terminal conditions in annual differences. Thus, the requirement of a constant level is expressed as $\hat{y}_t = \hat{y}_{t-4}$ and that of a constant growth rate as $\hat{y}_t/\hat{y}_{t-4} = \hat{y}_{t-4}/\hat{y}_{t-8}$. In Figure 2.5 we examine the impact of such alternative conditions, which we term 'seasonally adjusted conditions'. We show the results of using the existing LBS conditions, which are a combination of one level and two growth rate conditions; constant level conditions for all three variables; and constant growth rate conditions for all three variables. We also show results from these three possibilities expressed in seasonally adjusted form, giving six possibilities in all. We examine both the full solution period and a reduced period which is ten quarters shorter. It is seen that the three seasonally adjusted conditions are fairly closely grouped, with the variants that neglect seasonal influences (A–C) more widely spread. The sensitivity of the other endogenous variables in the model is also greatly reduced by the use of seasonally adjusted terminal conditions (D–F), with a maximum spread of only 0.08 per cent of GDP between the seasonal variants, compared with more than 1 per cent for the non-seasonally corrected alternatives. Thus, taking account of seasonality leaves the model much less sensitive to the type of condition employed.

We consider next the effectiveness of the various terminal conditions in

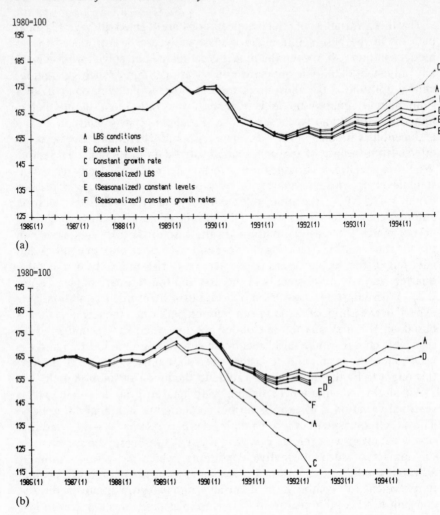

Fig. 2.5   Impact of alternative terminal conditions on the price of gilts in the LBS
forecast base. (a) Full solution period; (b) Reduced solution period.

the face of a shorter solution horizon. The constant growth conditions
based on quarter-to-quarter change (C) clearly do worst. They project the
downward trend of 1989(4)–1991(2) and in addition diverge further as the
solution ends in the second quarter. The fact that the stable growth path
for the model does not appear to be achieved until after 1991(2) leads us to
expect that all of the terminal conditions will be slightly distorted. However, the case identified above, together with the actual LBS conditions,
show the greatest divergence. The constant level conditions do better,

given that the long-run solution path becomes relatively flat after 1991(2) and the choice of the second quarter terminal date favours this condition when seasonal influences are present. Seasonally adjusted conditions (D,F) give much better performance than their unadjusted counterparts. Even the constant growth condition (F), which performs least well, shows divergence only over the last four quarters.

The LBS base solution extends to 1994(4), and this is used to generate a published forecast up to 1990(4). The overall length of the solution period is sufficient to ensure that it is a close approximation to the solution path and the base forecast would not be greatly altered with different terminal conditions. However, if terminal conditions were used that eliminated the seasonal fluctuations, then the base forecast could be produced from a solution period extending only to 1992(2), with consequent savings in computation time. In general, the use of such terminal conditions enables fewer solution periods to be discarded in order to analyse alternative long-run simulation paths of the model.

The NIESR model

The NIESR model contains forward expectations terms in 11 endogenous variables, with leads of up to four quarters on each variable. Definitions and descriptions of the terminal conditions used are given in Table 2.19.

Table 2.19 *Expectational variables and terminal conditions in the NIESR model*

Expectational variables
  Output index (GDP)
  Output index (manufacturing)
  Output index (other)
  Output index (mainly public)
  Consumer price index
  Wholesale price of manufactures
  Average earnings
  Personal disposable income
  Interest rate on local authority debt
  Nominal effective exchange rate
  Rate of employers' national insurance contribution
  (All have leads of up to 4 quarters ahead)
Terminal condition
  All use a constant rate of growth, quarter-on-quarter, except for the nominal effective exchange rate, which is calculated from

$$\log (EFFRAT_{T+1}PWMF_{T+1}/PF6_{T+1})$$
$$= \log (EFFRAT_{T0}PWMF_{T0}/PF6_{T0}) + 1.75\log (EX_T M_{T0}/EX_{T0}M_T)$$

  where $EFFRAT$ is the real exchange rate, $PWMF$ the wholesale price of manufactures, $PF6$ is exogenous world wholesale prices, projected at constant rate of growth, EX is total exports, M is total imports, T the last solution period, and $T0$ the last *historical* period.

With the exception of the exchange rate, these are all generated by a quarter-on-quarter growth rate. (This seems to be inappropriate for the local authority interest rate variable.)

The real exchange rate equation is crucial both to the model as a whole and to an analysis of the role of terminal conditions in this model. It can be written thus:

$$\ln \varrho_t = 0.102\ln \varrho_{t-1} + (1 - 0.102)\ln \varrho_{t+1} + 0.009 \, (\Delta i_t^{UK} - \Delta i_t^{W})$$

where ϱ is the real effective exchange rate, i^{UK} is the real UK interest rate, and i^W is the real world interest rate, with both interest rate variables exogenous. No other endogenous variable enters the exchange rate equation. It has a unit root, so the equation does not have a unique stable solution, neither backward-looking nor forward-looking, but simply defines a trajectory from a given initial condition to a given terminal state. With the former given by historical observations, the solution for the real exchange rate is entirely dependent on the terminal conditions.

One problem with the base solution is that the final period contains an additive residual for the real exchange rate. This is pre-recursive to the rest of the model, and an adjustment to the final period value is equivalent to a change in the terminal condition. Since the solution is so dependent on the terminal value, the whole solution trajectory for the real rate can be controlled by this method. The residual appears to have been chosen to ensure that the real exchange rate remains constant over the forecast horizon. The presence of a single residual at the end of the solution period creates difficulties in assessing the long-run solution path. One might usually assume that all exogenous variables and adjustments are themselves on stable trajectories immediately prior to the terminal date, otherwise the endogenous variables are unlikely to be on stable trajectories. If we change the solution period by one quarter, we find that the solution for the nominal exchange rate (e) in the final period falls by 20 per cent. This effect then dominates the analysis of sensitivity.

The residual on the real exchange rate cannot be removed independently of all other adjustments without the model failing to solve. Therefore we take a base solution one period shorter than the full forecast. All results are then presented as deviations from the base solution ending in 1990(4).

In Figure 2.6 we show the effects on the nominal exchange rate, GDP, and the price level of successively shortening the solution period. The results are quite striking in three ways. First, substantial deviations occur in every period for both GDP and the nominal exchange rate, including the first period. This is symptomatic of the unit root on the real exchange rate. The fact that there is an initial period difference which is smaller than the final period difference reflects the invariant initial condition and the coefficient on the forward expectation of the real exchange rate of 0.9 (as opposed to the lag coefficient of 0.1). Hence the terminal condition is

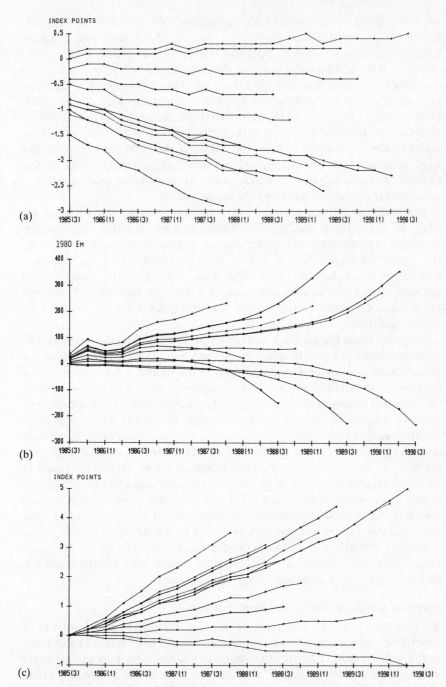

Fig. 2.6   Sensitivity of NIESR forecast base to terminal dates. (a) Effective
exchange rate; (b) GDP; (c) Price level.

relatively more important than the initial condition, although the solution path is tied down at both ends. Second, the size of the deviations from the base are substantial — up to 3 points on the nominal exchange rate, $\frac{1}{2}$ per cent for GDP, and up to 5 points on the price level, yielding an increase in the annual inflation rate of over $\frac{3}{4}$ per cent. Third, there is an even more pronounced seasonal pattern in the results than in the LBS model. Solutions ending in the third or fourth quarters produce relatively small differences in the nominal exchange rate, whereas those ending in the first or second show a substantial drop. For GDP, those solutions ending in the third or fourth quarters deviate substantially only in the last four or five periods, whereas solutions finishing in the first or second quarters show a much larger deviation, and over the whole period.

Explanations for the seasonal variations are very similar to those for LBS. In the NIESR model, all terminal conditions other than on the exchange rate are generated by quarter-on-quarter growth rates. Whatever the source of seasonality, it affects all the variables in a simultaneous system, as is evident in the NIESR base solution. For example, real personal disposable income has a distinct seasonal pattern and, in most years, shows a steep increase from the first quarter to the second (the budget quarter).

We now repeat the exercise conducted with the LBS model, namely, the substitution of seasonally adjusted growth rate terminal conditions for those conditions currently incorporated in the model. This is done for all expectational variables except the real exchange rate. As discussed above, this terminal condition plays a completely different role. The imposition of the new conditions on the solution ending in 1990(4) has a significant effect, reducing the nominal exchange rate by about two points. If we then compare these two types of terminal condition with solutions ending in 1989(2), we find that taking seasonality into account yields a deviation in the nominal exchange rate of no more than 0.36 point from its longer-run counterpart, whereas the figure is 2.5 points for the comparison with non-seasonally corrected conditions. The sensitivity of GDP is reduced from £387 to £105 million and for CPI from 4.4 to 0.4 percentage point. The remaining sensitivity of the model is due to the unit root on the exchange rate. The overall sensitivity of the model to different terminal dates is clearly reduced by taking seasonality into account.

Terminal conditions and simulation responses

We now turn from the sensitivity of the base solution to the sensitivity of simulation analysis, where we compare the results of a base solution and a perturbed solution. Clearly, the sensitivity with respect to the terminal date applies to both solutions, and the issue is whether or not any effect cancels out. We have already concluded that the base solution of the LPL model is insensitive to the terminal date. The main question for this model therefore is whether sensitivity may be induced in a simulation because of the equilibrium terminal conditions.

The main simulation exercise that we use is the government expenditure simualtion reported in Section 2.3, namely, an increase of £386 million per quarter (1980 prices), balanced equally between procurement and employment expenditure. For the NIESR and LBS models the financing assumption is one of fixed interest rates (real rates for NIESR). However, in examining the sensitivity of the LPL model to different terminal conditions we use a bond finance assumption. The reason for the different assumptions is that the permanent money finance rule in the LPL model automatically adjusts the terminal condition appropriately in the model and this is therefore an uninteresting case to explore.

In the LPL model, under bond finance the use of equilibrium conditions prompts the question as to whether a permanent government expenditure increase is consistent with these conditions. If it is not, then either the expenditure increase is required to be temporary or the terminal (equilibrium) conditions in the model need to be adjusted. We examine this issue by imposing an increase in government spending under existing LPL equilibrium conditions and then alternatively using constant-rate-of-growth terminal conditions. The two types of terminal condition both yield very similar answers to those shown in Table 2.3. This suggests that the permanent increase in government spending does not automatically violate the 'equilibrium' terminal conditions. Since bond financing is assumed, this implies that, when looking at the model as a whole, a simulation of permanent bond-financed government expenditure is not inconsistent with the equilibrium conditions of the model as embodied in the terminal constraints, at least over a 14-year time horizon. The possibility of instability under bond finance in theoretical macroeconomic models is well known: this is often charactertized by an accelerating increase in debt interest payments. In the case of the LPL model we observe a steady accumulation of real debt interest (11 per cent over the base level by 1998). This eventually leads to a fall in the GDP multiplier, but the effects are very sluggish. Although the behaviour of real debt interest itself is inconsistent with the equilibrium condition in the model (where it is required to rise in line with GDP), the effects of this transgression do not appear to be important for the rest of the model within this period. In contrast, simulations that generate conflict with the other terminal conditions, in particular the rate of inflation, are much more likely to cause major distortions in the model solution, because these other variables have a much more pervasive influence throughout the rest of the model.

For the LBS and NIESR models we compare the sensitivity of the simulation results when run over two different solution periods and then we consider how far we can reduce this sensitivity by taking account of seasonal influences. This yields four sets of results which are given in

Table 2.20   *Sensitivity of simulation results to terminal dates and seasonality: LBS*

Year	Short solution period		Long solution period	
	LBS conditons	Seasonal conditions	LBS conditions	Seasonal conditions
GDP (% difference from base run)				
1	0.64	0.66	0.67	0.66
2	0.83	0.90	0.92	0.89
3	0.95	0.99	1.01	0.98
4	1.00	0.96	0.99	0.97
5	0.99	0.91	0.97	0.92
6	0.96	0.85	0.92	0.86
7			0.85	0.83
8			0.77	0.79
9			0.71	0.73
Prices (% difference from base run)				
1	0.16	0.21	0.24	0.20
2	0.63	0.83	0.92	0.78
3	1.36	1.59	1.73	1.53
4	2.16	2.34	2.58	2.27
5	3.00	3.05	3.50	2.98
6	3.87	3.78	4.47	3.71
7			5.46	4.54
8			6.52	5.43
9			7.67	6.35
Unemployment (difference from base run, '000)				
1	−129	−133	−135	−137
2	−145	−156	−159	−154
3	−160	−173	−177	−170
4	−177	−183	−189	−181
5	−186	−179	−191	−178
6	−188	−172	−189	−172
7			−176	−161
8			−153	−145
9			−125	−122
Nominal exchange rate (% difference from base run)				
1	−1.99	−3.31	−3.71	−3.18
2	−3.23	−4.00	−4.19	−3.81
3	−4.41	−4.48	−4.89	−4.47
4	−5.08	−4.87	−5.73	−4.81
5	−5.80	−5.33	−6.58	−5.23
6	−6.16	−5.92	−7.10	−6.10
7			−7.69	−6.75
8			−8.53	−7.25
9			−9.69	−7.77

Table 2.21 *Sensitivity of simulation results to terminal dates and seasonality: NIESR*

Year	Short solution period		Long solution period	
	NIESR conditions	Seasonal conditions	NIESR conditions	Seasonal conditions
GDP (% difference from base run)				
1	0.72	0.72	0.70	0.70
2	0.73	0.73	0.69	0.71
3	0.75	0.74	0.69	0.71
4	0.74	0.74	0.67	0.69
5			0.63	0.66
Prices (% difference from base run)				
1	0.22	0.22	0.17	0.19
2	0.93	0.92	0.71	0.79
3	1.69	1.67	1.33	1.46
4	2.55	2.53	2.10	2.23
5			2.85	3.06
Unemployment (difference from base run, '000)				
1	−53	−53	−52	−52
2	−58	−58	−54	−55
3	−59	−58	−51	−54
4	−55	−54	−44	−48
5			−34	−38
Nominal exchange rate (% difference from base run)				
1	−0.86	−0.83	−0.49	−0.61
2	−1.45	−1.41	−0.90	−1.09
3	−2.04	−2.00	−1.37	−1.60
4	−2.69	−2.65	−1.92	−2.18
5			−2.53	−2.82

Tables 2.20 and 2.21, respectively. In both cases we observe quantitative differences between the simulation results when the solution period is shortened. How far these differences are regarded as important depends on the interpretation and use of the results, but differences of up to 0.1 per cent in GDP and 0.6 per cent in the price level do seem to be relevant in relation to the average impact effect observed in this simulation. Using the terminal conditions adjusted for seasonal effects largely removes the sensitivity of the simulations to the terminal date for the LBS model. In the NIESR case some sensitivity remains as a result of the unit root in the exchange rate, as discussed above.

It should be noted, however, that the long-period solution does produce different results when existing terminal conditions are used as opposed to seasonally adjusted conditions. These effects are particularly noticeable for the price and exchange rate effects. Given that the solutions with the existing terminal conditions are more sensitive to changes in the terminal date than those with seasonally corrected conditions, we expect the latter solution to be a closer approximation to the underlying solution path of the model.

2.6 Experimental design in rational expectations models

In the standard simulations reported in Section 2.2 it is usually assumed that all perturbations to policy instruments are permanent and unantici-pated. In this section we study the importance of these assumptions in the face of model-consistent forward expectations variables, considering first the distinction between permanent and temporary shocks, then that between unanticipated and anticipated shocks.

Permanent and temporary shocks

Conventional backward-looking models react no differently to permanent and temporary shocks during the period in which they are in force. Once a temporary shock is removed, however, such models tend back towards the original steady state, at a rate of adjustment depending on their intrinsic dynamics; thus there is clearly a long-run difference between the two kinds of shock. This effect is also present in models with forward expectation variables, but in addition they may react differently to a shock during the period in which it is in force, depending on whether it is known to be permanent or temporary. (We do not consider questions of credibility, such as whether a policy is believed to be one thing when it might in fact be another.) Differences in reaction may occur because forward-looking eco-nomic institutions essentially anticipate the future removal of the interven-tion, and this has an impact on their current behaviour.

In general, the models do not distinguish different reactions to perma-nent or temporary stimuli through the specification of individual equations. Although a consumption function might rest on a permanent income theory, for example, separate identification of permanent and transitory components of income does not occur. The difference between permanent and temporary shocks occurs through a complete model solution. It depends not only on the nature and role of the forward expectations variables, but also on the model's dynamic adjustment, since a protracted

---

Note to Table 2.22:
1. The shock is an increase in government expenditure of the equivalent of £386 million per quarter (1980) prices under fixed interest rates (LBS, NIESR). For LPL we examine money finance (under endogenous terminal conditions) and alternatively balanced finance (by changing the exogenous PSBR/GDP ratio).
2. The temporary shocks continue until the period denoted by a solid line. Subsequent periods do not contain the shock.

Table 2.22 *Comparison of temporary and permanent shocks*

Year	LBS Temp.	Perm.	NIESR Temp.	Perm.	LPL Bal. finance Temp.	Perm.	Money finance Temp.	Perm.
GDP (% difference from base run)								
1	0.65	0.67	0.66	0.69	0.11	−0.03	0.02	−0.09
2	0.87	0.92	0.59	0.67	0.41	0.25	0.33	0.21
3	0.96	1.00	<u>0.51</u>	0̈.66	0.40	0.20	0.23	0.06
4	0.96	0.99	−0.13	0.63	0.33	0.07	0.20	−0.02
5	<u>0.90</u>	0.97	−0.15	0.58	0.37	—	0.27	−0.10
6	0.23	0.92			<u>0.30</u>	−0.04	<u>0.21</u>	0.16
7	0.02	0.85			−0.11	−0.04	−0.10	−0.15
8	−0.08	0.77			−0.09	−0.04	−0.10	−0.05
9	−0.15	0.71			−0.07	−0.03	−0.08	−0.03
14					−0.01	0.01	−0.01	0.12
Prices (% difference from base run)								
1	0.16	0.24	0.05	0.14	2.01	2.23	1.90	2.00
2	0.68	0.92	0.23	0.58	3.74	4.08	3.60	3.78
3	1.37	1.73	<u>0.58</u>	1.14	5.45	5.92	5.34	5.64
4	2.11	2.58	0.88	1.80	7.09	7.77	6.96	7.48
5	<u>2.74</u>	3.50	0.82	2.50	8.51	9.58	8.34	9.29
6	3.24	4.47			<u>9.54</u>	11.34	<u>9.33</u>	11.06
7	3.62	5.46			9.52	13.06	9.24	12.82
8	3.83	6.52			9.50	14.76	9.21	14.52
9	3.98	7.67			9.48	16.47	9.19	16.15
14					9.39	25.20	9.09	24.53
Unemployment (difference from base run, '000)								
1	−132	−135	−50	−52	−103	−93	−76	−67
2	−151	−159	−44	−52	−149	−132	−130	−114
3	−166	−177	<u>−29</u>	−47	−132	−111	−124	−102
4	−177	−189	32	−39	−95	−71	−102	−72
5	<u>−175</u>	−191	37	−27	−71	−41	−86	−41
6	−50	−188			<u>−51</u>	−23	<u>−60</u>	−19
7	−24	−175			−20	−13	−21	−3
8	−12	−152			−6	−8	−5	3
9	8	−124			—	−5	1	1
14					—	−1	1	−8
Nominal exchange rate (% difference from base run)								
1	−2.84	−3.70	0.31	−0.29	−3.85	−4.31	−4.26	−4.52
2	−3.47	−4.19	0.27	−0.61	−4.85	−5.37	−5.30	−5.62
3	−4.29	−4.89	<u>0.09</u>	−1.00	−5.90	−6.51	−6.43	−6.86
4	−4.69	−5.73	−0.17	−1.49	−6.97	−7.76	−7.56	−8.20
5	<u>−4.19</u>	−6.58	−0.25	−2.04	−7.93	−9.08	−8.55	−9.59
6	−3.81	−7.10			<u>−8.62</u>	−10.40	<u>−9.23</u>	−10.94
7	−3.74	−7.69			−8.52	−11.71	−9.07	−12.28
8	−3.43	−8.53			−8.48	−13.01	−9.00	−13.55
9	−3.54	−9.69			−8.45	−14.28	−8.97	−14.74
14					−8.37	−20.43	−8.86	−20.53

period of lagged adjustment following the ending of a temporary shock will also have an impact on current behaviour through future expectations variables. Ideally, the temporary shock should end sufficiently far in advance of the terminal date that the terminal condition causes no additional distortion.

Although the LPL model does identify a separate exogenous variable called 'temporary monetary growth', there is no permanent counterpart in the model. This prompts the question of how long a government spending increase can be sustained, financed by temporary monetary growth, without causing a distortion in the model solution. In the bond finance case we simulate a sustained increase by using endogenous terminal conditions. We repeat this experiment for money finance by shocking the temporary monetary growth variable (and government spending) for different periods. The unsustained shock corresponds to the simulation reported in Section 2.2 and shown in Table 2.1. An alternative method of finance is via a balanced increase in money and bonds. This is achieved by changing the exogenous PSBR/GDP ratio in the model, and this automatically increases the level of government spending, for given tax rates. A sustained increase in spending under balanced finance is also reported in Section 2.2, and shown in Table 2.4. Here we examine the effects of an unsustained increase in spending under balanced finance. For the two quarterly models the simulation exercise corresponds to that described in Section 2.5.

The results of these simulations are shown in Table 2.22. Because of the differing solution periods, the temporary shocks are imposed over different time periods. This limits the comparability across the models, but by comparing results over the common period of temporary and permanent shocks we observe that the simulation effects for LBS and NIESR are in general smaller when the shock is temporary than when it is permanent, although the differences are not that substantial for the LBS model. Part of the explanation for the relatively small differences observed for LBS is provided by the rapid adjustment of the exchange rate, together with the sluggishness of domestic wages and prices, so that output effects persist for longer after the removal of the temporary shock than in the NIESR model, where there is a greater difference between the alternative forms of shock.

Under money finance in the LPL model, an unsustained shock generates larger output effects but weaker price effects than its sustained counterpart. On removal of the shock the level of output returns rapidly to its base' level. In the unsustained case the terminal condition for inflation is unchanged, and thus there is only a permanent shift in the price level. In the sustained case, however, this terminal condition is changed and a higher rate of inflation emerges. In turn, this reduces the level of output so that the effects of the sustained shock come close to the theoretical predictions of the new classical approach. Similar differences between the sustained and unsustained shocks are observed for the balanced finance case. In particular, the distinction between an increase in the price level and an increase in the rate of inflation carries over to this simulation. The effects on the price level are very similar to those for the money finance case since the monetary expansion is the same. The higher output effects under balanced finance arise since there is a revision to the equilibrium terminal condition, which also raises the equilibrium (and hence the actual) level of government spending.

In conclusion, we do find some differences between temporary and permanent shocks. In the quarterly models the temporary shocks tend to have weaker output and price level effects than their permanent counterparts, but the differences for the various shocks are not that great. In contrast, the LPL model generates larger output effects for an unsustained shock. Here the higher price effects generated by a sustained shock adversely affect output. All the models suggest that an unsustained money financed expansion of spending merely raises the price level, but a sustained increase generates a higher inflation rate.

Anticipated and unanticipated effects

Finally, we turn to the distinction between anticipated and unanticipated shocks. In the simulation results reported in Section 2.2 we assume that all shocks are unanticipated. Conventional backward-looking models react no differently to anticipated and unanticipated effects. If the shocks were anticipated with forward-consistent expectations, however, we might expect to observe a change in behaviour prior to the actual shock. As with the temporary/permanent distinction, in general models do not allow for different reactions to anticipated/unanticipated shocks through the specification of individual equations, and differences emerge only for complete model solutions. Simulation of anticipated effects is then typically achieved by shocking an exogenous variable at an intermediate point during the solution period, while solving over the entire solution period under consistent expectations. In the long run we would expect to observe the same effects as for unanticipated shocks, since the same steady-state growth path should be attained in both cases. A separate mechanism is incorporated in the LPL model whereby the reaction of economic agents to unanticipated inflation is modelled explicitly through a term in the real-wage equation (with a negative coefficient). Under consistent expectations, this term is identically zero for all except the first period, where the expectation is formed outside of the solution period and hence is not required to be consistent. In order to isolate the impact of this variable, we report results from the LPL model both including and excluding this term. (Note that the base run solution for LPL is of the unanticipated form.)

The simulation exercise is identical to that used to distinguish temporary and permanent shocks, namely, an increase in government spending under fixed interest rates or money finance. For the two quarterly models the

Table 2.23   *Comparison of anticipated and unanticipated shocks*

Year	LBS		NIESR		LPL (1)		LPL (2)	
	A	U	A	U	A	U	A	U
GDP (% difference from base run)								
1	0.02	—	0.04	—	−0.34	—	−1.17	−0.09
2	0.08	—	0.12	—	−0.17	—	0.01	0.21
3	0.74	0.64	0.73	0.67	−0.33	—	0.01	0.06
4	0.89	0.91	0.71	0.65	−0.29	—	0.04	−0.02
5	0.93	0.99	0.69	0.64	−0.07	−0.33	−0.10	−0.08
6	0.92	0.99			−0.05	0.29	−0.15	−1.00
7	0.88	0.97			−0.10	0.03	−0.14	−0.16
8	0.83	0.94			−0.09	−0.05	−0.03	−0.15
9	0.79	0.89			—	—	−0.02	−0.05
14					0.11	0.13	0.12	0.11
Prices (% difference from base run)								
1	0.07	—	0.06	—	0.22	—	3.03	2.00
2	0.34	—	0.25	—	0.40	—	4.69	3.78
3	0.76	0.21	0.56	0.11	0.81	—	6.31	5.64
4	1.34	0.86	1.21	0.33	1.55	—	7.94	7.48
5	2.10	1.65	2.00	0.68	3.22	2.12	9.59	9.29
6	2.93	2.54			4.89	3.81	11.25	11.06
7	3.80	3.51			6.52	5.89	12.93	12.82
8	4.74	4.59			8.10	7.51	14.56	14.82
9	5.78	5.78			9.64	9.23	16.15	16.15
14					17.58	17.47	24.44	24.53
Unemployment (difference from base run, '000)								
1	−3	—	−3	—	33	—	149	−67
2	−12	—	−12	—	29	—	66	−115
3	−146	−130	−66	−51	46	—	23	−102
4	−163	−152	−61	−50	48	—	12	−71
5	−171	−168	−50	−44	23	−34	11	−41
6	−173	−177			9	−80	11	−20
7	−165	−174			8	−60	13	−3
8	−151	−163			6	−38	11	3
9	−130	−143			1	−28	5	1
14					−1	−12	−8	−8
Nominal exchange rate (% difference from base run)								
1	−1.02	—	−0.45	—	−0.54	—	−3.34	−4.52
2	−1.99	—	−0.66	—	−0.69	—	−5.05	−5.12
3	−3.28	−3.51	−0.87	−0.11	−1.10	—	−6.50	−6.86
4	−4.07	−4.00	−1.29	−0.33	−1.86	—	−7.97	−8.20
5	−4.85	−4.77	−1.84	−0.68	−3.57	−4.88	−9.43	−9.59
6	−5.60	−5.68			−5.10	−5.87	−10.83	−10.94
7	−6.22	−6.51			−6.56	−7.09	−12.18	−12.28
8	−7.03	−7.45			−7.92	−8.34	−13.45	−13.55
9	−8.10	−8.51			−9.21	−9.56	−14.66	−14.74
14					−15.46	−15.60	−20.45	−20.53

effects of an anticipated shock in government spending lead to a greater effect on the main outcome variables (see Table 2.23) than an unanticipated shock, in the period in which the shock is introduced. This difference persists for several subsequent periods, the main exception being GDP in the LBS model. The impact on the price level in the LBS model shows clearly how both anticipated and unanticipated effects converge towards the long-run solution. This is not so apparent from the LBS results for GDP, nor is it from the NIESR results; in the NIESR model, however, there is not a unique long-run solution and the trajectory depends on the terminal condition for the exchange rate. The perfectly anticipated shocks support the idea that some effects may be felt in advance of the imposition of the shock. The impacts, although qualitatively significant, are not that quantitatively important for the quarterly models, and take place largely in the year before the shock is introduced.

In the comparable experiment, LPL(1), there are clearer signs that both anticipated and unanticipated solutions tend towards the same long-run solution, with the difference largely in terms of dynamics. As with the other models, the anticipated effects are stronger than in the unanticipated case in the year in which the shock is introduced, but this is quickly reversed. The pre-shock effects are far more significant for this model, however, and it is quite striking that GDP falls for several periods before the government expenditure shock is introduced. In the second set of LPL simulations the increase in spending occurs in the first period for both anticipated and unanticipated cases, and any difference in the solution is due entirely to the inclusion of the unanticipated inflation effect on real wages. This leads to a marked difference in the results for the period in which the shock occurs, but this is rapidly eliminated so that the two simulations coincide after about five years.

The results suggest, therefore, that the choice of unanticipated/anticipated shocks does matter for the models, but principally in terms of dynamic response. In the case of LPL, similar implications can be drawn from either anticipated or unanticipated variant after five or six years of the

---

Notes to Table 2.23:

1. The shock is a government expenditure increase under fixed interest rates (LBS, NIESR) or permanent money finance (LPL).

2. A: anticipated shocks; U: unanticipated shocks.

3. For LPL(1), NIESR, and LBS, the anticipated shock is introduced at a future period, and the model is solved from the current period. An unanticipated shock means that the model is resolved from the period in which the shock is introduced.

4. The horizontal lines dividing the solution period denote the period from which the shock is introduced.

5. LPL(2) gives results for a shock introduced in year 1, with the unanticipated inflation term appearing in the real-wage equation in year 1. This is set to zero in the anticipated case.

simulation, but the two quarterly models are more sluggish and conclusions regarding the general properties from relatively short solution periods are seen to be dependent on the nature of the shock. Differences also emerge in the LPL responses depending on whether the shocks are introduced in individual equations or through the overall model solutions.

2.7   Summary and conclusions

As in our previous simulation exercises, we have examined the properties of the latest vintage of the macroeconomic models under a variety of shocks. The models themselves have changed in varying degrees from the versions used in the earlier exercises. The LBS model now has forward-consistent expectations in its financial sector, and the NIESR model within the goods, labour, and exchange rate sectors. The NIESR model now also includes a new relationship between unemployment and employment. The current CGP model contains an endogenous exchange rate, and there have been some changes to the HMT model, particularly in respect of interest rate sensitivity. The CUBS and LPL models are little changed from their earlier versions, and we have examined the BE model for the first time.

The incorporation of forward expectations in the LBS model makes it more expansionary for a money-financed increase in government spending than the other models over a five-year horizon, since the exchange rate depreciates sharply in anticipation of rising inflation. Hence the implied government expenditure multiplier rises over time. Multipliers for the other quarterly models are all around unity, but decline over the simulation period. A distinctive feature of the NIESR model emerges in the unemployment consequences of higher government spending, whereby a lower propensity to register as unemployed for the non-manufacturing sector leads to a much smaller unemployment effect in this model compared not only with the other models, but also with the previous vintage of the NIESR model.

We also examine the sensitivity of the government spending results to the financing assumption. In general, the output response is weaker for bond finance than for money finance. Compared with our second review of the models, we find slightly more crowding-out in the HMT model under bond finance, but weaker effects for the LBS model. There is virtually no crowding-out in the BE model. Price level effects are typically very weak under bond finance, as compared with money finance. The results for the LPL and CUBS models are similar to each other under bond finance, but they diverge under balanced money and bond finance with far greater inflation effects for LPL.

When higher government spending is financed by higher income taxes so as to produce a balanced budget, we find that the multipliers diminish over time as the response to the tax cuts is less immediate than that for public spending. The LBS model generates a stronger output response than the other models, but this comes from a greater response for both government spending and tax rates than in the other models. The sharper increase in the price level in comparison with the other models, and with the previous version of the LBS model, reflects the sharp exchange rate depreciation. In contrast, the price level falls in the CGP model as lower taxes increase the target real wage, and hence diminish the pressure on nominal wages. Results for the remaining models are similar to those observed in our previous review. In the CUBS model there is an output effect of similar magnitude to that of HMT but only a temporary price rise. The LPL model has the smallest change in output of all the models.

Distinctive features of the simulation in which the rate of VAT is reduced include the rise in price level in the LBS and CUBS models and the fall in the level of output in the CGP model. The difference between the LBS and CGP models can be explained principally by the behaviour of the exchange rate in the two models: in the case of LBS it depreciates, whereas the reverse response occurs in the CGP model. Elsewhere output rises by around $\frac{1}{4}-\frac{1}{2}$ per cent in this simulation, with a somewhat larger effect for HMT.

As on previous occasions, we observe a strong contrast between the effects of reducing the rate of unemployment benefits in the LPL model and in the other two models where this variable appears. Important differences also emerge for the interest rate simulation where output and price responses are found to be very weak except for the LBS and HMT models. Neither does a clear consensus emerge from the oil price simulation. The LBS, CGP, and CUBS models imply that lower oil prices, *ceteris paribus*, are favourable to domestic output. In the case of CGP, a strong inflationary effect is observed as the exchange rate depreciates sharply. For the remaining models the effects on output and the price level are very weak.

Some of the models contain disaggregation of output and employment so that it is possible to analyse the implications for the distribution of output and employment between manufacturing and non-manufacturing for the range of shocks used to analyse the broad properties of the models. Although the methods of disaggregation adopted are similar for many of the models, the responses across the sectors vary considerably, both between models and between simulations. A key factor is the behaviour of the exchange rate, and the results are consistent with the Dutch disease debate in so far as the exchange rate is the main instrument of de-industrialization, where this is defined as a decline of the manufacturing sector; but the simulations imply that the distribution of output between the sectors can be influenced by monetary and fiscal policy.

Of the three models containing rational expectation terms, the LPL and LBS models appear to achieve unique stable solutions. The NIESR model, by design, does not have a unique stable solution for the real exchange rate and the solution for this variable is imposed via its terminal condition. It can be argued that the exchange rate cannot be forecast by an economic model and that the specification used by NIESR represents a true picture of reality — we make no judgement on such a claim in this exercise.

The LPL model solution is insensitive both to solution period and to the type of terminal condition, at least for the base forecast. The LBS and NIESR models are both sensitive to the terminal date, largely owing to a neglect of seasonality in their specifications of terminal conditions. If we impose conditions that do take seasonality into acount, we find that the sensitivity is largely removed. In the NIESR model, the whole solution is sensitive to the exchange rate terminal condition, and one cannot therefore search for a solution that is independent of terminal values. If one discards the last five quarters in the LBS model, the solution is relatively insensitive to the types of condition imposed.

From the simulation exercises we find similar effects. The NIESR and LBS simulations both show signs of sensitivity with respect to the length of the simulation period. In the LBS model this sensitivity is removed when seasonality is taken into account. In the NIESR model we can reduce the sensitivity but not eliminate it because of the dependence on the real exchange rate terminal conditions. The removal of seasonal effects allows much more of the solution to be used for analysis of model properties. We find that permanent bond financing is feasible in the LPL model, at least for a 14-year period, since, although the behaviour of real debt interest is inconsistent with the equilibrium conditions of the model, the effects of this are not important for the rest of the model.

In general, we find that experiments comparing temporary and permanent shocks or anticipated and unanticipated shocks yield changes to the dynamic response path. We find that a temporary shock has a smaller impact than a permanent shock in the two quarterly models over the common period of shock. These findings are not repeated for the LPL model, where the output and unemployment responses are stronger for an unsustained shock. The LPL model produces a typical new classical result when government spending is financed by sustained monetary growth. There is more than one way of simulating anticipated shocks for the LPL model. These lead to quite different dynamic responses. In general, however, we find that anticipated and unanticipated shocks have the same long-run effect in the LPL model, with the anticipated shock shifting some of the response forward in time. This finding is not so clear from the quarterly models, as the time horizons for model solution are not sufficiently long to obtain full, long-run solutions, although the empirical results tend towards the theoretical conclusions. The effects in the NIESR and LBS models tend not to be very large because there are no explicit mechanisms within the model structure that distinguish between temporary/permanent or anticipated/unanticipated shocks. In the LPL model there is such a treatment, and this produces more marked effects than simply altering the date at which shocks are entered or removed. Whereas we have previously emphasized the importance of stating the underlying policy assumption when analysing simulation results, the findings from the models with rational expectations suggest that further assumptions, such as the nature and dating of the terminal conditions and the setting of the exogenous shock, need to be clearly stated as well.

Chapter 3

Forecast Comparisons

3.1 Introduction

In this chapter we present our third systematic analysis of *ex ante* forecasts. *Ex post* analysis over 1984 and 1985 of the forecasts made in 1983 is now possible and is presented in Chapter 4. As in the case of the previous *ex ante* comparisons, we consider four forecasts from different model teams, all made at approximately the same time — autumn 1985 — so ensuring that differences in the information available to the forecasters are minimized as far as possible. Differences between the forecasts are explained in terms of the different assumptions regarding exogenous inputs, the influence of residual adjustments, and the differences between the underlying economic models.

This analysis is based on the set of models and their input and adjustment files supplied to the Bureau by the model teams. Some may wish to distinguish their conditional projections of the economy from forecasts of future outcomes, and the term 'forecast' is used loosely to cover both. The set of four forecasts remains the same as in the earlier exercises: namely, two quarterly forecasts (LBS and NIESR) and two annual forecasts (CUBS and LPL). In the general descriptions of forecasts we also include the forecast based on the Cambridge Growth Project model (annual), but as it is prepared privately by Cambridge Econometrics Ltd (CE) it is not included in the formal analysis. The annual models tend to have longer forecast horizons than the quarterly models, which limits comparability, but on this occasion all the forecasts extend until at least 1990. Her Majesty's Treasury also produces model-based forecasts, but only selected elements are published (for example, there is no published unemployment forecast), with only an 18-month horizon. There is no publicly available account of exogenous assumptions or residual adjustments, and so this forecast is not included in our comparative analysis.

In the next section the forecasts themselves are briefly outlined. We also contrast the development of the three successive *ex ante* forecasts discussed in this and earlier reviews. Section 3.3 then examines the projections of exogenous variables that underlie the forecasts and considers the effect on the differences between the forecasts of choosing a set of consistent (standardized) assumptions about exogenous variables. In Section 3.4 the role of residual adjustments in explaining the differences between the forecasts is considered. Three out of the four models analysed in this chapter contain forward-consistent expectations, and some consideration is given to the use of residual adjustments in these models in general and in the NIESR forecast in particular. In Section 3.5 an accounting framework is presented that relates forecast differences to variations in exogenous assumptions, in residual adjustments, and in the models themselves.

It would be misleading to suggest that residual adjustments represent the sole impact of 'judgement' in the preparation of a forecast. Some degree of judgement is present in the specification of the formal model through the choice of its structure and its statistical representation. This form of judgement varies between model teams and is reflected in the relative weights they attach to economic theory and statistical performance. A second form of judgement arises from the choice of values for the exogenous variables. Thus, a forecaster who is unhappy with a model-based forecast may change parameters (or even whole equations) of the model, or may modify the projections of exogenous variables, without necessarily adjusting residuals. In some cases, moreover, a new explicit external factor may be incorporated into the model by modifying an equation residual, as an alternative to introducing a new exogenous variable. An example of this type of adjustment is an allowance for the effects of privatization on the private/public sector composition of fixed investment.

In general, it is comparatively rare for model teams to respecify a model once a forecasting round is under way, although current developments in software are bringing this within the realm of possibility. There is a greater freedom in revising exogenous variable projections, but this freedom may be limited by the need to maintain a view of exogenous developments that is not too distant from the consensus of other forecasters and of economic commentators. This is supported by findings in our first and second reviews, where differences in exogenous assumptions accounted for only a minor part of differences between forecasts. In the absence of published information regarding the reasons for making residual adjustments, all these adjustments are treated equally, in that they are additions to the model that are not verifiable by standard statistical procedures.

3.2 Summary of the forecasts

The various forecasts of seven key variables are presented in Table 3.1 and the inflation–unemployment forecasts are also plotted in Figure 3.1. The forecasts start from different estimates of the base year (1985) because these figures are themselves forecasts, based on perhaps as little as six months' information for that year. Those forecasts that predict a falling level of unemployment combined with a falling rate of inflation can be classed as relatively optimistic and are depicted in Figure 3.1 by a movement towards the south-west quadrant. Such forecasts are those of CUBS and LPL, with the LPL forecast the most optimistic, predicting that the level of unemployment will fall to around 1 million by the late 1990s in

Table 3.1   *Forecasts compared*

		1985	1986	1987–88	1989–90	1991–98
GDP growth (% p. a.)						
LBS	(output)	3.6	2.4	2.1	1.5	
	(expenditure)	3.8	2.5	2.2	1.5	
NIESR	(output)	3.5	1.9	1.1	1.3	
	(expenditure)	3.8	2.0	1.1	1.4	
CE	(output)	3.4	1.4	1.2	1.2	
	(expenditure)	3.4	1.3	1.3	1.2	
CUBS	(output)	4.1	3.7	4.0	2.6	1.8
LPL	(expenditure)	3.4	3.0	3.3	4.8	2.8
Average	(output)	3.7	2.4	2.2	1.7	
	(expenditure)	3.6	2.2	2.0	2.2	
Inflation (% p. a.)						
LBS		4.8	4.3	4.3	3.5	
NIESR		4.9	3.3	3.7	3.7	
CE		4.8	5.0	5.9	4.5	
CUBS		4.3	3.6	4.9	6.3	3.8
LPL		4.3	3.6	2.9	2.4	2.5
Average		4.6	4.0	4.2	4.1	3.2
Unemployment (millions)						
LBS		3.2	3.1	3.0	2.9	
NIESR		3.2	3.0	3.0	3.0	
CE		3.2	3.4	3.6	3.7	
CUBS		3.1	2.8	2.2	1.4	1.6
LPL		3.1	3.1	2.9	2.3	1.2
Average		3.2	3.1	2.9	2.7	1.4
PSBR (£b)						
LBS		7.7	8.3	7.1	7.6	
NIESR		8.4	8.5	8.0	7.6	
CE		9.9	9.7	12.9	12.7	
CUBS		8.5	12.1	8.7	2.3	5.8
LPL		10.2	7.7	8.4	8.3	1.3
Average		8.9	9.3	9.0	7.7	
Money supply growth (% p. a.)						
LBS	M0	5.4	7.1	2.3	3.3	
	£M$_3$	11.6	9.9	6.0	2.0	
NIESR	£M$_3$	13.8	16.1	15.3	15.1	
	M$_1$	14.7	14.3	16.2	11.2	
CE	£M$_3$	10.7	7.5	7.4	5.8	
CUBS	M0	4.7	5.0	5.0	3.9	3.7
LPL	M0	5.6	5.0	4.0	4.6	3.4
Nominal effective exchange rate growth (% p. a.)						
LBS		−0.6	−1.5	−1.3	2.8	
NIESR		−0.4	2.3	0.9	−0.2	

Table 3.1 *(continued)*

	1985	1986	1987–88	1989–90	1991–98
CE	−1.8	2.0	−3.6	1.2	
CUBS	0.1	5.7	5.2	−3.8	1.6
Short-term interest rate					
LBS	12.1	9.8	8.1	8.0	
NIESR	11.9	7.7	5.7	5.2	
CE	12.0	10.5	11.4	9.3	
CUBS	11.9	9.9	9.3	16.4	5.4
LPL	11.5	8.9	8.2	5.3	5.8

combination with a declining rate of inflation for most of that forecast period.

The CUBS forecast shows falling unemployment and inflation in the short term (i.e. to 1987) but then a steady rise in the inflation rate to 1991. At this point the predicted decline in unemployment ceases and the rate of inflation falls sharply to a low point of under 1 per cent in 1995. The final three years of the forecast however reveal a deterioration in both inflation and unemployment.

The LBS forecast is one of modest optimism with the level of unemployment declining gently (to just under 3 million by 1990) while the rate of inflation eases to around $3\frac{1}{2}$ per cent. Little change in the current conjuncture is predicted by the NIESR forecast. The CE forecast is the most pessimistic of those considered here: it predicts an increase in the level of unemployment with rising inflation until 1988.

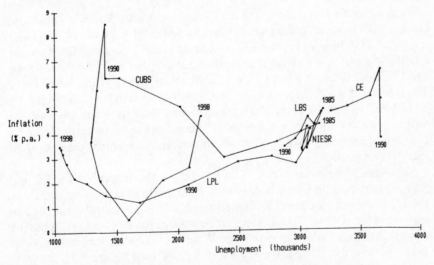

Fig. 3.1 Unemployment and inflation in the 1985 forecasts.

With the exception of LPL, forecasts of GDP show a tendency for growth to decline over the forecast horizon and for the average level of growth to be well below that experienced in 1985, which was boosted by the miners' strike. In 1986 output pessimism is greatest in the case of CE and optimism greatest for CUBS, but all the forecasts suggest a weakening of growth relative to estimates of the growth experienced in 1985. A greater degree of divergence between the forecasts is apparent in later years. CUBS and LPL predict a return towards 1985 growth for 1987–88 whereas LBS and CE forecast a continuation of the 1986 rate of growth. In contrast, NIESR predict further weakening in growth. In the LPL forecast GDP growth accelerates sharply in 1989–90 and then remains just below 3 per cent per annum through the 1990s. In all the remaining forecasts the rate of GDP growth either remains steady or falls after 1988, making the LPL forecast much more of an outlier than in earlier years. While direct comparisons are difficult, the HMT forecast appears to be relatively optimistic as regards output growth for 1986 and about average for inflation; no information is available on the unemployment forecast.

As the average growth of GDP across the forecasts declines with the length of the forecast horizon, so the dispersion of the individual forecasts increases. In 1987–88 the range of the output growth forecasts is 2.9 per cent, from a minimum of 1.1 per cent (NIESR) to a maximum of 4 per cent (CUBS), against a mean forecast of 2.2 per cent; and by 1989–90 the range is 3.4 per cent (1.4 per cent, NIESR, to 4.8 per cent, LPL) compared with an average remaining at 2.2 per cent. The dispersion of the inflation forecasts is similar to that of GDP growth, and it also increases over time. However, the range of inflation forecasts is less than their average, unlike the case of output.

Some of the financial aspects of the forecasts are also shown in Table 3.1. Up to 1990 the broad consensus appears to be that the PSBR will lie in the region of £7–9 billion, similar to the estimated 1985 outturn. Outliers are CUBS, who suggest a sharp decline in the PSBR between 1988 and 1990, and CE, who forecast a level of the PSBR closer to £13 billion after 1986. The narrowness of the range of the PSBR forecasts, which might be considered to have a greater degree of uncertainty than the forecasts of output growth and inflation, probably stems from a fairly high degree of unanimity regarding assumptions about government policy over most of the forecast period.

Measures of monetary growth vary between the forecasts. CUBS and LPL concentrate on M0, whereas £M_3 is the main monetary aggregate in the other models. In general, monetary growth is projected to decline in the forecasts, but the NIESR forecast stands out from the others in having a much higher absolute growth rate. Whereas the other forecasts predict constant velocity, NIESR forecasts a sharp rise (see Figure 3.2).

The development of the nominal exchange rate is shown in Figure 3.2.

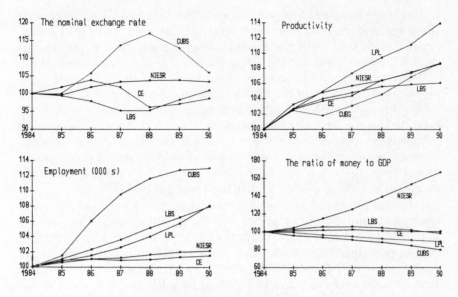

Fig. 3.2   Further aspects of the published forecasts.
Index 1984 = 100
Money is M0 for LPL and CUBS and £M₃ for LBS, NIESR, and CE.

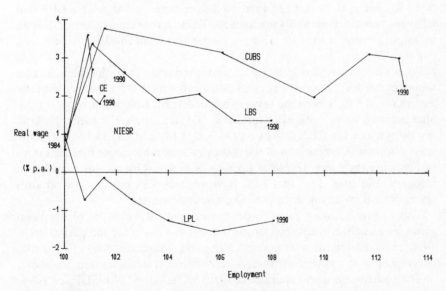

Fig. 3.3   Real-wage growth and employment in the forecasts.
Index 1984 = 100

Little change is expected in the NIESR forecast, whereas CUBS forecasts a sharp appreciation until 1988, after which the rate returns to a level not far above that of 1985. LBS also predict a level of the exchange rate close to the 1985 level by 1990, but this follows a period of depreciation until 1988.

Implications for productivity are also shown in Figure 3.2. Most rapid growth is experienced in the LPL forecast and weakest growth in that of LBS. Although CUBS forecast a fall in the level of productivity in 1986 it is predicted to recover subsequently, so that by 1990 the forecast level of productivity coincides with that of NIESR and CE. All the forecasts envisage rising employment over the period to 1990, and all predict some general slowing down of real-wage growth (Figure 3.3). However, with the exception of LPL, real-wage growth itself remains positive.

Table 3.2 presents successive forecasts of output growth, inflation, and unemployment from 1983 together with the actual outturns. The relationship between forecasts and outturns is analysed in the following chapter. It does appear that those teams that are relatively pessimistic on output growth, such as LBS and NIESR, have revised their forecasts for 1985 and 1986 *upwards* over successive forecasts, as have CE for 1985. There is less evidence of systematic revisions in the 1985 forecasts of both CUBS and LPL, but CUBS forecasts of output in 1986 have clearly been revised in an upward direction, whereas those of LPL (who have been relatively optimistic concerning output growth on average) have been revised down. An obvious factor in the revision of the 1985 forecasts is the allowance for the rebound from the miner's strike. Longer-term forecasts for NIESR appear to have been increased over time, but those for LBS and CE have remained basically unchanged. There has been an average decline in output optimism for LPL over the longer term, but this has not occurred evenly.

Forecast revisions for inflation are more striking. There has been a clear tendency for forecasts to be revised downwards for 1985 and 1986, with the exception of LPL where the reverse has occurred. Inflation prospects have also become more optimistic for LBS, NIESR, and CE for the 1987–90 period but not for CUBS. After 1996 both LPL and CUBS have become less optimistic. Comparison of the successive unemployment forecasts does not indicate the same degree of revision of views as for output growth and inflation, but it is clear that LPL have become less optimistic over prospects for unemployment in their successive forecasts.

This examination of successive forecasts indicates that there has been some movement towards consensus in forecasts made for the period up to 1990, even though the average of the forecasts has changed relatively little. The dispersion of inflation forecasts in particular has fallen quite markedly.

The contributions of expenditure items to the growth in GDP for 1985–90 are shown in Figure 3.4. The CUBS model does not have an income–expenditure framework and so cannot be described in these terms. The

Table 3.2 *Successive forecasts of output, inflation, and unemployment*

Forecast for:			1982	1983	1984	1985	1986	1987–90	1991–95
GDP growth (% p. a.)									
Forecast made in:									
LBS	1983	O		1.8	2.4	2.4	1.7	1.1*	
		E		2.5	1.9	2.4	1.7	1.1*	
	1984	O			2.3	3.1	2.1	1.7**	
		(E)			(2.2)	(2.7)	(2.1)	(1.7)**	
	1985	O				3.6	2.4	1.8	
		(E)				(3.8)	(2.5)	(1.8)	
NIESR	1983	O		2.2	2.0	1.0			
	1984	O			2.0	3.3	1.4	1.2***	
	1985	(O)				(3.5)	(1.9)	(1.2)	
		E				3.8	2.0	1.2	
CE	1983	E		2.5	2.5	1.6	1.5	1.3	
	1984	E			2.0	2.1	1.2	1.4	
	1985	E				3.4	1.3	1.3	
CUBS	1983	O		2.2	4.9	3.3	0.2	2.1	1.9
	1984	O			1.8	2.9	2.9	3.4	1.3
	1985	O				4.1	3.2	3.3	1.9
LPL	1983	E		3.6	3.5	3.0	4.3	4.7	4.0
	1984	E			2.4	3.5	3.4	3.8	2.6
	1985	E				3.4	3.0	4.0	3.1
Actual									
October 1983		O	1.5						
		E	2.3						
October 1984		O	2.0	2.9					
		E	1.4	3.4					
October 1985		O	1.9	3.0	3.0				
		E	1.5	3.4	1.4				
March 1986		O	1.8	3.0	3.2	3.4			
		E	1.9	3.7	1.7	3.3			
Inflation (% p. a.)									
Forecast made in:									
LBS	1983			5.6	5.9	6.3	6.9	7.5	
	1984				4.9	5.2	4.9	4.8**	
	1985					4.8	4.3	3.9	
NIESR	1983			5.5	5.8	6.1			
	1984				4.9	6.3	5.9	7.2**	
	1985					4.9	3.3	3.7	
CE	1983			6.7	8.0	7.9	7.2	6.3	
	1984				5.8	7.2	6.9	6.5	
	1985					4.8	5.0	5.2	
CUBS	1983			6.1	6.8	8.3	5.7	3.7	2.9
	1984				5.1	4.5	5.3	3.2	5.5
	1985					4.3	3.6	5.1	3.0

Table 3.2   *(continued)*

Forecast for:		1982	1983	1984	1985	1986	1987–90	1991–95
LPL	1983		4.6	3.4	2.1	0.9	−0.4	−0.8
	1984			4.5	3.1	2.2	1.2	−0.8
	1985			4.3	3.6	2.9	2.4	2.1
Actual								
October 1983		8.4						
October 1984		8.3	5.1					
October 1985		8.6	5.1	5.1				
April 1986		8.6	5.2	4.6	5.4			

Unemployment (millions) — new basis
Forecast made in:

LBS	1983		2.9	3.0	2.8	2.7	2.6*	
	1984			3.0	3.1	3.3	3.3**	
	1985				3.2	3.1	3.0	
NIESR	1983		2.9	3.1	3.4			
	1984			3.0	3.2	3.3	3.3***	
	1985				3.2	3.1	3.0	
CE	1983		2.9	3.1	3.3	3.5	3.7	
	1984			3.0	3.1	3.4	3.6	
	1985				3.2	3.4	3.6	
CUBS	1983		2.9	2.6	2.4	2.3	1.6	1.9
	1984			3.1	2.9	2.5	1.6	1.9
	1985				3.1	2.8	1.8	1.4
LPL	1983		2.9	2.7	2.4	1.9	1.4	0.8
	1984				3.1	3.0	2.3	1.1
	1985				3.1	3.1	2.6	1.3
Actual								
March 1986		2.7	2.9	3.0	3.2			

Notes:
 * 1987 only
 ** 1987–88
*** 1987–89

O is the output measure
E is expenditure measure: brackets indicate that less emphasis was placed on this measure on the forecast publication.

decomposition is purely an accounting exercise, describing differences between expenditure components of the forecasts, and cannot be interpreted causally. Changes in the trade balance contribute negatively in general, with the effects being strongest for LBS. Most growth, and most variation between forecasts, occurs in the components of domestic final demand. Stronger output growth for LPL in the period 1985–87 is in terms of public expenditure, but between 1987 and 1990 these effects are dominated by buoyant growth in non-durable consumption and other private sector expenditure. LBS has a more optimistic outlook for

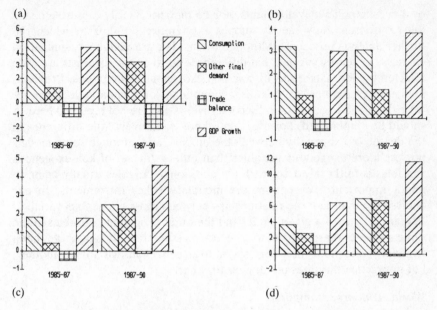

Fig. 3.4 Expenditure contributions to GDP growth (% p. a.).
(a) LBS; (b) NIESR; (c) CE; (d) LPL.

consumption than the remaining forecasts, with CE having the least optimistic. Differences in consumption largely account for the different output growth forecasts for 1985–87, but for the following period (1987–90) LBS is more optimistic than both CE and NIESR in terms of most categories of final demand.

3.3 Exogenous assumptions

We first describe the various exogenous assumptions, which are classified into three groups, relating to the world economy, the domestic economic policy, and other areas of the models such as the North Sea sector and the labour market. This description does not reveal how one forecast differs from another unless the relative importance of each assumption for the different forecasts is known. Accordingly, we then recompute the forecasts on the basis of a set of common assumptions about the exogenous variables.

The set of common assumptions is generally based on a mean or median value of the various forecast assumptions and is constructed in order to produce a forecast to set alongside the published forecast to enable the role of the different exogenous assumptions to be assessed. The common assumptions do not represent any independent view of the role of external or domestic policy developments, nor do they necessarily capture a plausible consensus: they merely supply a reference point from which the further analysis proceeds. Although the models are nonlinear, simulation exercises generally suggest that differences between the forecasts are little affected by alternative sets of common exogenous assumptions. Problems in defining common exogenous assumptions for comparative purposes were discussed in our first and second reviews and are not repeated here. It should be emphasized, however, that there is relatively little difference in the degree of exogeneity between the models, and although some models possess more exogenous variables than others, the set of key exogenous variables is fairly standard, with the additional variables usually being of minor importance: exceptions are monetary policy instruments. In our analysis we maintain the relationships between those exogenous variables that are unique to a given model and the other exogenous variables in the same model that are subject to a common assumption. It is possible that a residual in one model may correspond to an exogenous variable in another, but in practice this does not appear to occur.

World economy assumptions

The first set of assumptions, summarized in Table 3.3, concerns developments in the world economy. The LBS model contains a formal sub-model of the world economy with a larger range of world variables than the other models, but the overall system is essentially block-recursive and this subsystem is causally prior to the domestic economy. For the purposes of this exercise, variables within this sector are treated as predetermined.

Table 3.3 *Principal exogenous assumptions: world economy*

		1985	1986	1987–88	1989–90	1991–98
			% per annum			
World trade						
LBS:	manufactures	5.9	5.1	4.4	3.9	
NIESR:	manufactures	5.1	5.2	5.2	5.3	
	total	4.0	4.1	4.3	4.4	
CUBS:	total	5.9	5.3	4.6	3.5	3.5
LPL:	total	6.5	5.0	5.0	5.0	5.0
Common assumption:						
	total		4.8	4.6	4.3	4.3
	manufactures		5.8	5.6	5.3	
World prices ($)						
LBS:	export prices	−0.9	14.2	11.9	7.4	
	wholesale prices (world currency)	4.0	4.5	5.3	5.2	

Table 3.3 *(continued)*

		1985	1986	1987–88	1989–90	1991–98
NIESR:	export prices	1.6	22.0	5.5	5.0	
	wholesale prices	3.6	2.3	4.8	3.6	
CE:	wholesale prices	0.6	8.0	6.4	4.4	
CUBS:	wholesale prices	4.5	4.5	5.3	4.7	4.8
LPL:	wholesale prices[a]	3.8	3.5	3.4		
Common assumption:						
	export prices		19.4	8.7	6.5	
	wholesale prices		4.6	5.0	4.5	4.5

World (non-oil) commodity price, relative to wholesale prices ($)

	1985	1986	1987–88	1989–90	1991–98
LBS (world currency)	−2.2	0.9	1.5	−0.4	
NIESR	−10.9	8.2	0.4	0.3	
CUBS	−2.3	1.0	1.4	0.1	—
Common assumption		3.4	1.1	—	—

World oil price, relative to wholesale prices ($)

	1985	1986	1987–88	1989–90	1991–98
LBS	−6.2	−15.2	−10.1	−7.3	
NIESR[b]	−12.9	−2.5	−2.9	−1.4	
CE	−6.1	−8.0	−4.4	2.7	
CUBS	−3.8	−20.8	−5.0	−2.2	—
Common assumption		−9.3	−4.4	−1.5	

Real interest rates (%)

		1985	1986	1987–88	1989–90	1991–98
LBS[c]		3.6	3.0	2.2	2.3	
NIESR		6.7	4.8	2.8	2.5	
CUBS[c]		7.6	8.6	9.2	10.4	5.8
LPL:	long rate	5.0	3.3	3.1	3.0	3.0
	short rate	4.5	4.0	3.3	3.0	3.0
Common assumption						
	short rate		5.1	4.4	4.6	4.4
	long rate		5.1	4.4	4.6	4.4

[a] shown for comparative purposes: this variable is not part of the formal model
[b] import price
[c] implied from nominal interest rates and world (wholesale) price inflation

As noted in analyses of forecasts in our first two reviews, the forecasts of world trade show considerably less variation than do the forecasts of domestic output. This may reflect the fact that the assumptions are often based on similar sources. The forecasts suggest a slowdown in the pace of world activity in 1986 followed by steady growth, and this feature is reflected in the common assumption adopted. There is greater difference between the various assumptions regarding world prices. The common assumption chosen is one of a fairly constant rate of inflation of world prices of manufactured goods. Real oil prices in dollar terms are assumed to decline sharply in 1986 with a further more moderate decline until 1990.

Domestic policy and other assumptions

Some details of the assumptions made regarding domestic policy are shown in Table 3.4. Although the forecasts all adopt assumptions that are broadly consistent with the Medium Term Financial Strategy (MTFS) while it is in operation, both the policy rules assumed and the values of the policy instruments chosen differ between models. After the end of the formal period of MTFS the policy rules change in some of the model forecasts (e.g. CUBS). In the NIESR forecast it is assumed that policy is unchanged, with tax rates held constant, allowances and indirect tax duties indexed for inflation, and public expenditure interpreted from official government expenditure plans. There is, therefore, no fiscal adjustment to bring the PSBR into line with MTFS plans. The monetary policy rule adopted in the NIESR forecast is that the nominal short-term interest rate adjusts to

Table 3.4   *Principal exogenous assumptions: domestic economy policy and North Sea oil*

	1985	1986	1987–88	1989–90	1991–98
Standard rate of income tax (%)					
LBS	30.0	30.0	30.0	30.0	
NIESR	30.0	30.0	30.0	30.0	
CE	30.0	30.0	30.0	30.0	
CUBS	30.0	28.5	27.0	27.0	27.0
LPL[a] (overall tax rate)	31.8	31.2	30.5	30.3	30.3
Common assumption	30.0	30.0	30.0	30.0	30.0
Current government expenditure (% p. a.)					
LBS	1.3	1.5	0.8	0.8	
NIESR	1.4	1.1	0.6	—	
CE	2.1	0.5	0.6	0.7	
CUBS	—	—	—	1.0	1.0
Common assumption		0.8	0.5	0.6	0.5
Capital (non-housing) general government expenditure (% p. a.)					
LBS	−3.4	0.8	−0.5	—	
NIESR	−13.7	−6.1	−0.5		
CE	−0.7	—	0.6	1.2	
CUBS	—	—	—	—	—
Common assumption		−1.8	−0.1	—	—
Rate of unemployment benefit					
LBS	Unchanged in real terms				
LPL	Constant				
CUBS	Constant				

Table 3.4   *(continued)*

	1985	1986	1987–88	1989–90	1991–98
Standard rate of VAT (%)	Constant rate				
Tax allowances (% p. a.) LBS	+ 6.75% in real value in 1986				
Others	Indexed for inflation				
National insurance contributions					
Employers: LPL	11.8% fall in rate in 1986				
Employees: CUBS	Fall in 1986, rises in 1989 and 1994				
LPL	Rate falls 15% 1986, 10% 1987, 11% 1988; all others constant				
Common assumption	No change				
Corporation tax rate (%)					
LBS	41.25	36.25	35.0	35.0	
NIESR	41.25	36.25	35.0	35.0	
CUBS	23.5	23.0	22.5	22.5	22.5
Interest rates (real)					
LBS[b]	7.3	5.4	3.8	4.5	
NIESR	7.0	4.4	2.0	1.5	
CE[b]	7.2	5.5	5.5	4.8	
CUBS[b]	7.6	6.3	5.3	10.1	1.6
LPL[c]	7.9	6.2	5.3	4.7	3.1
Common assumption		5.6	4.5	4.5	2.3
North sea oil production (% p. a.)					
LBS	0.7	0.9	−3.2	−3.4	
NIESR	—	3.3	−3.9	−4.5	
CE	1.3	−5.9	−7.6	−3.3	
CUBS	1.4	−7.6	−1.0	−5.5	−8.9
Common assumptions		−2.3	−3.9	−4.2	−5.0
Policy rules					
CUBS: money base growth	4.7	5.0	5.0	n.a.	n.a.
LPL: PSBR/GDP ratio (%)	1.5	1.5	1.75	2.75	3.0
Temporary money growth	4.1	3.5	2.2	1.8	0 after 1994
LBS and CE	Nominal interest rate exogenous				
NIESR	Real rate exogenous				
Common assumptions:					
CUBS: Money base growth rate		5.7	3.8		
LPL: PSBR/GDP ratio		2.5	2.0	1.6	1.0
Temporary money growth		3.2	1.8	1.0	1.0 to 1994

[a] aggregate tax rate, income, and expenditure
[b] implied from nominal rate
[c] endogenous; shown for comparative purposes

maintain a given profile for the real interest rate. The LBS forecast allows
for some accommodation to MTFS plans for the PSBR by adjusting
personal tax allowances in 1986; otherwise the stance is one of fixed policy
instruments. (The policy assumption regarding tax allowances is made
through a residual adjustment, but in this exercise is treated as an exogenous variable change.) The monetary policy assumption embedded in the
forecast is that the nominal short-term interest rate is exogenous. The
CUBS forecast is similar to that of LBS in that tax allowances are assumed
to adjust to be consistent with the MTFS. The main difference from LBS is
that the monetary base is exogenous for the duration of MTFS and
assumed to grow at the centre of the MTFS target range. Thereafter (i.e.
from 1988), government deficits are assumed to be financed by money base
expansion and debt creation in balanced proportions. National insurance
contribution rates are assumed to rise in 1989 and 1994 in order to finance
the national insurance fund. In the LPL framework the equilibrium PSBR/
GDP ratio is exogenous and determines the rate of monetary growth and
inflation, apart from the exogenous influence of 'temporary' monetary
growth. Public expenditure is then determined as a residual item from the
assumption on the average tax rate and the PSBR/GDP ratio. In the
forecast the equilibrium PSBR/GDP ratio is set at 1.5 per cent (below the
MTFS targets) in 1986 and is then increased in subsequent years, but this
effect on monetary growth is augmented by another variable, which represents (additional) 'temporary' monetary growth and which is assumed to
occur until 1994. The LPL forecast assumes tax cuts which continue until
1988; this allows a more rapid expansion of public spending than is
assumed in the other forecasts.

Our common assumption for domestic economic policy is one of
unchanged fiscal policy instruments, so that tax rates, allowances, and
national insurance contribution rates remain constant over the forecast
horizon. Government expenditure is assumed to grow by around 0.5 per
cent per annum for current spending throughout. Capital spending is
assumed to fall in 1986 and 1987 but remain constant thereafter. Real
interest rates are assumed to average $4\frac{1}{2}$ per cent from 1987 to 1990.
Monetary base growth in the CUBS model, and the PSBR/GDP ratio and
temporary monetary growth in LPL, are set to be consistent with the other
models.

North Sea oil production is assumed to decline at an increasing rate until
1990, though individual forecasts show considerable short-term
divergence.

Results under common assumptions

The results of recomputing the forecasts using this set of common exogenous assumptions (shown in Table 3.5 and Figures 3.5 and 3.6) are of
interest principally for their influence on the differences between forecasts,

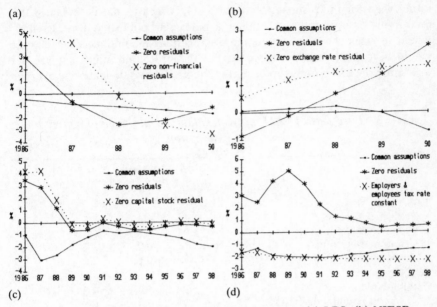

Fig. 3.5   Effects on GDP of alternative assumptions. (a) LBS; (b) NIESR;
(c) CUBS; (d) LPL.

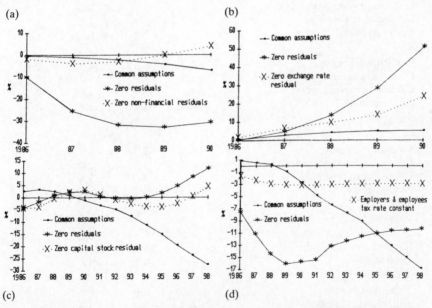

Fig. 3.6   Effects on prices of alternative assumptions. (a) LBS; (b) NIESR;
(c) CUBS; (d) LPL.

rather than for their impact on a particular forecast; that is to say, if the exogenous assumptions underlying a particular published forecast happened to coincide with our common exogenous assumptions, no change would be expected in the forecast. For example, one might expect that averaging the exogenous inputs across the models would leave the average

Table 3.5 *Forecasts of GDP growth, inflation, and unemployment under various assumptions*

	1986	1987–88	1989–90	1991–98
GDP (% p. a.)				
LBS				
Published forecast	2.5	2.5	1.5	
Common assumptions (CA)	2.0	1.8	1.2	
CA and zero residuals	5.1	−0.7	2.2	
Zero residuals	5.5	−0.6	2.2	
NIESR				
Published forecast	1.9	1.1	1.3	
Common assumptions (CA)	2.1	1.1	0.9	
CA and zero residuals	1.5	2.3	2.3	
Zero residuals	1.2	1.8	2.2	
CUBS				
Published forecast	3.7	4.0	2.6	1.8
Common assumptions (CA)	2.7	3.1	3.4	1.6
CA and zero residuals	6.2	2.0	2.4	1.7
Zero residuals	7.3	2.8	1.7	1.8
LPL				
Published forecast	3.0	3.3	4.8	2.8
Common assumptions (CA)	1.3	3.3	3.9	3.2
CA and zero residuals	4.4	3.9	3.8	2.7
Zero residuals	6.1	4.0	3.8	2.7
Inflation (% p. a.)				
LBS				
Published forecast	4.3	4.3	3.5	
Common assumptions (CA)	4.0	3.3	1.0	
CA and zero residuals	−6.6	−9.6	3.6	
Zero residuals	−6.3	−9.2	4.4	
NIESR				
Published forecast	3.3	3.7	3.7	
Common assumptions (CA)	4.0	5.5	6.7	
CA and zero residuals	5.0	15.1	23.2	
Zero residuals	2.5	10.5	19.6	
CUBS				
Published forecast	3.6	4.9	6.3	3.8
Common assumptions (CA)	6.4	3.9	4.3	−0.2
CA and zero residuals	1.8	6.7	5.0	0.7
Zero residuals	−0.8	6.8	7.1	4.9

Table 3.5   *(continued)*

	1986	1987–88	1989–90	1991–98
LPL				
Published forecast	3.6	2.9	2.4	2.5
Common assumptions (CA)	4.6	2.5	0.8	0.5
CA and zero residuals	−3.2	−1.4	−0.3	1.1
Zero residuals	−4.2	−1.0	1.5	3.3
Unemployment (millions)				
LBS				
Published forecast	3.1	3.0	2.9	
Common assumptions (CA)	3.1	3.0	3.0	
CA and zero residuals	2.9	2.7	2.6	
Zero residuals	3.0	2.7	2.5	
NIESR				
Published forecast	3.0	3.0	3.0	
Common assumptions (CA)	3.0	3.0	3.1	
CA and zero residuals	2.9	2.8	2.6	
Zero residuals	2.9	2.8	2.6	
CUBS				
Published forecast	2.8	2.2	1.4	1.6
Common assumptions (CA)	3.0	2.7	1.9	2.0
CA and zero residuals	2.4	1.7	1.8	2.1
Zero residuals	2.0	1.2	1.5	1.8
LPL				
Published forecast	3.1	2.9	2.3	1.2
Common assumptions (CA)	3.1	3.5	3.2	1.8
CA and zero residuals	3.3	2.9	2.0	1.3
Zero residuals	3.3	2.3	1.3	0.7

outcomes very much the same, while reducing the spread around the average, if the effects of changes in exogenous variables are the same across the models; but the analysis of Chapter 2 shows that there are some marked differences in the models with respect to certain important exogenous variables. We should not therefore expect average outcomes to be unaffected by averaging exogenous inputs. Nevertheless, we find that, on this occasion, the average of the GDP growth forecasts is changed little, although there is a lower average growth forecast for 1986. The ranking of forecasts changes in 1986, with LPL now the most pessimistic, but in later years there is little change in the ranking. The lower growth of output in the LPL forecast results from projecting a constant value for the employee and employer tax rates instead of the gradual reduction which is part of the published forecast. This finding is similar to that of the analysis of the 1984 LPL forecast in our second review.

The effects on inflation do not follow the same line of reasoning. As with output, the average inflation forecast is little altered, but now the dispersion of inflation forecasts is greater than in the published forecasts, particularly for the period 1989–90. This is largely due to the very different model responses to the world oil price as discussed in Chapter 2. CUBS and NIESR now generate the more pessimistic inflation forecasts as against CUBS and LBS in the published forecasts.

3.4 Residual adjustments

In this section we analyse the impact of the forecaster's adjustments to the model as reflected in the assignment of non-zero residuals. Major residual adjustments in the four forecasts are shown in Tables 3.6–3.9. We assess the effects of these interventions by recomputing the forecasts with all residuals set to zero, giving what are sometimes called 'mechanical' or 'hands-off' forecasts. The recalculation of forecasts starts in 1986 in order to avoid the ragged edge present in 1985, where data are partially observed and partially forecast. Whereas using common exogenous assumptions reduces the divergence between the GDP forecasts, the use of zero residuals in addition increases forecast dispersion between 1986 and 1988 but lessens it between 1988 and 1990. Moreover, average output growth is much higher than in the published forecasts, especially in 1986 (see Table

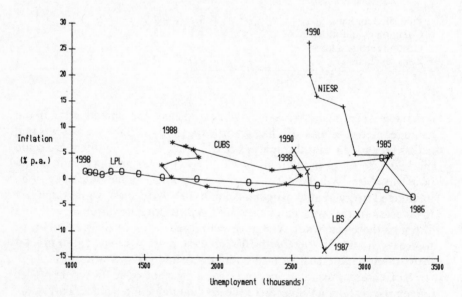

Fig. 3.7   Inflation–unemployment relationships in the common assumptions/zero residuals forecasts.

3.5). The effects on the dispersion of inflation forecasts are quite striking, as dispersion (relative to the published forecasts) is substantially increased through the forecast period.

The effect of 'standardizing' the forecasts in terms of the treatment of exogenous variables and projection of residuals is shown in inflation–unemployment space in Figure 3.7. This figure can be compared with Figure 3.1, which presents the results from the published forecasts. The general optimistic tendency of the LPL forecast does not seem to be markedly altered. Inflation is on average slightly lower and unemployment levels very similar to those in the published forecast (with the exception of 1986). Nor is the general shape of the CUBS forecast much changed, the major difference here being the slightly higher average level of unemployment. More significant changes occur for the LBS and NIESR forecasts. In its published forecast LBS predicts a small movement towards the south-west quadrant, that is, lower unemployment and inflation. In the recomputed forecast there is a sharp fall in the *price level* in 1986 and 1987, with the unemployment level in 1990 somewhat lower than in the published forecast. In the case of the NIESR published forecast there is very little movement in unemployment–inflation space. The recomputed forecast shows a sharp rise in inflation over the forecast period coupled with a small fall in the level of unemployment.

Average output growth is increased in these mechanical forecasts, especially for 1986. The individual forecasts most affected are LBS, where output growth is now predicted to be 5 per cent, and CUBS, whose forecast of output growth also rises by $2\frac{1}{2}$ per cent. There is a substantial impact on inflation in the mechanical forecasts. In three of the forecasts (LBS, LPL, and CUBS) inflation is now predicted to be considerably lower in 1986, and in the first two of these lower for most of the forecast period. In contrast, inflation now accelerates rapidly in the NIESR forecast.

In the case of the LBS model, the sensitivity of the forecast in the 'hands-off' exercise is associated with the response of the exchange rate. This more than doubles in the first quarter of the mechanical forecast and hence results in lower domestic inflation. The exchange rate change is in turn a consequence of effects in the financial model, where significant residuals are included in order to bring back on track a heavily calibrated sector of the model. The effect of removing residuals elsewhere in the model and maintaining a constant value for the residuals in the financial model effectively eliminates most of this exchange rate effect, but leads in turn to a very rapid increase in output in 1986. On the other hand, the impact on prices, while still negative, is much less than in the case where the financial sector residuals are removed. Two adjustments that appear to be particularly influential in the financial model are those on overseas bank loans and holdings of overseas equity and debenture holdings (AOL and AOE, respectively, in Table 3.6). We conclude that the exchange rate and

Table 3.6   *Major residual adjustments in the LBS forecast*

Quarter	AEM	KIID	KIIM	PXMAN	PMMAN	INPOX	C	AOL	AOE
1985(3)	1.1	−100	−900	−6.6	−6.3	300	−200	−8500	350
(4)	3.15	−150	−950	−4.0	−3.0	300	−200	−6200	400
Forecast									
1986(1)	3.19	−150	−950	−4.0	−3.0	600	−400	−6300	250
(2)	2.75	−150	−950	−4.0	−3.0	−300	−400	−6700	500
(3)	2.29	−200	−950	−4.0	−3.0	0	−400	−6720	500
(4)	2.70	−200	−950	−4.0	−3.0	0	−400	−6620	500
1987(1)	2.60	−250	−1000	−4.0	−3.0	0	−400	−6620	500
(2)	2.50	−250	−1000	−4.0	−3.0	150	−400	−6620	500
(3)	2.40	−250	−1000	−4.0	−3.0	150	−400	−6620	500
(4)	2.30	−250	−1000	−4.0	−3.0	150	−400	−6620	500
1988(1)	2.20	−250	−1000	−4.0	−3.0	150	−400	−6620	500
(2)	2.10	−250	−1000	−4.0	−3.0	150	−400	−6620	500
(3)	2.00	−250	−1000	−4.0	−3.0	150	−400	−6620	500
(4)	1.90	−250	−1000	−4.0	−3.0	150	−400	−6620	500
1989(1)	1.80	−250	−1000	−4.0	−3.0	150	−400	−6500	500
(2)	1.70	−250	−1000	−4.0	−3.0	150	−400	−6500	500
(3)	1.60	−250	−1000	−4.0	−3.0	150	−400	−6500	500
(4)	1.50	−250	−1000	−4.0	−3.0	150	−400	−6500	500
1990(1)	1.40	−250	−1000	−4.0	−3.0	150	−400	−6500	500
(2)	1.30	−250	−1000	−4.0	−3.0	150	−400	−6000	0
(3)	1.20	−250	−1000	−4.0	−3.0	150	−400	−6000	0
(4)	1.10	−250	−1000	−4.0	−3.0	150	−400	−6000	0
Value of variable in 1985									
	163	16,759	31,490	143.7	142	37,278	6705	−32,342	25,618

Key: AEM, average earnings in manufacturing (index, 1980 = 100); KIID, stock level, distribution (1980 £m); KIIM, stock level, manufacturing (1980 £m); PXMAN, price of manufacturing exports (index, 1980 = 100); INPOX, private non-housing, non-oil GDFCF (1980 £m); C, consumers' expenditure; AOL, overseas bank loans, (£m); AOE, overseas equity, debenture holdings (£m).

domestic inflation implications in the LBS forecast are highly dependent on the calibration of the financial sector of the model (see Figure 3.6), but that this affects real output to a much lesser degree. Rather, the adjustments to the remainder of the model, in particular those to stock levels, condition the forecasts of real output (see Figure 3.5).

In the NIESR forecast the adjustment to the exchange rate in the final period is of prime importance to the published forecasts of output and, particularly, inflation. The real exchange rate in the forecast is dependent only on initial and terminal values and on exogenous variables (relative world and UK real interest rates). The nominal exchange rate is then dependent on the real exchange rate and relative wholesale prices (largely constant). The real exchange rate does not appear in any other equation. In practice, therefore (see Chapter 2), the nominal exchange rate is largely determined by its own terminal value. Imposing a residual on the real (or nominal) exchange rate in the final period is equivalent to adjusting the terminal value, and using either of these methods to control the exchange rate is tantamount to exogenizing the variable. In the forecast a residual of 10 per cent is added to the real exchange rate in the final period, perhaps to ensure that the real exchange rate remains at its historical level. Whatever the reason for the adjustment, the result is that the trajectory of the exchange rate has been determined by the judgement of the forecaster rather than by the model structure (where this includes the specified

Table 3.7 *Major residual adjustments in the NIESR forecast*

Quarter	QDKMF	QMMF	EMPOTH	BLOPER	QDKRST	OMF
1985(3)	−90	26	−87	170	293	3.75
(4)	−35	108	−90	−5243	374	2.5
Forecast						
1986(1)	151	346	−120	−5010	206	1.0
(2)	−432	79	−111	−668	284	3.0
(3)	−220	−77	−106	−6547	262	3.8
(4)	−96	44	−112	−6626	334	4.5
1987(1)	−124	−78	−123	−7433	223	4.5
(2)	−133	−3	−125	−2872	349	4.5
(3)	−133	35	−117	−8861	318	4.5
(4)	−130	31	−115	−8761	423	4.5
1988(1)	−134	58	−119	−9316	310	4.5
(2)	−139	68	−118	−4915	415	4.5
(3)	−138	59	−122	−10465	353	4.5
(4)	−139	83	−126	−10151	417	4.5
1989(1)	−130	103	−126	−10911	301	4.25
(2)	−129	80	−161	−5504	411	4.25
(3)	−135	154	−159	−12149	355	4.0
(4)	−142	136	−163	−11807	428	4.0
1990(1)	−145	142	−164	−12471	321	3.75
(2)	−150	163	−153	−7209	428	3.75
(3)	−152	215	−172	−13609	373	3.75
(4)	−157	206	−174	−13088	444	3.75
Value of variable in 1985						
	1493	11053	8755	37684	1835	102.6

Key: QDKMF, manufacturing investment, (1980 £m); QMMF, imports of manufactures (1980 £m); EMPOTH, employment in private non-manufacturing ('000); BLOPER, bank lending to the personal sector (£m); QDKRST, other private investment (1980 £m); OMF, output in manufacturing (index, 1980 = 100).

terminal conditions). Although the real exchange rate is effectively predetermined in the forecast, the nominal rate can vary between simulations,
but only if relative wholesale prices change; thus, feedback from the model
to the exchange rate is limited.

It is not possible to remove the residual on the expected exchange rate
while maintaining all the other adjustments in the NIESR forecast, as this
results in a negative value for bank lending to the personal sector and
hence model solution fails. This problem can be avoided by simultaneously
removing the large adjustments to bank lending (see Table 3.7). Although
this adjustment is critical in achieving model solution for alternative values
of the adjustment on the exchange rate, its main influence on the model
forecast itself is solely in terms of the growth of the stock of money ($£M_3$).
Removal of the bank lending adjustment increases the money stock by 150
per cent by 1990, but there are no feedbacks from this higher monetary
growth to the remainder of the model. It is clear therefore that the main
purpose of this residual is to lower directly the already rapid growth of
money in the published forecast (and that very large adjustments are
required to do this). This would suggest that some degree of caution should
be attached to monetary developments in this particular forecast. Removing the terminal adjustment of the exchange rate, together with that on
bank lending, lowers the exchange rate by 9 per cent in 1986 and by 20 per
cent in 1990, thus raising the growth forecast and inducing an acceleration
in the inflation rate (see Figures 3.5 and 3.6). The exchange rate is, in
effect, treated as an exogenous variable in this forecast, and the published
forecast should consequently be seen as conditional on this particular view
of exchange rate developments.

We have suggested on earlier occasions that, in practice, residual adjustments may be made as part of an iterative process whereby a forecast run
made with an initial set of residuals is used to revise these, depending on
the plausibility and consistency of the model outcomes in the eyes of the
forecaster. This is an example of interaction between the model and the
forecaster. If, however, the latter has a very strong prior view as to the
value of a particular forecast variable, this can in practice be imposed, the
model being used to generate the implied residual necessary to achieve this
result (via a Type 1 fix). If this were applied to large numbers of variables,
one could only conclude that the role of the model in producing the
forecast was minor, merely ensuring a degree of internal consistency in a
forecast largely based on judgement. Our inspection of the residuals in the
NIESR forecast (see some examples in Table 3.7) suggests that many
important residuals were not decided independently by judgement or by
some mechanical rule, but were instead produced by the model in order to
generate particular values of the forecast variables. We would normally
expect either a constant level or a smooth path for residuals, but here the
pattern in many cases is uneven (for comparison see the projected LBS

Table 3.8 *Major residual adjustments in the CUBS forecast*

	MQK	EER	MQ	LSUP	AET
1985	−7200	−2.0	2600	600	3.0
1986	−7500	—	1500	750	2.0
1987	−7300	—	1000	500	—
1988	−3500	—	—	300	—
1989	−1000	—	—	—	—
1990	—	—	—	—	—
1991–98	—	—	—	—	—
Value of variable in 1985					
	287,347	82.1	147,253	24,628	153.7

Key: MQK, capital stock of marketed output sector (1980 £m); EER, nominal exchange rate; MQ, marketed output, (1980 £m); LSUP, labour supply ('000); AET, average earnings (index, 1980 = 100).

residuals in Table 3.6). Some of these adjustments affect key endogenous variables in the model. This strongly suggests that the NIESR published forecast was to a large extent imposed upon the model.

The CUBS forecast of GDP appears to be little affected by either common assumptions and/or zero residuals by the early 1990s although the contribution of common assumptions becomes more important towards the end of the forecast period. However, there are substantial short-term effects. Zero residuals alone would increase the output forecast substantially in 1986 and 1987 and the principal residual responsible is that on

Table 3.9 *Major residual adjustments in the LPL forecast*

	ZG[a]	XXM	ZRL	ZEG[a]	CNR[a]	ZRW[a]
1985	0.07	600	0.015	−0.015	−0.015	0.015
1986	0.002	−1200	0.015	−0.043	−0.015	0.015
1987	—	—	0.01	−0.04	−0.015	0.010
1988	−0.02	—	0.01	−0.065	−0.015	0.005
1989	−0.055	—	0.01	−0.08	−0.015	—
1990	−0.05	—	0.01	−0.075	−0.015	—
1991	−0.04	—	0.005	−0.07	−0.015	—
1992	−0.03	—	—	−0.065	−0.015	—
1993	−0.02	—	—	−0.06	−0.015	—
Value of variable in 1985						
	695,646	619	0.079	61,202	119,678	1.06

Key: ZG, private sector stock of goods (1980 £m); XXM, trade balance (1980 £m); ZRL, real long rate of interest; ZEG, government expenditure (1980 £m); CNR, non-durable consumption expenditure (1980 £m); ZRW, real earnings (index, 1980 = 1).

[a] These residuals are multiplicative.

capital stock (MQK) (see Table 3.8). In contrast, common assumptions alone would reduce the CUBS GDP forecast in those years. In the case of the CUBS price forecast it is the longer-term effects that are more apparent. The residual adjustment on capital stock acts to reduce prices in 1986 and 1987, but the pattern thereafter results from the oscillatory behaviour of the model.

In the case of LPL, some of the major change in the common assumption/zero residual variant occurs when the exogenous tax variables are revised. There is very little difference in the LPL forecast of GDP when computed under the zero residual assumption, but the price level is considerably lower.

3.5 Decomposition of the forecasts

A systematic way of recording the effects of exogenous assumptions and residual adjustments on the distribution of forecasts is provided by the accounting framework shown in Table 3.10 and Figures 3.8 and 3.9. This is achieved by breaking down the difference of each forecast from the average of all the forecasts into component parts: differences in exogenous assumptions, differences in residual adjustments, and differences in the models. The last is defined as the balancing item after calculating the parts of the forecast differences arising from the first two. Difficulties in exactly matching exogenous variables and residual adjustments imply that the allocation of the remaining element to model differences can be only very approximate.

The various contributions are measured in the following way. Let P be a particular published forecast of a variable and let A be the average of all the forecasts, then $P - A$ is the total difference to be explained. If CA is the model forecast based on a set of common exogenous assumptions, then the contribution of differences in exogenous variable projections to the forecast difference is $P - CA$. If CAR is the model forecast using both common exogenous assumptions and zero residuals, then the contribution of the forecaster's residual adjustments is $CA - CAR$. The difference in the published forecast from the average owing to model difference is then defined as $CAR - A$. The differences shown are expressed as a percentage of the average forecast.

The LBS forecast is more pessimistic than average in terms of the level of GDP. For 1986–87 this is due largely to the influence of the equation residuals (in both the financial and the non-financial sectors) with a small expansionary effect from exogenous assumptions. But between 1988 and 1989 it is the model itself that provides the pessimism with partial offsetting influences from the residuals and exogenous variables.

The NIESR is the most pessimistic of the GDP forecasts in this section.

Table 3.10 *Decomposition of forecasts**
(% of average forecast)

	Total difference[a]			Contribution of exogenous variables[b]			Contribution of residuals[c]			Contribution of models[d]		
	1986–87	1988–89	1998	1986–87	1988–89	1998	1986–87	1988–89	1998	1986–87	1988–89	1998
GDP forecasts												
LBS	−0.67	−1.73	—	0.70	1.18	—	−1.32	1.72	—	−0.06	−4.63	—
NIESR	−1.65	−4.36	—	−1.10	−0.09	—	−0.06	−2.31	—	−1.50	−1.96	—
CUBS	1.79	3.98	−5.60	2.06	2.31	1.95	−3.11	−0.24	0.43	2.84	1.91	−7.95
LPL	0.47	2.00	5.60	1.48	1.97	1.47	−2.72	−4.70	−0.50	1.72	4.73	4.63
Price forecasts												
LBS	1.22	1.59	—	0.85	3.37	—	17.85	30.57	—	−17.48	−32.35	—
NIESR	−0.20	−0.83	—	−1.69	−4.61	—	−4.81	−21.94	—	6.30	25.71	—
CUBS	−0.42	1.56	9.57	−2.93	−1.65	30.12	3.11	−1.62	−8.14	−0.60	4.81	−12.41
LPL	−0.61	−2.32	−9.57	−0.76	0.34	15.06	9.29	14.88	9.31	−9.14	−17.53	−33.94

* Components may not sum to totals owing to rounding.
[a] the difference between the published forecast and the average of all the forecasts, expressed as a percentage of the average forecast
[b] that part of the total difference resulting from a comparison of the published forecast with the common assumption forecast
[c] that part of the total difference resulting from a comparison of the common assumption forecast with that based on common assumptions and zero residuals
[d] the remaining part of the total difference

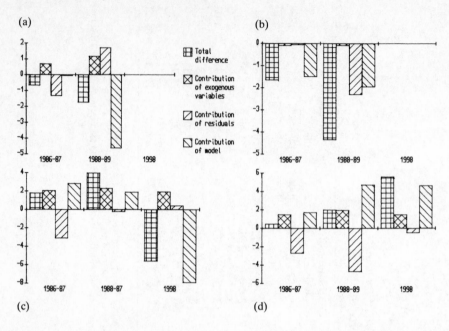

Fig. 3.8   Decomposition of GDP forecasts (% of average forecast). (a) LBS; (b) NIESR; (c) CUBS; (d) LPL.

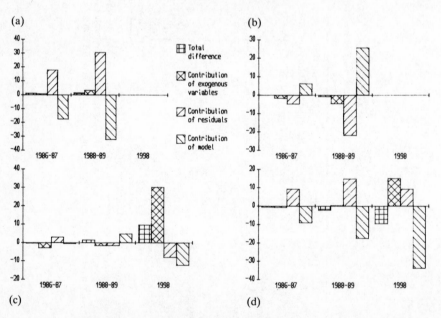

Fig. 3.9   Decomposition of price forecasts (% of average forecast). (a) LBS; (b) NIESR; (c) CUBS; (d) LPL.

For 1986–87 this is due entirely to the model, but for 1988–89 residual adjustments add to the pessimistic influence of the model itself.

CUBS and LPL are relatively optimistic up to 1989. Exogenous variables play some part in this. For 1986–87 the residuals reduce the optimistic tendency of the model but residual effects are very weak thereafter. Optimism over GDP is also due to the model in the case of LPL, but here the effect of residual adjustments in reducing the degree of optimism is more sustained through the forecast period.

Divergences of individual inflation forecasts from the average are relatively minor in 1986–87. In the case of LBS and LPL the residual adjustments broadly offset the tendency of the model to generate a more optimistic forecast, whereas the residual adjustments operate so as to counteract the pessimistic influence in the NIESR model.

Although forecast divergences remain fairly small in the following two-year period to 1989, they mask very large compositional effects. As noted earlier, the removal of the residual adjustments in the financial sector of the LBS model produces a fall in the price level, which is clearly captured in Figure 3.9, where the residual adjustments can be seen to offset a very large model effect. In the case of NIESR it is the exchange rate residual that is eliminating the model's tendency to generate rapid inflation. In the LPL forecast residual adjustments also operate to offset some of the model influence — in this case a tendency towards optimism over inflation. As we found in our first two reviews, the CUBS forecast is one where residual influences are weakest except in the first two years of the forecast, suggesting that the forecasters are content to allow the model to operate fairly freely.

The scale of the compositional effects in the price forecasts in this analysis is far greater than we observed in our first and second reviews of *ex ante* forecasts, but the overall forecast divergences of inflation from the average are smaller than the 1984 forecasts. The discussion above noted the tendency of inflation forecasts to diverge even more when residual adjustments were removed. This is largely due to the opposite tendencies in the two quarterly forecasts: in one (LBS) the financial sector adjustments are holding up the price forecast, whereas in the other (NIESR) the exchange rate adjustment is holding it down.

Our first two reviews of *ex ante* forecasts concluded that exogenous variables played a minor part in explaining forecast differences. That conclusion is supported by this third study, although exogenous influences do appear to be fairly important in explaining divergences of the CUBS and LPL forecasts. The role of residuals in masking very real differences in the models themselves is brought out clearly in the present LBS and NIESR forecasts of prices. Thus, the apparent consensus of published forecasts of inflation may be misleading. The evidence from the two annual forecasts (CUBS and LPL) suggests that these are fairly free of residual adjustments in the longer term.

3.6 Summary and conclusions

This is our third successive study of *ex ante* forecasts. Throughout these reviews we have found two annual forecasts, CUBS and LPL, to be considerably more optimistic in terms of inflation and output prospects than the two quarterly models (LBS and NIESR). Another repeated finding is that the dispersion of output growth forecasts is high relative to the mean of the forecasts, but although the dispersion of the inflation forecasts increases over the forecast horizon, it remains less than the average forecast.

With the exception of the tax rate effects in the LPL forecast, we find yet again that exogenous assumptions play a fairly small part in explaining forecast differences. The use of equation residuals appears to mask some of the basic differences between the models so that pure model-based forecasts show even greater dispersion than is evident from the published forecasts. The CUBS forecast remains the forecast that is least affected in this way. Residual adjustments are also less important in the long-term development of the LPL forecast. In the current analysis we find that the exchange rate is effectively exogenized in the NIESR forecast at its historical value, and this assumption is critical to the inflation forecast. There also appears to be some indication that the residual adjustments were in fact calculated in order to be consistent with a given model solution, and to this extent their forecast can be regarded as more judgementally based than the others. In the case of LBS, the calibration of the financial sector is critical to the inflation forecast, and the residuals in this sector operate on inflation in a different direction from the exchange rate residual in the NIESR forecast. Whereas the NIESR inflation forecast relies heavily on the adjustment to the exchange rate, that of LBS is dependent on the skill of the forecaster in calibrating the financial sector of the model.

Chapter 4

Analysis of the Autumn 1983 Forecasts

4.1 Introduction

Several studies have been published describing the forecast performance, *ex post*, of UK macroeconomic models. In general these are limited to comparisons of forecasts with outturns, and little analysis of the major sources of forecast error is available. Independent analysts of forecasts have not been able to recompute the forecasts under alternative assumptions using the exact model underlying each forecast. The Bureau however has taken successive deposits of models and their associated forecasts since autumn 1983, and archived this information. With the availability of actual data up to 1985, it is now possible to begin *ex post* analyses of forecast performance.

In Section 4.2 we outline some of the main methodological issues in *ex post* forecast analysis. This is followed in Section 4.3 by a comparison of the autumn 1983 forecasts of LBS, NIESR, CUBS, and LPL with current estimates of the outcomes for 1984 and 1985, focusing on output, inflation, and unemployment. In Sections 4.4–4.6 forecast errors are then decomposed into contributions arising from the exogenous variables, residual adjustments, and model error, using a similar framework to that developed in our studies of the *ex ante* forecasts. The effects of data revision are considered in Section 4.7. Comparisons with forecasts based on a vector-autoregressive model are presented in Section 4.8, and comparisons across models based on combinations of the results for different variables are described in Section 4.9. The main findings are summarized in Section 4.10. Some forecast teams (e.g., CUBS) present a set of conditional projections for the economy rather than a single forecast: in these cases we have chosen their central projection for analysis.

4.2 Methodological considerations

Assessment of UK economic forecasts is not new. The model teams themselves regularly publish accounts of their own forecast performance, and occasionally contrast this with that of other groups. There have also been several independent studies of forecast performance across models, for example, Ash and Smyth (1973) and Holden and Peel (1983). These studies are limited to a descriptive account of forecast errors, both over time and across models, typically consisting of the calculation of root mean square forecast errors, or other summary statistics, for certain variables from a series of forecasts. In addition, regression analysis may be used to compare actual and forecast data; for example, Holden and Peel (1985) use this approach to test for bias, efficiency, and consistency in the NIESR forecasts.

Another approach to the comparative evaluation of forecasts emanates from the idea of combining forecasts (Nelson, 1972; Granger and Newbold, 1977, p. 283). If a combined forecast has an error variance that is not significantly smaller than that of an individual forecast, then the competing forecast appears to offer no additional useful information. (Seeing whether the forecasts of one model explain another model's forecast errors is used by Chong and Hendry (1986) as part of the encompassing approach to model evaluation, of which more in Chapter 5.) There is little emphasis in the literature on the various sources of forecast error, an exception being Osborn and Teal (1979), who consider the role of residual adjustments and exogenous variable error; their study is restricted to two forecasts from one model (NIESR).

As forecasts are the joint product of the forecaster and the economic model, analysis based only on sequences of forecasts and forecast errors cannot reveal their relative contributions to forecast performance; nor can comparison of forecast data with actual outcomes distinguish between alternative models and alternative forecasters.

These approaches to forecast evaluation require data on a series of forecasts over time, but as yet we have only one forecast that can be compared to actual data. As we accumulate more *ex ante* forecasts and more data on actual outcomes, so we shall be able to conduct forecast evaluation exercises utilizing these techniques. The present exercise, however, is limited to forecasts made at a single point in time. On the other hand, the information available on the construction of the forecasts permits an analysis of why forecast errors arise, using a similar approach to Osborn and Teal, and allows a comparative analysis of forecasts produced by the different model teams. In the remainder of this section we discuss some of the general issues in forecast evaluation as they apply to the present study.

The first issue concerns the assessment of the forecast error in a given variable. Since there is no absolute measure of the forecastability of a variable, various comparative criteria have been suggested. First, forecast errors may be compared to the model errors experienced in the sample period over which the model was estimated. In addition to the danger that a model may be estimated in such a way as to produce a spuriously high degree of fit, this rests on the assumption that the sample period and forecast period are homogeneous. On the other hand, through various random events or systematic changes, the economy may be harder to forecast in certain periods. If the forecaster's skill leads to good predictions of these events, then small forecasting errors will result, now representing a joint measure of model and forecaster no longer directly comparable with model estimation errors.

A further form of comparison considers forecast errors across models, which is the main approach used here. A possible criticism (see McNees, 1981) is that different models may have different degrees of exogeneity and so cannot be compared directly. If actual exogenous data are used to evaluate forecast error, then one might expect a relatively open model with a greater number of exogenous variables to perform better than a model with a much lower degree of exogeneity. To compare models it is then necessary to standardize the exogenous information set in some way. However, in the models with which we are concerned there are very few differences in the classification of variables, and this particular difficulty does not arise.

A second issue arises from the dynamic, multivariate nature of the forecasts. Macroeconomic forecasts consist of predictions for several economic variables over several time periods. One model may forecast one variable relatively well and another relatively badly, or may be relatively successful at forecasting one year ahead but relatively poor at longer-term forecasts. In order to evaluate forecasts formally, a loss function that weights the relative importance of different variables or time periods is required. In most of our discussion we concentrate on three variables which receive considerable attention in the public discussion of forecasts, namely, GDP, prices, and unemployment, without attempting to weight these three main outcomes; and it is possible that consideration of an alternative set of variables might reach different conclusions regarding forecast accuracy. In Section 4.9, however, we present an illustrative calculation of a loss function and discuss the comparative possibilities.

A third question is whether errors should be measured in terms of levels or growth rates. In a two-year forecast period, as here, it is possible that a particular model can forecast growth rates for the two individual years badly yet be quite accurate in its prediction of the level of the variable at the end of the period. Alternatively, a single growth error in either year will produce a poor forecast of the level after two years, perhaps accompanied by a good estimate of growth in the other year of the forecast. This is again an instance where some loss function is required. Public attention usually focuses on the growth rate of output, the rate of inflation, and the level of unemployment, but we present both level and growth errors in our analysis.

Finally, we have the problem of data revision, which affects many macroeconomic variables. Major data revisions occur annually following the publication of the National Income and Expenditure Blue Book, with minor revisions occurring more frequently. Less frequently, reconstruction of the real national accounts data using revised relative price weights (as happened in late 1983, when the weights were changed from a 1975 to a 1980 base) can lead to very substantial revision of data, going back perhaps to the origin of the data series. Such revisions can change both the level of the series and the growth rates between given time periods. Further discussion of this issue takes place below. Whereas quantity data are perhaps subject to greatest regular revision, price data are less liable to revision, except for the periodic change of the base year of index numbers; and certain variables such as interest rates are rarely revised. Changes in definition or method of measurement affect other variables such as the level of unemployment, and in the present exercise it is necessary to adjust the current outcomes for unemployment to be consistent with the series that the models were attempting to forecast in 1983. We assume that the final revised figure is most accurate and that the objective is to forecast this rather than the first announced figure. Our estimates of the actual outcome are based on March 1986 data (April 1986 for inflation), but, given that data for 1984 and 1985 may be further revised, our conclusions should be regarded as preliminary. The forecasts for 1985 may appear in a different light when viewed from a later year.

Data revisions have two main effects on the assessment of forecasts. First, changes to estimates of the data for the forecast period affect any measures of forecast accuracy based on a comparison of the forecast with estimates of the actual outcome. This effect is fairly easily calculated, however, once the revision process is complete. Second, and less susceptible to quantification, data revisions to the recent past alter the initial conditions for the forecast. It is reasonable to suppose that a different view of the current situation would lead to a different forecast. Typically, forecasters examine the performance of their model over the recent past prior to forecasting, and the results of this examination often influence their projections of model residuals through the forecast period. Changes to data over the recent past may alter their perception of the performance of the model and hence the necessary adjustment to be made in the forecast period. Likewise, they may take a different view of likely outcomes for the exogenous variables during the forecast period, particularly in respect of policy variables. Thus, a full assessment of the effects of data revisions would require simulation of the behaviour of the forecaster when faced with a different information set. We cannot hope to replicate such behaviour, but in Section 4.7 we describe an attempt to allow for some element of data revision by making some simple adjustments to residuals over the forecast period.

We now turn to a description of our methodology for explaining the main sources of forecast error. A general expression for the forecast error in a linear model is (see, for example, Salmon and Wallis, 1982)

$$y_{T+j} - \hat{y}_{T+j} = \hat{\Pi}(z_{T+j} - \hat{z}_{T+j}) - (\hat{\Pi} - \Pi)z_{T+j} + v_{T+j}$$

where y_{T+j} is the vector of endogenous variables in period $T + j$, z_{T+j} is the vector of predetermined variables, Π are the true reduced-form coeffi cients of the model, and the carets denote estimated or forecast values. The first term relates to the effect due to a divergence of the exogenous variables from their projected values, the second to coefficient estimation error, and the third term represents the random disturbance, v_{T+j}, in the forecast period. Although the standard approach is to assume that the optimal forecast of the disturbances is their unconditional mean value of zero, in practice, various adjustments to the forecast are made via the predictions of the residuals. Whereas this decomposition is usually presented on the assumption that the model is correctly specified, model misspecification can be treated as part of the second term, with coefficients either erroneously equated to zero when the true value is non-zero, or assigned a non-zero value when the true value is zero. Errors in model specification due to the wrong functional form are also implicit in this term. We estimate the contribution of the exogenous variables to forecast error by recomputing the forecast using the actual exogenous data. By additionally setting residual adjustments to zero, we estimate this influence on the forecast. The remaining element, representing the contribution of model error, therefore includes errors of specification, functional form, and the influence of random errors in the forecast period. A large 'model' forecast error may indicate the presence of a random shock within the forecast period rather than a poorly specified model. This term also includes any effect of data revisions not explicitly accommodated elsewhere.

The term 'exogenous variable error' is used loosely, since some of the forecasts analysed may be one of several possible variants, and the one selected for analysis is therefore merely conditional on one particular set of exogenous variables. The exogenous variables may not have the status of variables that forecasters are aiming to predict. For example, some groups (NIESR) present forecasts conditional on unchanged policy. In such a case an 'unsatisfactory' prospect for the economy may lead to a change in policy and hence to an exogenous variable error in the sense defined above. Our calculation of forecasts under actual exogenous variable values places models and their forecasts on an equal footing in the sense that they are conditional on this same exogenous data set.

The two quarterly forecasts are based on data for 1983 which is a mixture of actual and forecast. The published forecasts were computed from the fourth quarter of 1983, although various temporary exogeneity switches were present for this period. In order to ensure comparability with the annual models we recompute the forecasts from the first quarter of 1984 to the end of 1985. Separate problems arise for the LPL forecast, which is based on forward expectations and so depends on the whole future profile of the model and its exogenous assumptions. Ideally, we would wish to incorporate the information regarding future exogenous variables contained in the now available actual data for 1984 and 1985, and we approximate this by using the future values from the most recent (i.e., autumn

1985) LPL forecasts on the assumption that this incorporates the latest information.

4.3   Forecasts and outturns

In Chapter 3 successive forecasts of output, inflation, and unemployment are presented, and these suggest that there has been some systematic revision of forecasts over time, presumably in part owing to the emergence of forecasting errors. In this chapter we are concerned solely with the analysis of one particular forecast: that made in autumn 1983 or, in the case of LPL, early 1984. For the purpose of this section we use data consistent with the March 1986 issue of *Economic Trends* to form the set of actual outcomes. Information on the consumer price index was taken from the April issue as full 1985 data were not available in March. These data enable us to calculate forecast errors for 1984 and 1985. Although most of the forecasts were made in late 1983, at that time data for many of the variables were available only for the first six months of the year, although some preliminary information was known for other variables for perhaps ten months of the year. The estimates for 1983 that formed part of the published forecasts are therefore a mixture of actual and forecast, and forecast errors are also shown for this year.

We note above that, around the time the forecasts were made, national accounts data were rebased using 1980 relative price weights instead of the then existing 1975 price weights. The main effects on the estimates of GDP arise from the fact that the oil sector has a larger weight in total output in 1980, given it had been expanding rapidly as North Sea oil came on stream. The revised 1980-based GDP growth estimated in late 1983 was now 12 per cent between 1980 and 1982 for the expenditure measure, in comparison with a fall of 0.8 per cent for the 1975-based measure. The revised (1980-weighted) output measure of GDP still indicates a decline of 0.6 over this period, slightly less than the 1.4 per cent reduction for the 1975-weighted index. Although the new 1980-based data were available to the forecasters at the time of the forecast, the time lag was too short for them to rescale their models completely to take account of this change. Consequently, forecasts were prepared using 1975-based versions of the models, although typically these forecasts were subsequently rescaled to a 1980 price base in the published discussion.

The actual GDP data, against which we wish to compare the forecasts, are on a 1980 price base, and so some rescaling of the 1975-price-based forecasts is necessary. We have already observed that the growth rate of GDP when computed at 1980 relative price weights differs from that using 1975 weights over the period up to the preparation of the forecasts. However, the degree of divergence in growth rates over the forecast period appears to be very minor. The LBS, in their published review, gave a comparison of the two sets of growth rates and showed the difference to be only of the order of 0.1 per cent per annum for 1983–85 growth rates. These relatively small differences reflect the levelling out of oil production over the forecast period. We have not made any correction to the forecasts for the rebasing effect, for the following reasons. First, the rebasing effects identified by LBS are quite trivial in comparison with the forecast errors reported later in this chapter, and their order of magnitude is such as to make no change to our conclusions in respect of relative forecast accuracy. Such corrections would require a re-weighting of each forecast separately, since oil production forecasts differ, so these minor adjustments would differ across forecasts. Further, one forecast (LPL) does not distinguish oil production separately, and therefore we are not able to make a model-specific correction in this case. We have therefore simply rescaled the forecasts by the difference between the 1975-based series and the 1980-based series for the first half of 1983 (the latter appearing in the October 1983 edition of *Economic Trends*). Since the forecasters had access to these data, we assume that it is the same information set as in their forecasts (thus there is no forecast error for the first half of 1983). The derived scaling factor is then used to convert forecast levels of GDP throughout the forecast. This preserves the growth rates implicit in the forecasts. A similar procedure is adopted for the consumer price index, although here there are no complications arising from reweighting.

Separate problems arise for the unemployment outcomes. There was a classification change to the series owing to measures announced in the 1983 Budget, when certain older men, mainly aged over 60, no longer needed to sign on at an unemployment benefit office. This effect came into operation in August 1983, and although the change was known at the time of forecast some of the teams made no adjustment within their models, but reported the potential impact in their published discussion. In our analysis the information is taken from the forecast deposit, and hence some adjustment for the revised definition of unemployment needs to be made if the information is to be compatible with the official data. For this we use the official estimates of the effects of the change and adjust the old series (i.e., that used in the forecasts) downwards by 156,000 throughout the forecast period. The definition of unemployment adopted is the annual average of wholly unemployed, excluding school-leavers.

As noted above, three particular outcomes are usually emphasized: GDP, the rate of inflation, and the level of unemployment. Forecasts of these variables compared with outcomes are presented in Table 4.1.

Before examining this information, we need to discuss an event that has had a bearing on the recorded estimates of the behaviour of the economy over the period in question. This was the miners' dispute, which lasted from March 1984 to March 1985, and which was unanticipated at the time of the forecast. (Even subsequent forecasts, once the strike had begun, were uncertain as to its duration.) This is an example of a random event which the models were not expected to incorporate but which affects the data against which their performance is monitored. One possibility would be to adjust the actual data for the effects of the strike and hence compare the forecasts with a 'strike-adjusted' outcome. However, we have not attempted to do this formally for two main reasons. First, there are no official estimates that give the total effect of the dispute. The official statisticians note that the *direct* effect of the dispute, using estimates of lost coal production, was to reduce output growth by around 1 per cent in 1984, and to increase it by around 1 per cent in 1985; but no estimates for other variables of interest are attempted. No official measures of the total (direct and indirect) effects are given, although indications are that the indirect impact was minor. The forecasting teams have at times indicated how they judge the impact of the strike, and it is clear from this that the principal direct effects were on output, imports, exports, stockbuilding, and the PSBR. Second, the estimates that are available suggest that the impact of the dispute was largely one of timing, with, for example, the effects on GDP estimated to be almost completely offsetting in the two years 1984 and 1985, and so our conclusions on forecast error over the whole period are largely unaffected. Errors for the individual years do, however, reflect this dispute, and to aid interpretation we include some very approximate adjustments for the strike (based on official estimates) in the comparison of forecast errors. It is obvious from inspection of the forecast errors, however, that, although the miner's strike might represent a common cause of error, there is not a common pattern of error in the forecast residuals.

We now turn to the discussion of the forecasts. Some basic statistics on forecasting accuracy are given in Table 4.1. We illustrate four particular variables: the level and growth of GDP, the rate of (consumer price) inflation, and the level of employment. LBS and NIESR forecast more than one measure of GDP; we have chosen the measure emphasized in the published report of the NIESR forecast (output), but for LBS, where no clear preference is indicated, we report both measures. Inspection of Table 4.1 reveals that the choice of GDP measure is important, as the output measure is now estimated to have grown by over 3 per cent in 1984 as against only $1\frac{3}{4}$ per cent for the expenditure measure.

Taking GDP growth first, it appears from the table that the NIESR forecast was consistently over-pessimistic. A different picture emerges for the LBS depending on whether the output or expenditure measure is used. Forecast performance was superior using the expenditure measure to that based on the output measure, where the under-prediction for 1984 was quite large in comparison with the strike-adjusted actual data, and was not compensated by a corresponding over-prediction for 1985. LPL and CUBS were optimistic for 1984, even when strike effects are taken into account, and this optimism carries over to 1985 but on a weaker level. Only LPL

Table 4.1   *The autumn 1983 forecasts, and outturns, 1983–85*

	1983	1984	1985
GDP growth (% per annum)			
(i) Output measure			
Forecasts: LBS	1.8	2.4	2.4
CUBS	2.2	4.9	3.3
NIESR	2.2	2.0	1.0
Actual	3.0	3.1	3.4
Actual (adjusted for miners' strike)*		4	2½
(ii) Expenditure measure			
Forecasts: LBS	2.5	1.9	2.4
LPL	3.6	3.5	3.0
Actual	3.7	1.7	3.3
Actual (adjusted for miners' strike)*		2¾	2½
Inflation (% p. a.)			
Forecasts: LBS	5.6	5.9	6.3
NIESR	5.8	5.8	6.1
CUBS	6.1	6.8	8.3
LPL	4.6	3.3	2.1
Actual	5.2	4.6	5.4
Unemployment (millions)			
Forecasts: LBS	2.9	3.0	2.8
NIESR	2.9	3.1	3.4
CUBS	2.9	2.6	2.3
LPL	2.9	2.7	2.4
Actual	2.9	3.0	3.2

* Estimates based on *Economic Trends*, April 1985 and April 1986 issues.

came close to forecasting the outcome for the base year of the forecast (1983), but this forecast was made some three months later than the others. The size of forecast error for this year made by the other teams is at least as great as the errors made for subsequent years. Data revisions affect the estimates of the growth rate in 1983 depending on the measure of GDP used (see Section 4.7).

Problems of data revision are far less acute for estimates of the inflation rate, and there is a relatively small dispersion of estimates for the base year (1983). LBS, NIESR, and CUBS were all consistently over-pessimistic over inflation, with CUBS producing the most pessimistic forecast. In contrast, LPL can be seen to have been over-optimistic.

Only one group overestimated the level of unemployment by 1985, namely, NIESR. This error is clearly related to the underprediction of output. However, NIESR are closer to the eventual outturn in 1985 than the other groups. Even though LBS underpredicted output growth in 1985, it underpredicted the level of unemployment. The unemployment forecasts of LPL and CUBS projected a falling level in both 1984 and 1985 but the actual experience has been a slight increase. In consequence, both underestimated the 1985 level of unemployment by around $\frac{3}{4}$ million.

Table 4.2 shows the size of forecast errors in the levels of the three main outcome variables. Both LBS and NIESR show an increasing size of GDP forecast error over time, despite the miners' strike, and all of the forecasts imply an increasing absolute percentage error in the price level and in the level of unemployment to 1985. The forecast errors for GDP in 1985 are smallest for LPL, followed by CUBS and LBS (expenditure measure). The largest forecast errors occur for NIESR and LBS (output measure).

Table 4.2   *Forecast errors: GDP, prices, and unemployment*
(actual − forecast)

	1983	1984	1985
	(% of actual unless otherwise stated)		
GDP			
LBS — output	1.57	2.42	3.36
LBS — expenditure	0.92	0.67	1.53
NIESR — output	1.63	2.69	4.99
CUBS — output	0.19	−1.57	−1.52
LPL — expenditure	0.62	−1.11	−0.82
Price level			
LBS	0.16	−1.08	−1.93
NIESR	0.18	−0.97	−1.61
CUBS	−0.86	−2.91	−5.52
LPL	0.55	1.68	5.00
Unemployment ('000)			
LBS	−7	63	372
NIESR	−28	−86	−253
CUBS	−22	398	917
LPL	80	392	751

Table 4.3 shows the forecast errors of other important endogenous outcomes in the forecasts. The comparison of employment errors with those of unemployment (Table 4.2) reveals some interesting results. The LBS forecast for 1985 underpredicted the level of employment by some 80,000 jobs but overpredicted the level of unemployment by 370,000. In contrast, the size of the employment forecast errors for NIESR for both 1984 and 1985 greatly exceed the equivalent unemployment errors. These forecasting errors arise as a result of changes in the employment–unemployment relationship rather than errors in labour supply forecasts, although these play a part in the unemployment error. (The errors have led to changes in model specification in the latest versions of these models.) With the exception of CUBS in 1984, the CUBS and LPL employment forecast errors are broadly the same as those for unemployment but of opposite sign.

Table 4.3   *Forecast errors: employment, exchange rate, and PSBR*

	1983		1984		1985	
	'000	%	'000	%	'000	%
(a) Employment (difference from actual)						
LBS	132	0.63	95	0.45	−81	0.38
NIESR	124	0.59	161	0.76	483	2.27
CUBS	−237	−1.13	−281	−1.33	−924	−4.34
LPL	−48	−0.23	−360	−1.70	−719	−3.38
(b) Exchange rate (% of actual)						
LBS	−0.34			−2.43		−0.71
NIESR	−0.48			−2.36		2.30
CUBS	−1.70			−4.69		−1.61
Actual	83.3			78.8		78.7
(c) PSBR (difference from actual, £m)						
LBS	746			1889		900
NIESR	3774			378		−2641
CUBS	4328			9001		13153
LPL	2993			3759		2506
Actual	11609			10150		7568

Forecast errors for the nominal effective exchange rate are also shown in Table 4.3. LBS, NIESR, and CUBS all underestimated the magnitude of the fall in the exchange rate in 1984, but as it stabilized in 1985 so the size of forecast error diminishes and the direction of error varies between the forecasts. Errors in exchange rate forecasts explain very little of the forecast errors of output and prices for the period under considertion.

Finally, we show forecast errors relating to the PSBR. In general, errors are quite large in relation to the magnitude of the variable being forecast. Revisions to 1983 data lead to a considerable under-forecast in the base year, but the scale of underprediction increases in 1984 for all the forecasts except NIESR. Here there is a clear indication of effects from the miners' dispute. The scale of the errors for CUBS and LPL is very large in relation to the actual outturn. LBS are closest to the actual figure in 1985, even allowing for an effect for the miners' strike, and NIESR overpredict the size of the PSBR. Whereas the size of the LPL error falls, that of CUBS becomes extremely large.

The effect of revisions to the main expenditure components of GDP are discussed below, but we note here that there has been a substantial upward revision to the data on gross fixed investment since late 1983, largely owing to a re-classification of expenditure on consumption. It is not surprising, therefore, that both LBS and NIESR reveal a large degree of underprediction in this variable throughout their published forecasts (see Table 4.4). What is perhaps more interesting is that they share other errors in forecasting the components of GDP. Both make large errors on trade, with exports and imports underpredicted by large margins. The net effect is to overpredict the contribution of net trade to output in both forecasts. Significant overprediction also occurs for stockbuilding for 1984 (partly as an effect of the miners' strike), thus offsetting some of the underprediction arising from errors on fixed investment. The stockbuilding error remains quite large for NIESR for 1985 but largely disappears for LBS. Both LBS and NIESR forecast the level of consumption quite accurately for 1984, but NIESR make an underestimate of $3\frac{1}{2}$ per cent for 1985.

Table 4.4   *Expenditure components of GDP*
(% per annum unless otherwise stated)

	Published forecast		Actual exog. assump- tions(AE)		AE + zero residuals		Actual	
	1984	1985	1984	1985	1984	1985	1984	1985
Consumers' expenditure								
LBS	2.0	1.8	2.4	2.8	3.1	2.1	1.8	2.8
NIESR	0.6	0.2	1.2	0.9	2.6	1.5		
Gross fixed investment								
LBS	4.4	3.4	6.7	−4.5	14.9	0.8	7.9	0.9
NIESR	3.8	0.8	7.1	−7.0	6.9	−5.7		
Stockbuilding (1980 £m)								
LBS	678	742	769	806	2378	1858	−142	878
NIESR	1233	1171	1434	1185	3575	3393		
Exports of goods and services								
LBS	3.1	4.5	6.7	5.4	7.5	7.5	7.2	6.0
NIESR	3.9	4.8	9.6	3.1	11.6	0.9		
Imports of goods and services								
LBS	3.8	2.7	7.3	4.5	10.7	4.3	9.5	3.0
NIESR	4.1	2.7	8.4	1.1	5.3	0.7		
Factor cost adjustment								
LBS	3.0	2.1	2.1	2.7	1.8	1.4	3.7	2.8
NIESR	4.0	2.0	7.2	−0.5	4.6	—		

One might ask whether an average of the forecasts would have produced a smaller forecasting error than selecting any particular forecast. This is true for the level of GDP for 1984 and for the price level for both 1984 and 1985, but it is not true of GDP for 1985 or of the level of unemployment in either year. This result occurs since we have in general two relatively optimistic forecasts (LPL and CUBS) and two relatively pessimistic forecasts (LBS and NIESR), and the degrees of optimism and pessimism roughly cancel out for GDP and prices. However, for unemployment the degree of optimism of CUBS and LPL is not matched by an equal degree of pessimism by the other two forecasts.

4.4   Exogenous assumptions

In order to condition the forecasts on the same set of exogenous information, we recompute the forecasts using estimates of the actual behaviour of these variables. These estimates are taken from the latest forecasts deposited at the Bureau in autumn 1985. Since final data on these variables for 1985 were not then available, there is inevitably some degree of forecast still remaining in these estimates, corresponding to the forecasting groups' views of likely developments in late 1985. Changes from 1975 to 1980 price weights may lead to some rebasing effects here, as for the main endogenous variables. Generally, the set of exogenous variables in each model has stayed unchanged between 1983 and 1985, although some variables have switched from an exogenous to an endogenous classification over this period (for example, nominal interest rates in the NIESR model). This causes no problems for this exercise, but difficulties do arise where variables have been dropped from the models since 1983, or have substantially changed definition. Examples of such changes are the elimination of the variable measuring OPEC oil balances in the LBS model, and the revised definition of public sector investment in the NIESR forecast. Where variables have disappeared, it has usually been possible to use official data sources to estimate the actual values of the variables. In the case of revisions to definitions, it has usually been possible to relate the two series together in some reasonably simple manner. This exercise is concerned with the principal exogenous assumptions; therefore some minor exogenous variables are ignored.

Before examining the implications for the forecasts of using a revised set of exogenous assumptions corresponding to current knowledge, we describe the main exogenous assumptions made in the 1983 forecast. These are shown in Table 4.5. The most important exogenous variables in the models under consideration cover two areas — the world economy, and domestic economic policy — and actual and projected values of key variables from the two quarterly models are shown in Figures 4.1 and 4.2. Although some forecasts were conditional on unchanged domestic policy (e.g. NIESR), it appears that actual policy was fairly close to that assumed in the forecasts, and that the main differences in exogenous variables occur in the world economy. However, it should be noted that slightly different definitions of exogenous variables lead to a difference in estimates of actual outcomes. (For example, LBS project world commodity prices in world currency, whereas other forecasts use a dollar price definition.) Although the LBS model contains an endogenous representation of world economy variables, these are wholly recursive to the domestic economy and are hence regarded as exogenous.

All the forecasts underprojected the buoyancy of world demand in 1984 and, to a much lesser extent, in 1985. The LBS and NIESR forecasts also

Table 4.5   *Forecasts of principal exogenous variables*
(% per annum)

		1983	1984	1985
World trade				
LBS:	Forecast	—	4.7	5.1
	Actual	3.5	11.1	5.9
NIESR:	Forecast	1.1	4.5	4.8
	Actual	3.2	10.3	5.1
CUBS:	Forecast	7.4	5.8	4.8
	Actual	4.8	8.5	5.7
LPL:	Forecast	3.0	5.7	6.2
	Actual	3.0	8.8	6.5
World wholesale prices ($)				
LBS:	Forecast	6.1	7.0	6.8
	Actual	4.4	5.5	4.0
NIESR:	Forecast	1.4	4.0	4.6
	Actual	4.1	4.1	3.6
CUBS:	Forecast	5.0	5.0	5.0
	Actual	3.9	4.7	4.5
World oil prices ($)				
LBS:	Forecast	−10.7	1.3	9.0
	Actual	−12.0	−2.4	−5.7
NIESR:	Forecast	−10.3	5.8	4.0
	Actual	−6.9	−1.0	−9.3
CUBS:	Forecast	−10.0	5.0	5.0
	Actual	−12.4	−2.9	−2.4
World commodity prices (LBS, world currency; NIESR, CUBS, $)				
LBS:	Forecast	4.5	10.5	6.8
	Actual	5.4	7.9	1.9
NIESR:	Forecast	−1.6	5.6	4.6
	Actual	−3.9	−2.2	−7.3
CUBS:	Forecast	5.0	5.0	5.0
	Actual	−7.8	−5.3	−0.8
North Sea oil output				
LBS:	Forecast	7.0	4.8	3.4
	Actual	11.1	9.9	0.9
NIESR:	Forecast	8.2	0.8	—
	Actual	12.8	9.6	−0.1
CUBS:	Forecast	9.6	4.4	—
	Actual	9.6	6.9	1.2

appear to have underestimated the level of world demand in 1983. Some of this can be attributed to a revision of the estimates of world demand in early 1983, but it is also clear that both forecasts underprojected the

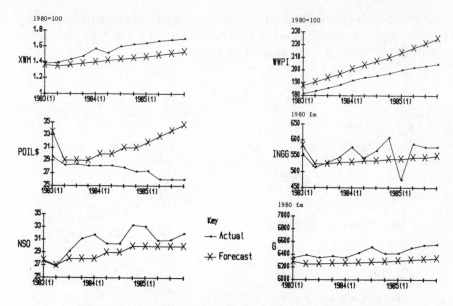

Fig. 4.1   Exogenous variables from the LBS 1983 forecast.
XWM, volume of world trade; POIL$, world oil price; NSO, North Sea output of oil
(m tons); WWPI, world wholesale prices ($); INGG, public sector investment;
G, general government consumption

growth in world demand in the second half of the year. In contrast, the
CUBS forecast was conditioned on a level of world demand that was higher
than the outcome for 1983. Whereas the forecasts, in general, were conditioned on a lower level of demand than actually occurred, the reverse holds
for world price inflation in 1985, although projections of world inflation
were quite close to the outturn in 1984. The implication of the demand and
price forecasts together is that the combinations of world demand and price
projections may have characterized a different relationship from that
subsequently observed. For example, in 1984, when inflation projections
were quite close to the outturn, world demand grew far more strongly than
projected, whereas for 1985 reasonably close estimates of demand growth
were accompanied by lower inflation than projected. A possible reason for
this pattern is the behaviour of world oil prices. These fell in each of the
three years 1983–1985, but all the forecasts were conditioned upon rising
oil prices in 1984 and 1985. Differences in oil price assumptions from the
actual outturn were quite substantial for LBS and NIESR for 1985. Note
that LPL do not require projections of either world wholesale prices or
world oil prices for their model forecast. Although low oil prices may be a
partial explanation for the difference between the observed and projected
relationship between world demand and inflation, they do not seem able to
supply a complete explanation. For example, the fall in oil prices in 1984

occurred in the second half of the year, and while this might explain why world inflation forecasts were reasonably accurate for 1984, it cannot explain the strong growth in world demand.

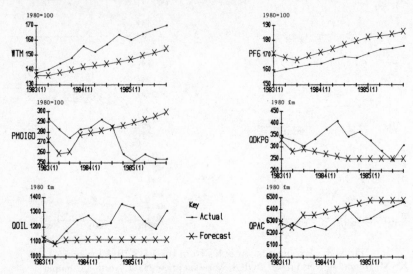

Fig. 4.2 Exogenous variables from the NIESR 1983 forecast.
WTM, volume of world trade; PMOIGD, world oil price ($); QOIL, North Sea output of oil; PF6, world wholesale prices ($); QDKPG, public sector investment; QPAC, general government consumption

As with oil prices, projections of the rate of inflation of the price of world non-oil commodities were also higher than the outturn, although comparisons between the models here are complicated by different definitions. Both the LBS and NIESR projections of world interest rates were close to the observed outcome for 1984 and, for the LBS, for 1985, when NIESR missed the fall in the Eurodollar rate. The exogenous interest rate variables in the LPL model are real US long and short rates. Both have turned out to be considerably higher in 1984 than was assumed in the 1983 forecast but fairly close to the actual outcome for 1985.

As remarked above, domestic policy assumptions were in general close to what actually occurred. All the forecasts were based on an interpretation of the Medium Term Financial Strategy (MTFS), and hence projected a low rate of growth in government current consumption. However, government investment in 1985 fell by more than was assumed in the forecasts. LBS, NIESR, and CUBS assumed a constant standard rate of income tax, whereas LPL posited a reduction in the overall tax rate in both 1984 and 1985. Income tax allowances were assumed to be inflation-indexed with the exception of CUBS, where some additional increase was incorporated, and this has proved to be closer to the actual outcome. Only

LBS and NIESR explicitly incorporated any allowance for the employers' national insurance surcharge. LBS projected that the surcharge would be phased out in 1984 whereas NIESR did not. LPL embodied a gradual reduction in both employer and employee tax rates over the forecast period. There are relatively few exogenous monetary policy variables in the models. In the case of CUBS, money base growth has turned out to be higher than was assumed in the forecast. Both LBS and NIESR assume that domestic interest rates are exogenous. The NIESR projection of the Treasury bill rate coincides with the actual outturn in 1984, but the increase in the rate in 1985 is not forecast. The LBS published forecast assumed a decline in the short-term interest rate in 1984 with no further change in 1985, and thus the level of the rate is underpredicted for both 1984 and 1985.

Results using actual exogenous variables

The forecasts are recomputed using revised values of the exogenous variables from the beginning of 1984; thus no attempt is made to explain the forecast error for 1983. This reflects the difficulties in doing this as a result of the ragged edge which is present in the quarterly forecasts.

The effects on the size of forecast errors for GDP, the price level, and the level of unemployment are shown in Table 4.6 and implications for growth rates in Table 4.7. In the case of the LBS forecast, the use of actual values of the exogenous variables raises the forecast level of GDP for 1984. However, in the following year the growth is almost exactly offset so that the level of GDP is very close to that of the published forecast, although the average error in GDP is reduced. The output estimate is affected in the same way as that of expenditure, but it has a higher absolute error on average. Thus, the effects of using actual exogenous variables would change the distribution of GDP growth in the LBS forecast without influencing its level at the end of 1985. The principal factors underlying higher output in 1984 are higher levels of private consumption and fixed investment, which offset the negative influence of net trade. The forecasting error on fixed investment diminishes in size but that on consumption increases. However, whereas the consumption level error persists into 1985, the contribution of fixed investment reverses direction and, together with the effects from net trade, removes the positive effect on output.

Thus for 1985 the error on fixed investment is larger than in the published forecast and the absolute errors on imports and exports have decreased, although their net effect on the GDP error is little changed. In its published forecast LBS overpredicted the price level and inflation rate for both 1984 and 1985. With the revised exogenous assumptions, the LBS model underpredicts the inflation rate for 1984 and 1985. The exchange rate was overestimated for 1984 in the published forecast but by the end of 1985 was quite accurately forecast. The scale of overestimation is now reduced for 1984, with the rate being underforecast in 1985 (6 per cent by the end of the year). Thus the reduction in the inflation rate is in spite of, rather than due to, the effects on the exchange rate. The published LBS forecast predicted a fall in the level of unemployment for 1985 which did not occur. Although output is now higher for 1984 and remains at the published forecast level in 1985, the unemployment error for both 1984 and 1985 reverses sign. This effect follows from the effects on employment. Both employment and unemployment were underforecast originally, but employment is now reduced using the actual values of the exogenous variables, despite higher output in 1984. Thus the level of productivity (which was underforecast in the published version) is now overpredicted in 1984 but hits the actual level of productivity for 1985. This suggests that, for 1985 at least, the forecast error for employment derives from the underprediction of output. Finally, we consider a financial aspect of the forecast, by looking at the forecast errors of the PSBR. In the published forecasts the level of the PSBR was understated. This error now increases in magnitude, probably as a result of the lower inflation rate in the forecast using actual values of the exogenous variables.

Table 4.6   *Forecast errors of output, prices, and unemployment under various assumptions*

	1983	1984	1985	Mean error 1984–85
GDP (% of actual)				
LBS (expenditure)				
Published forecast	0.92	0.67	1.53	1.10
	(1.57)	(2.42)	(3.36)	(2.89)
Actual exog. variables (AE)		−0.62	1.51	0.45
		(1.16)	(3.40)	(2.47)
AE and zero residuals		−3.28	−1.92	−2.60
		(−1.37)	(−0.02)	(−0.71)
NIESR (output)				
Published forecast	1.63	2.69	4.99	3.84
Actual exog. variables (AE)		1.57	5.04	3.31
AE and zero residuals		−3.16	0.21	−1.48
CUBS (output)				
Published forecast	0.19	−1.57	−1.52	−1.55
Actual exog. variables (AE)		−3.54	−4.84	−4.19
AE and zero residuals		−1.12	−3.85	−2.49
LPL (expenditure)				
Published forecast	0.62	−1.11	−0.82	−0.97
Actual exog. variables (AE)		−1.36	−4.74	−3.05
AE and zero residuals		−3.23	−7.79	−5.51

Table 4.6   *(continued)*

	1983	1984	1985	Mean error 1984–85
Price level (% of actual)				
LBS				
Published forecast	0.16	−1.08	−1.93	−1.51
Actual exog. variables (AE)		0.83	2.43	1.63
AE and zero residuals		−1.73	−6.40	−4.07
NIESR				
Published forecast	0.18	−0.97	−1.61	−1.29
Actual exog. variables (AE)		−1.19	−0.06	−0.63
AE and zero residuals		0.56	3.45	2.01
CUBS				
Published forecast	−0.86	−2.91	−5.52	−4.22
Actual exog. variables (AE)		0.53	−0.43	0.05
AE and zero residuals		4.31	6.20	5.26
LPL				
Published forecast	0.55	1.68	5.00	3.34
Actual exog. variables (AE)		0.30	3.99	2.15
AE and zero residuals		7.38	15.38	11.38
Unemployment ('000)				
LBS				
Published forecast	−7	63	372	218
Actual exog. variables (AE)		−127	−134	−131
AE and zero residuals		−190	−127	−159
NIESR				
Published forecast	−28	−86	−253	−170
Actual exog. variables (AE)		−164	−543	−254
AE and zero residuals		300	153	227
CUBS				
Published forecast	−23	398	917	658
Actual exog. variables (AE)		723	1433	1078
AE and zero residuals		797	2953	1875
LPL				
Published forecast	80	392	751	572
Actual exog. variables (AE)		480	1218	854
AE and zero residuals		796	1640	1218

Note: Figures in brackets for LBS denote GDP (output) forecast errors.

We now turn to the NIESR forecast. In the published forecast growth was underestimated, particularly for 1985. Using the actual values of the exogenous variables increases growth for 1984, but the revised forecast now predicts a slight fall in the level of output for 1985 and also predicts a level of output that is close to that recorded in the published forecast (as in the case of LBS). Thus the changed exogenous variables merely redistribute growth from the published forecast. Consumption expenditure and net exports are higher in both years, but the increase in fixed investment and stockbuilding is reversed for 1985. Using actual exogenous assumptions reduces the forecasting errors in exports and imports but exports by more than imports, so that the net effect is to worsen the GDP error. The investment error increases in size for 1985 whereas the forecast error for consumption in this year is reduced, but not by much. The error in forecasting the price level increases a little for 1984 but the rate of inflation is underpredicted for 1985, bringing the forecast of the price level very close to the recorded outturn. The exchange rate was too high for 1984 in the published forecast and too low for 1985. The revised level is very similar for 1984 but is now too high for 1985. Nor is the level of unemployment changed much for 1984, but the error increases for 1985 so that greater overprediction of unemployment is associated with a higher level of output for 1984 and an unchanged level for 1985. Likewise, the underprediction of the level of the PSBR is unaltered for 1984, but this variable is overforecast by a greater extent for 1985 despite a lower price forecast.

Table 4.7   *Forecasts of output growth, inflation, and unemployment under various assumptions*

	1983	1984	1985	Average 1984–85
GDP (% p. a.)				
LBS (expenditure)				
Published forecast	2.5	1.9	2.4	2.2
	(1.8)	(2.4)	(2.4)	(2.4)
Actual exog. variables (AE)		3.3	1.2	2.2
		(3.8)	(1.2)	(2.5)
AE and zero residuals		5.9	4.6	5.3
		(6.4)	(2.0)	(4.2)
Actual	3.7	1.7	3.3	2.5
	(3.0)	(3.1)	(3.4)	(3.2)
NIESR (output)				
Published forecast	2.2	2.0	1.0	1.5
Actual exog. variables (AE)		3.1	−0.2	1.5
AE and zero residuals		6.1	1.9	4.0
Actual	3.0	3.1	3.4	3.2
CUBS (output)				
Published forecast	2.2	4.9	3.3	4.1
Actual exog. variables (AE)		7.1	4.5	5.8
AE and zero residuals		4.5	6.3	5.4
Actual	3.1	3.1	3.4	3.2
LPL (expenditure)				
Published forecast	3.6	3.4	3.0	3.2
Actual exog. variables (AE)		3.7	6.3	5.0
AE and zero residuals		5.6	7.9	6.7
Actual	3.7	1.7	3.3	2.5

Table 4.7   *(continued)*

	1983	1984	1985	Average 1984–85
Inflation (% p. a.)				
LBS				
Published forecast	5.6	5.9	6.3	6.1
Actual exog. variables (AE)		3.9	3.7	3.8
AE and zero residuals		6.6	10.6	8.6
Actual	5.2	4.6	5.4	5.0
NIESR				
Published forecast	5.5	5.8	6.1	5.9
Actual exog. variables (AE)		5.0	4.2	5.1
AE and zero residuals		4.2	2.5	3.3
Actual	5.2	4.6	5.4	5.0
CUBS				
Published forecast	6.1	6.8	8.3	7.5
Actual exog. variables (AE)		3.1	6.4	4.7
AE and zero residuals		−0.6	3.5	1.4
Actual	5.2	4.6	5.4	5.0
LPL				
Published forecast	4.7	3.4	2.1	2.7
Actual exog. variables (AE)		4.8	1.6	3.2
AE and zero residuals		−2.1	−1.9	−2.0
Actual	5.2	4.6	5.4	5.0
Unemployment (millions)				
LBS				
Published forecast	2.9	3.0	2.8	2.9
Actual exog. variables (AE)		3.2	3.3	3.2
AE and zero residuals		3.2	3.3	3.2
Actual	2.9	3.0	3.2	3.1
NIESR				
Published forecast	2.9	3.1	3.4	3.2
Actual exog. variables (AE)		3.2	3.7	3.4
AE and zero residuals		2.7	3.0	2.8
Actual	2.9	3.0	3.2	3.1
CUBS				
Published forecast	2.9	2.6	2.3	2.4
Actual exog. variables (AE)		2.3	1.8	2.1
AE and zero residuals		1.6	0.2	0.9
Actual	2.9	3.0	3.2	3.1
LPL				
Published forecast	2.9	2.7	2.4	2.5
Actual exog. variables (AE)		2.6	2.0	2.3
AE and zero residuals		2.3	1.6	1.9
Actual	2.9	3.0	3.2	3.1

Note: Figures in brackets for LBS refer to the GDP (output) measure.

The LPL growth forecast is too optimistic for 1984 even allowing for the effects of the miners' strike. This optimism continues for 1985. When the actual data on exogenous variables are used (derived from the autumn 1985 forecast) the growth error worsens a little for 1984, but more importantly a substantial overprediction of growth occurs for 1985, with a forecast of $6\frac{1}{3}$ per cent, contrasting with the estimated outturn of $3\frac{1}{3}$ (or $2\frac{1}{2}$ per cent adjusted for the miners' dispute). In 1984 there is a switch in the factors responsible for growth, with lower non-durable and durable consumption expenditure offset by higher government spending and net exports. The main influences behind the higher growth forecast for 1985 are durable expenditure and government spending. The published forecast underpredicted the inflation rate for both 1984 and 1985, but particularly for 1985. The forecast error is now largely removed for 1984 but the inflation error increases for 1985. However, the estimate of the price level in 1985 is closer to the actual than the published forecast. The underprediction of unemployment was quite substantial in the original 1983 forecast (700,000 for 1985); this error now increases, with a forecast prediction of 2 million unemployed for 1985. The general tendency for the 1984 errors to improve a little when new exogenous assumptions are used in this model but for the 1985 errors to increase is matched by the behaviour of the PSBR.

As in the case of LPL, CUBS overforecast the rate of growth of GDP in 1984 and in 1985 (on a strike-adjusted basis). However, when actual values of the exogenous variables are used the forecast error for 1984 increases substantially and a further sizeable error is introduced for 1985, thus producing an overestimate of nearly 5 per cent in the level of GDP for 1985. Unlike LPL, the published CUBS forecast was too pessimistic in terms of the rate of inflation. The revised exogenous assumptions lower the inflation forecast so that inflation is now underpredicted for 1984 with an overprediction remaining for 1985. However, the price level error is only $\frac{3}{4}$ per cent in absolute value for both years. The original published forecast was too optimistic over prospects for the level of unemployment, with an error of nearly 1 million for 1985. Changed exogenous assumptions widen the error, with an underprediction of $\frac{3}{4}$ million for 1984 and nearly $1\frac{1}{2}$ million for 1985 (the forecast level of unemployment for 1985 is 1.8 million).

Rather than narrow the relative forecast errors of GDP made by the model teams in their 1983 forecasts, the substitution of actual exogenous variables produces the opposite effect. In the case of the two quarterly models the distribution of growth between 1983 and 1985 is changed with little effect on average growth, and hence both still underpredict the level of GDP for 1985. For the two annual models the degree of overestimation of growth increases. There is however a tendency for the forecast errors of the price level to diminish when actual values of exogenous variables are used. The previous overprediction in the LBS model now becomes one of underprediction. The inflation forecast errors improve for both CUBS and LPL on average and there is a far greater convergence towards the actual outturn than in the case of the GDP forecasts. With the exception of LBS, noted above, the unemployment consequences follow those of output quite closely (but in the opposite direction). The range of unemployment forecasts for 1985 when correct exogenous values are used turns out to be far greater than the differences between the published forecasts. We must therefore conclude that, at least as far as output and unemployment are concerned, the observed forecast errors cannot be explained by errors in the projections of the exogenous variables. Whether the forecast errors can be explained by interventions made by the forecaster or by the model itself are considered next.

4.5 The influence of residual adjustments

In our previous discussions of *ex ante* forecasts we have attempted to isolate the influences of the forecasters' interventions on the forecasts by recomputing the forecasts with all residual adjustments set to zero. In this section we apply the same procedure, and recompute the forecasts using the correct values of the exogenous variables and zero residual adjustments. In some sense the results can be regarded as pure model forecasts, and they allow a decomposition of the forecast error.

We first consider the LBS forecast. In the previous section we noted how the insertion of actual exogenous values merely changed the distribution of GDP growth between 1984 and 1985 but changed the inflation forecast from one that was pessimistic to one that was over-optimistic. Using zero residuals in addition boosts the growth rate in both years so that LBS GDP forecast becomes too optimistic. The forecast error of the level of GDP (expenditure) is some $3\frac{1}{4}$ per cent in 1984 and nearly 2 per cent for 1985. The average error for 1984–85 is $-2\frac{1}{2}$ per cent compared with the 1 per cent in the published forecast. If we look at the output estimate, however, the error in the level of GDP is much larger on average in the published forecast, so that the effect of making the adjustments to exogenous variables and residuals produces an average overestimate of $\frac{3}{4}$ per cent, with the level of GDP being predicted almost exactly for 1985. If we were concerned with the level of the output measure we might conclude that this mechanical forecast was an improvement on the published version. However, in this case a large part of the initial error comes from a base-year effect (revision of the output estimate), and if we inspect the figures for growth (Table 4.7) we observe that the mechanical forecast is no better than the published version in its growth rate predictions for 1984 and 1985. These differences emphasize the sensitivity of *ex post* assessment to the precise measure of GDP used. The forecast errors on the price level (and the inflation rate) also increase in size, and the price level error for 1985 is over 7 per cent. The proximate source of these effects is the behaviour of the exchange rate, which is some 25 per cent below the actual outcome by the end of 1985. In our study of the *ex ante* (as it was then) 1983 forecast, we analysed the effects of removing the equation residuals and concluded that the absence of a residual on earnings led to an inflationary spiral. This is the reaction that we observe here. We also noted in the *ex ante* study that the residuals on imports and investment had important effects on the forecast of output. Despite an increase in the error on output, we find that the error on unemployment remains small. This is a result of the overestimation of productivity under this residual assumption. Most of the components of GDP have smaller forecast errors than in the published forecast, most notably fixed investment. However, the error on stockbuilding increases markedly.

In the case of NIESR the mechanical forecast also produces rapid output growth for 1984 but then a small decline in growth for 1985. The forecast error of the level of GDP is negligible for 1985. Unlike the case of LBS, there is no tendency in this variant forecast for the individual GDP component errors to be reduced. The error on consumption for 1985 is largely removed but the remaining errors on investment, stockbuilding, imports, and the factor cost adjustment are similar in magnitude to those derived from the published forecast. The stockbuilding error, in particular, is very large. The inflation forecast falls so that the forecast error signifies underprediction of the price level by nearly 3 per cent for 1985, and the unemployment forecast errors show a small underprediction in contrast with the overprediction in the published forecast. The main equation residuals responsible for the shift in the forecast under the assumption of zero residuals are those on exports, imports, and stockbuilding. The first two induce an increase in the exchange rate which leads to the inflation effects observed, and the trade effects themselves boost final demand, as does the removal of the stockbuilding residual. The slowdown in growth for 1985 reflects the easing of the beneficial effect on trade as the exchange rate appreciates.

The CUBS forecast errors on output remain stubbornly ones of overprediction, although the removal of the equation residuals does diminish the size of the errors induced by using actual values of the exogenous variables. The inflation errors now worsen as the forecast gives estimates of the rate of inflation for 1984 and 1985 that are far below the actual outturn. Unemployment in this variant approaches only 200,000 for 1985. The main non-zero adjustments in the CUBS published forecast are those to private sector employment, the exchange rate, prices, and real wages. The observed unemployment effect arises as a result of the removal of the employment residual.

One problem with the recomputation of the LPL forecast is the distinction between exogenous monetary data and money supply residuals. The

principal exogenous monetary variable in the model is the long-run PSBR/
GDP ratio, which sets the permanent growth in the money stock. However, in this version of the model allowance is made for 'temporary'
monetary growth through a residual term. (This variable has become an
exogenous variable in subsequent versions of the model.) In setting zero
residuals we have allowed the LPL forecast to incorporate the correct

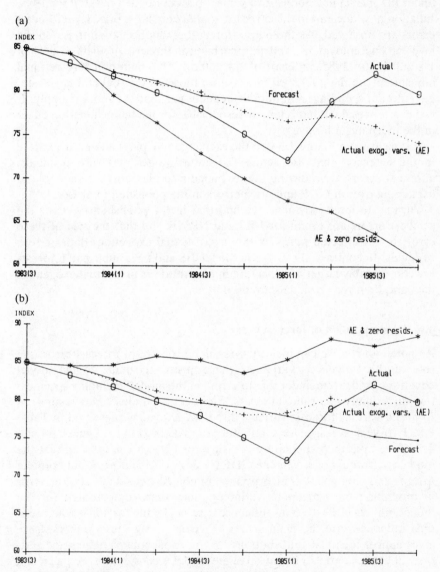

Fig. 4.3 Forecasts of the exchange rate under alternative assumptions,
1975 = 100. (a) LBS; (b) NIESR.

exogenous value of money using an appropriate combination of the PSBR/ GDP ratio and a residual effect, but we remove any additional money supply residual effects. Since the inflation rate is determined by monetary growth in the model, the resulting forecast errors essentially reflect errors in the M0−price relationship. The LPL results show that the forecast also remains one of overprediction of output, with the forecast error increasing under the mechanical forecast to some 7 per cent of actual GDP for 1985. Inflation now declines in this forecast, so that very large price level forecast errors are observed. As the output forecast errors rise so do those on the level of unemployment, and the mechanical forecast predicts a level of 1.8 million for 1985, an error of 1.4 million. The main non-zero residual adjustments in the published forecast are those on the real exchange rate, government spending, non-durable expenditure, and the money supply. It is the latter residual that is largely responsible for the falling inflation effect in the mechanical forecast.

It is clear from Figure 4.3 that the exchange rate plays an important role in the forecasts that use actual exogenous values and zero residuals, although errors in predicting the exchange rate play only a minor role in explaining overall GDP and price errors in the published forecasts.

Turning to unemployment, we find that in the published forecasts the smallest errors are found for LBS and NIESR and that the size of these errors is not affected much by the use of actual exogenous data or zero residuals. In contrast, the errors in the CUBS and LPL published forecasts are considerably larger and increase in magnitude as first actual exogenous data and then zero residuals are used.

4.6　Decomposition of forecast error

As noted above, we can identify three main sources of forecast error: the role of the exogenous variables, the adjustments made to the model equations, and a remainder due to errors in the model, including specification uncertainty and random errors. Their contributions can be estimated from the various forecast variants discussed above, as presented in Table 4.8. Two-year averages for GDP and prices are shown in Figures 4.4 and 4.5. If we take the expenditure measure for LBS, it can be seen that the model itself would overestimate GDP for both 1984 and 1985, but both the forecaster's judgement as incorporated in non-zero residuals and the error in projecting the exogenous variables more than compensated for the model influence. Exogenous influences are negligible for 1985, when residual influences are the main source of error. Using the output measure gives almost identical contributions for the exogenous variables and residuals, but the degree of optimism in the model is considerably reduced and the residuals are the major source of forecast error. For NIESR the relative contributions are very similar to those for the LBS output measure, but the scale of overall error and the contribution of the residuals is more marked. Exogenous variable effects are more important for the two annual models, especially for 1985. In the case of CUBS, residual adjustments compound the error and more than offset the tendency to underpredict GDP as a result of values of the exogenous variables other than those now recorded as actual. Residual adjustments in the LPL forecast act to counter the excessive optimism over GDP arising from the model.

Table 4.8 *Decomposition of forecast errors*

	Forecast error (% of actual)		Contribution of exog. variables		Contribution of residuals		Contribution of model	
	1984	1985	1984	1985	1984	1985	1984	1985
(i) GDP								
LBS*	0.67	1.53	1.29	0.04	2.59	3.40	−3.21	−1.91
LBS**	2.42	3.36	1.29	0.05	2.57	3.45	−1.44	−0.14
NIESR	2.69	4.99	1.12	−0.05	4.72	4.83	−3.15	0.21
CUBS	−1.57	−1.52	2.04	3.55	−2.54	−1.09	−1.07	−3.98
LPL	−1.11	−0.82	0.26	3.92	2.51	2.69	−3.88	−7.43
(ii) Price level								
LBS	−1.08	−1.93	−1.90	−4.39	2.58	9.28	−1.75	−6.82
NIESR	−0.97	−1.61	0.23	−1.57	−1.74	−3.42	0.54	3.38
CUBS	−2.91	−5.52	−3.52	−5.08	−3.79	−6.60	4.40	6.16
LPL	1.68	4.00	1.35	0.93	−6.63	−9.85	6.96	13.92

* expenditure measure
** output measure

Turning to the price level (Figure 4.5), we find some role for the exogenous variables in explaining overall forecast errors for all the models, with the effect greatest for 1985. In general, differences between the actual and projected values of the exogenous variables lead to overprediction of the price level, the exception being LPL. The countervailing influences of residual errors and model errors is clearly observed, with the model error in LBS in the opposite direction to the other forecasts.

Drawing together the results of this section with those of the preceding section leads to the following observations. LBS and LPL appear to have the smallest average error among the published forecasts of GDP, both being around 1 per cent of the actual level. In the case of LBS this comes from an average underprediction, whereas for the LPL published forecast the error is in the opposite direction. The larger GDP errors for CUBS and NIESR may partly reflect the greater revision of the output measure for GDP in the base year (1983) although the CUBS error is far smaller than that of NIESR. Similarly, when the GDP output measure is used LBS is seen to be far less accurate. LBS has the best performance in terms of average GDP growth (the margin is smaller when the output measure is used), and NIESR the worst. Rerunning the forecasts using correct values of the exogenous variables does not lead to any great improvement in forecast performance. Errors in the level of GDP are slightly reduced on average for both LBS and NIESR but are substantially increased for CUBS and LPL, thus widening the dispersion of forecast errors between the forecasts. In two cases a pure mechanical forecast (i.e., correct exogenous values and zero residuals) produces a result that improves upon the published forecast of GDP; this occurs for NIESR, and for LBS when the output measure of GDP is used. In the latter case, however, growth performance is not improved. Further, these results do not carry over to the price level and inflation rate. In all the other models the forecast errors increase, with the impact the greatest for LPL. One interesting feature of these results is that the mechanical forecasts unanimously overpredict GDP.

Whereas NIESR has the worst forecasting error on GDP in its published forecast, it has the smallest average inflation error (although with only a small margin over LBS). The LPL forecast is the only one in which the forecast has proved too optimistic. The use of actual exogenous values improves forecasting performance in general for the forecasts, unlike the case of output. This undoubtedly reflects the errors made in the forecasts

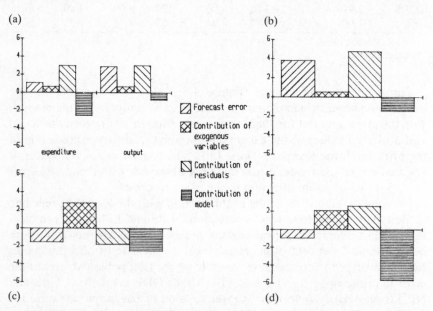

Fig 4.4   Decomposition of *ex post* GDP errors — average of 1984 and 1985, % of actual. (a) LBS; (b) NIESR; (c) CUBS; (d) LPL.

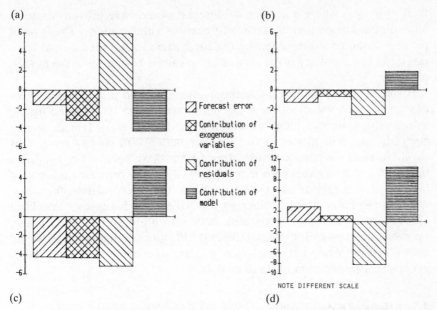

Fig. 4.5 Decomposition of *ex post* price errors — average of 1984
and 1985, % of actual. (a) LBS; (b) NIESR; (c) CUBS; (d) LPL.

of world oil prices and also of world non-oil commodity prices. But it
cannot be the case with LPL, where these variables do not enter. The
CUBS forecasts of the price level, using actual exogenous data, are
extremely accurate on average, although this is the result of an underestimate for 1984 balanced by an overestimate for 1985. Even with actual
exogenous data, the LPL forecast error remains positive. Introducing zero
residuals (the mechanical forecast) weakens forecast performance, especially for LPL. The smallest effects are for NIESR, where the error in the
mechanical forecast is close to that of the published version, but in the
opposite direction.

We conclude that the use of actual values of the exogenous variables
has played some role in explaining errors in the forecasts of GDP and
prices. However, in some cases the contribution of the exogenous variables
goes in the wrong direction to explain the observed forecast errors, for
example for the CUBS GDP forecasts. It must also be noted that in many
cases the forecaster, through non-zero residual adjustments, has compensated for errors in the model and therefore reduced the scale of forecast
error. Forecasters have appeared to have contributed some value-added to
the 1983 forecasts in the sense that pure model-based forecasts would have
performed less well than the published judgementally influenced forecast.
The main exceptions here are the NIESR and LBS forecasts of the level of

GDP (output), where a mechanical forecast would have proved considerably more accurate than that using forecasters' interventions. The general picture is one of value-added by the forecasters to the accuracy of forecasts, but the corollary is that less reliance can be placed upon the models alone.

By recalculating the forecast without any residual adjustments but allowing the forecast values of the exogenous variables to be replaced by the actual values, we can judge whether the models are misspecified, since a correctly specified model should forecast better with correct exogenous data. No clear conclusion can be drawn from these results. For the LBS, introducing actual exogenous data worsens the GDP forecast (in terms of both level and growth rates) but improves the price/inflation forecasts, whereas the reverse result emerges for NIESR. This suggests that both models are misspecified in the link between output and inflation but in opposite directions. Both the CUBS and LPL forecast errors for GDP and prices worsen when actual exogenous data are used, suggesting more general misspecification of these models.

4.7   Effects of data revisions

In this section we examine some of the major revisions to the initial conditions on which the forecasts were based and conduct an exercise on the two quarterly models (LBS and NIESR), projecting new values of the model residuals as a result of these revisions.

A full account of the revision process and its effects on GDP is given by Kenny (1985). Although he concludes that data revisions have tended to be upwards, this has not been invariably so. Table 4.9 presents some of the data revisions covering the period from 1982 to the middle of 1983, some of which were a result of the rebasing exercise described in Section 4.2. These represent changes to the forecasters' data set at the time of the forecast. The importance of the preferred measure of GDP in practical forecasting is apparent from this table. Although both output and expenditure were revised upwards in 1982 by similar amounts, the degree of revision for the output measure was much more marked for the first half of 1983. Thus, use of the revised expenditure measure would suggest that the economy was expanding less rapidly, but in contrast, the use of output resulted in an acceleration in the pace of activity relative to previous information. If we assume, heroically, that the effect of revisions for 1983 as a whole could be approximated by the effects in the first half of the year, we might revise *down* the forecast growth rate for expenditure GDP by just under $\frac{1}{2}$ per cent and revise up the growth rate for output by a similar margin.

The effects on the 1983 estimates of growth are shown in Table 4.10(a). NIESR and CUBS would now predict growth of 2.7 per cent, and they would therefore both be more accurate in their estimate of GDP in the

Table 4.9   *Major data revisions to the base-year data*
(Difference between March 1986 and October 1983 estimates; % unless otherwise indicated)

	1982 year	1983 1st half
GDP		
Expenditure	0.6	0.2
Output	0.8	1.3
Consumers' expenditure	−0.9	−1.1
Durables	4.3	2.5
Non-durables	−1.5	−1.5
Gross fixed investment		
Total	6.6	9.5
Private dwellings	75.0	78.7
Manufacturing	5.6	7.8
Stockbuilding (1980 £m)		
Total	−23	188
Distributive trades	127	−71
Exports	—	0.6
Imports	1.3	0.8
Employment ('000)	159	119
Unemployment ('000)	−124	−115
PSBR (£m)	−572	472

base year (1983). The LBS and LPL expenditure-based forecasts would however make greater errors than in their published forecasts for 1984 and 1985, since the downward revision would increase the underprediction of GDP growth. On the other hand, the error would be smaller for the LBS output measure. On the strong assumption that growth in subsequent years of the forecast remained unaltered but there was a constant level effect, we would now conclude that LPL had the smallest average forecast error on GDP for 1984 and 1985. The LBS (expenditure) forecast would still be ranked high in terms of forecast accuracy but less high than without this correction. The NIESR forecast would improve, but not sufficiently to change its ranking, while the forecast error would increase for CUBS.

Table 4.9 shows that within total GDP (expenditure) there have been some major changes to components. In particular, estimates of fixed investment have been revised upwards by very large amounts, the bulk of the revision taking place in private dwellings. This followed a reclassification of non-grant-aided housing improvement expenditure from consumers' expenditure to dwellings investment. Consequently, consumers' expenditure has been revised downwards. The revisions to the price level have been very minor. Employment data have been revised up for 1982 and early 1983 and unemployment data revised down. The latter reflects changes to the method of counting described earlier and incorporated in our calculation of forecast errors.

This approach to incorporating data revisions is very limited in that it does not take account of how the forecaster's understanding of the model of the economy may be revised, leading to other changes in the forecast. In order to make some adjustment for this, we have conducted an exercise on the two quarterly models in which the effects of data revisions on the model residuals in the period 1982(1)–1983(2) have been calculated and then projected forward to give revised residuals in the forecast period. Relatively few model residuals appear to be affected to any significant degree by the use of revised data and in most cases it seems appropriate to change the residuals in the forecast by a constant amount, starting from 1984(1). The effects on the forecast are shown in Table 4.10(b), with the changes in the residuals given in Table 4.11.

Table 4.10   *Data revisions and forecast errors*

(a) Effects assuming a permanent level effect on (i) GDP expenditure of −0.5 per cent; and (ii) GDP output of +0.5 per cent

	Growth 1983			Average forecast error 1984–85	
	Published forecast	Adjusted forecast	Actual	(% of GDP) Published forecast	Adjusted forecast
LBS (output)	1.8	2.3	3.1	2.9	2.4
LBS (expend.)	2.5	2.0	3.7	1.1	1.5
NIESR	2.2	2.7	3.1	3.8	3.3
CUBS	2.2	2.7	3.1	−1.6	−2.0
LPL	3.6	3.1	3.7	−1.0	−0.6

(b) Forecast errors allowing for model residual changes, 1984–85 average

	GDP (% of actual)		Price level (% of actual)		Unemployment (difference from actual, '000)	
	1984	1985	1984	1985	1984	1985
LBS (expenditure)						
Published forecast	0.67	1.53	−1.08	−1.93	63	372
Adjusted forecast	−1.62	0.11	−0.77	−1.05	62	278
NIESR						
Published forecast	2.69	4.99	−0.97	−1.61	−86	−253
Adjusted forecast	1.56	4.27	−1.19	−2.20	−219	−335

Table 4.11   *Revisions to key model residuals*
(average levels over periods noted)

LBS	INPOX	KIID	M	CND		
Historical residuals[a]						
Original	133	—	−155	−77		
Revised	88	96	−253	−168		
Projected residuals[b]						
Original	−225	−150	132.5	−50		
Revised	−75	−100	32.5	−150		
Change as % of level of variable*	1.8	0.6	−0.6	−1.1		

NIESR	QDKPD	QDSDT	QDKPM	QMMF	QAFC	OMP
Historical residuals[a]						
Original	−16	−111	125	398	−130	−5.86
Revised	152	−14	90	612	198	−4.61
Projected residuals[b]						
Original	1	−125	125	450	140	−5
Revised	150	—	90	650	200	−4
Change as % of level of of variable*	31.6	64.5	−1.9	3.9	2.0	0.9

Key:
LBS: INPOX, fixed investment, private sector; KIID, stock level distributive trades; M, imports of goods and services; CND, consumer expenditure on non-durables.
NIESR: QDKPD, private sector housing investment; QDSDT, stock building in distributive trades; QDKPM, investment in plant and machinery; QMMF, imports of manufactures; QAFC, adjustment to factor cost; OMP, public sector output.

Notes:
[a]   1982(1)–1983(2)
[b]   1984(1)–1985(4)
*   % of 1983(2) level

No startling changes to the forecasts are observed when the revised residual assumptions are made. The LBS adjusted forecast is worse for GDP for 1984 but much more accurate for 1985, leading to a small improvement on average for both years. The price forecast is clearly better but there is little difference to the unemployment forecast. The NIESR GDP forecast error is improved, although not dramatically, but price level errors worsen, as do those for unemployment.

Our conclusion from these exercises is therefore that not a great deal changes when these effects of data revisions are taken into account. If a significant part of the forecast error does arise from inaccurate base data, then its influence on the forecast must operate in a more complex fashion than we are able to capture.

4.8   Comparison with forecasts based on a vector autoregressive model

An alternative approach to dynamic modelling currently receiving much attention is one in which the reduced form of the system is specified directly as unrestricted dynamic equations that form a vector autoregressive (VAR) model. In order to provide a benchmark for the *ex'post* forecasts generated by more conventional structural econometric models, comparable forecasts were generated from VAR models for a selection of the key macroeconomic variables used in the LBS and NIESR forecasts.

VAR models differ from conventional structural models both in the way they are constructed and in the way in which they are typically used for forecasting. In the estimation of a VAR model all variables are treated as endogenous, with none being determined outside the model. Because a VAR model does not distinguish between exogenous and endogenous variables, it can be used to generate an 'unconditional' forecast. The forecast does not depend on an explicit assumption about the future behaviour of those variables which are deemed to be exogenous. The forecast derived from a traditional structural model, on the other hand, is a 'conditional' forecast since it is dependent upon the particular time profile chosen for those variables that are regarded as strictly exogenous to the model.

There are variables in a structural model that are often considered to be strongly influenced by forces outside the scope of the model, and hence are treated as exogenous. The user of a structural model may therefore have additional information which is not available to the model, which can be incorporated into the forecast of these variables and so improve the forecast of the variables that are treated as being determined endogenously by the model. Forecasts based on a VAR are based on the implicit assumption that the past behaviour of all variables in the system over the sample period used for estimation provides the optimum forecast of their behaviour in the future. Expectations of 'off-model' events which may influence the forecast are not incorporated.

If the user of a structural model has accurate information on these non-model factors which are not reflected in the sample data used to estimate the VAR model, then the conditional distribution of the endogenous variables in the structural model, given these forecasts of exogenous variables, will be much narrower and more stable than their unconditional distribution. If an appropriately specified structural model uses accurate extraneous information, we should therefore expect the *ex post* dynamic forecasts from this structural model to be more accurate than the *ex post* forecasts based upon a VAR model. This informational advantage of the structural model may be reinforced by the VAR modeller's need to employ restrictive linearity assumptions in the estimation of the VAR model.

VAR models are typically small, covering only a few of the variables contained in a large-scale structural model. A lack of degrees of freedom also restricts the length of the lag distribution of the included variables. There are therefore implicit priors in the choice of variables to include and their lag length.

Practical experience in forecasting with an unrestricted VAR suggests that over-parameterization often leads to a poor post-sample predictive performance, since coefficients tend to be imprecisely estimated and sensitive to changes in the specification of the VAR. Litterman (1986) has pioneered the use of Bayesian prior information about the likely value of coefficients to reduce the degree of over-parameterization in unrestricted VAR models, and to improve forecasting performance. Unlike a structural model which uses (over-identifying) restrictions derived from economic theory and data analysis to obtain forecasting equations, a Bayesian vector autoregressive (BVAR) model uses information on the statistical characteristics of the variable in question to shape the lag distributions of the variables in each equation. Litterman suggests that, since the behaviour of most macroeconomic time series can be specified as a random walk around an unknown deterministic component, it is therefore reasonable to specify a prior distribution in which the coefficients on all other variables but the first lag of the dependent are close to zero. This is formalized using normal prior distributions with mean zero and small standard errors on those variables other than the lagged dependent variable.

In effect, the use of a prior distribution allows variables to enter an equation at the margin if they have high explanatory power. The BVAR modeller is not forced arbitrarily to include or exclude particular variables or their lags to reduce over-parameterization; variables with low explanatory power are assigned coefficients that are close to zero. Given the apparent success of BVAR models for forecasting, the forecasts we report were made using a BVAR model rather than an ordinary VAR model. An unrestricted VAR model was in fact estimated, but it produced forecasts that diverge explosively from the actual data and are not reported.

The BVAR model consists of nine equations explaining, respectively, the logs of real GDP, the consumer price index, the £M$_3$ money stock, average earnings in manufacturing, employment, the exchange rate, government expenditure, the ratio of the PSBR to the £M$_3$ money stock, and the three-month Treasury bill rate. The high percentage of redundant coefficients in the unrestricted VAR model and the high autoregressive component in each equation leads us to specify a tight prior distribution on all variables other than their own first lag in each equation.

Each equation was specified to include four lags of each variable, a constant, and a time trend. The estimation period was 1967(1)–1983(1). This end-point was chosen since it was the last period for which a full data set was available for the variables in the BVAR model when the quarterly forecasts under consideration were made. Data for 1983(2) were available for the effective exchange rate, the short-term interest rate, and earnings in manufacturing when the forecasts were made. In order to take account of all information available for forecasting the other variables for this period, the equations of the BVAR model were modified to exploit any contemporaneous correlation among the model innovations, and so improve the one-step-ahead forecast performance, according to the suggestion of Wallis (1986). The results are shown in Table 4.12.

Table 4.12   *Forecasts from a Bayesian vector autoregressive (BVAR) model*

	1983	1984	1985
GDP (expenditure)			
Forecast	209507	219885	229005
Actual	206742	210210	217182
% error	−1.3	−4.6	−5.4
Price level			
Forecast	127.0	136.4	156.3
Actual	127.4	133.5	139.9
% error	0.3	−2.2	−11.7
Employment			
Forecast	21439	21975	22590
Actual	21061	21182	21279
% error	−1.8	−3.7	−6.2
Exchange rate			
Forecast	79.3	69.1	63.7
Actual	83.3	78.8	78.7
% error	4.8	12.3	19.1
Money stock			
Forecast	96729	110301	125474
Actual	98775	107755	121493
% error	2.1	−2.4	−3.3
Short rate			
Forecast	10.02	11.20	13.00
Actual	9.79	9.52	11.96
error	−0.23	−1.68	−1.04
PSBR			
Forecast	11319	14686	16352
Actual	11609	10150	7568
error	290	−4536	−8784

The BVAR forecast for output in 1984 and 1985, like the mechanical forecasts from all the structural models, is too optimistic. The BVAR forecast lies towards the top of the range for 1984, being the highest if the structural models use actual values of the exogenous variables, and marginally lower than the NIESR using the projection of exogenous variables in the published forecast. In 1985 only the LPL model prediction based on actual exogenous variables is more optimistic.

The BVAR again overpredicts the actual price level in both 1984 and 1985. With the exception of LBS and NIESR, the BVAR model produces the smallest absolute forecast error for 1984 when the structural models are given the actual exogenous variables. The BVAR lies in the middle of the range when projected exogenous variables are used, LBS and LPL having larger absolute errors. In 1985, the absolute error from the BVAR model is larger than all the structural models with the exception of LPL, irrespective of whether actual and projected exogenous variables are employed.

In comparison with the published forecasts, the BVAR model has the greatest absolute error on both output and the price level in both 1984 and 1985. While our comparison is based on only one set of published forecasts, the relative accuracy of the forecasts based on the models in comparison to the BVAR forecast points to the importance of the forecasters' judgemental interventions for forecast accuracy.

4.9 Loss functions

In the foregoing discussion no explicit loss function or decision criterion is specified, although it might be argued that an informal loss function is implicit in our selection of variables to discuss. In this section we present an illustration of the questions that arise in constructing a weighted combination of forecast errors of several variables to give a single index of forecast performance for each model.

Forecasts of a single variable are usually assessed through a squared error loss function, so that positive and negative deviations are penalized equally (and for reasons of analytic tractability). In a multivariate setting, given a vector of forecast errors, e_t, the natural generalization is the quadratic form $e_t' K e_t$, where K is a symmetric weighting matrix. Non-zero off-diagonal elements of K indicate that there is a cost incurred by forecast errors in particular variables in combination; these terms contribute to the usual decision criterion, namely, the expected value (in theoretical work) or time average (in empirical work) of such quadratic forms, unless the forecast errors are uncorrelated. The choice of K depends on one's view of what is important; in what follows we ignore trade-offs between possibly correlated forecast errors and restrict attention to a diagonal matrix. The choice of weights to be attached to the squared forecast errors in each individual variable remains.

For illustrative purposes we consider four variables: the level of GDP, the growth of GDP, the inflation rate, and the unemployment rate. We calculate the mean square forecast error for each variable and each model, taking a simple average of the two years of the forecast period. These individual mean square errors are then expressed as a ratio of their average for a given variable across all the models, in order to standardize the comparison in respect of the degree of difficulty in forecasting that variable. The resulting relative mean square errors are plotted in Figure 4.6 in a four-quadrant diagram. Each quadrant is bounded by two axes along which the relative mean square errors are plotted (growth and output in a negative direction). Thus, a point within the quadrant represents the relative mean square errors of a pair of variables. On joining the points to form a rectangle we gain an impression of each model's forecast accuracy over all four variables, and the use of the same scale for each axis implies that the four variables are weighted equally in this comparison. Thus, if each variable is given a weight of one quarter, and the relative mean square errors are combined with these weights to give a total loss, then the average forecast has a loss of one, equal to one-eighth of the perimeter of the rectangle. The square formed by joining the points (1, 1) represents average performance in respect of each of the variables being forecast, and a rectangle lying within this square represents better-than-average performance on all variables. Likewise, comparing two models, one rectangle lying entirely within the other represents superior performance across all four variables. Changing the weights can be represented as a rescaling of the axes, but if one rectangle lies entirely within another this is unaffected by different weights, and the relative values of the loss function, and hence the ranking of the forecasts, is independent of the weighting scheme. Where rectangles overlap, however, a different scaling representing different weights in the loss function will affect the ranking of the forecasts. In

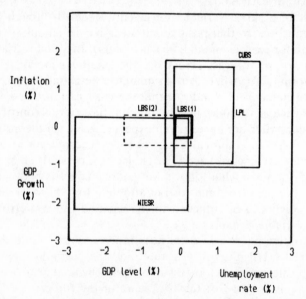

Fig. 4.6   Relative mean square errors.

Figure 4.6 we observe that the LBS(1) rectangle, using the expenditure measure of GDP, lies within the LPL rectangle, which in turn lies within the CUBS rectangle, giving an unambiguous ranking both under this set of relative weights and under any alternative set.

Turning to the intersecting rectangles, we see that with equal weights the NIESR and CUBS forecasts are ranked equal, and the LBS(2) forecast using the output measure of GDP is ranked higher than that of LPL. By changing the weights in the loss function, however, it is possible to alter the ranking of these forecasts. Thus, the NIESR forecast would improve its ranking if GDP level and growth errors were penalized weakly and if inflation errors had a higher relative weight, and the LBS forecast using the GDP output measure would similarly improve its position if growth errors had a low relative weight. Finally, we report that the VAR forecast rectangle would lie entirely outside the LBS, CUBS, and LPL forecasts, and is therefore inferior to these forecasts for all sets of relative weights assigned to the variables. It is also inferior to the NIESR forecast under this set of relative weights, but as it would intersect the NIESR forecast, which has a higher relative mean square error for GDP growth, this ranking is not independent of the choice of weights.

Comparing the mechanical forecasts from the different models, we find that the smallest loss value is recorded for NIESR, followed by LBS. Both of these forecasts are superior to that of LPL, independent of the choice of relative weights. However, the ranking between NIESR and LBS and rankings involving the CUBS model cannot be made unambiguously. Comparing each individual mechanical forecast with the corresponding published forecast, we find that the former always has a higher loss under equal weights. For three of the forecasts — LBS (expenditure), CUBS, and LPL — the superior performance of the published forecast is invariant to the choice of relative weights, thus supporting the conclusions of Section 4.6. Finally, we note that the VAR forecast is inferior to both LBS and NIESR mechanical forecasts, independent of the weighting scheme. It has a higher loss value than the CUBS mechanical forecast if we assume equal relative weights, but performs slightly better than the LPL mechanical forecast.

4.10 Summary and conclusions

In this chapter we analysed the sources of error in four model-based forecasts, by comparing forecasts for 1984 and 1985 with the March 1986 estimates of the actual outcomes. It should be noted that this was one of the very first published forecasts with the CUBS model. Both LBS and LPL have the smallest average forecasting errors for the level of GDP, but LBS is more accurate in terms of GDP growth. Contrary to the results of Matthews *et al.* (1985), this particular LPL forecast does not outperform the others in forecasting either the price level or inflation. LBS and NIESR do better, although they overpredict the price level, while LPL underpredict. LBS and NIESR are also more accurate than either CUBS or LPL in their forecasts of the level of unemployment, although LBS and NIESR make large errors in the relationship between employment and unemployment. Forecast errors for the PSBR on average are quite large in relation to the size of the PSBR over the forecast period. The exchange rate, often thought to be difficult to forecast, is predicted with reasonable accuracy.

Selecting an average of the published forecasts for 1984 would have been more successful for GDP and prices than using any one individual forecast, but this would not have been so for GDP in 1985, or for the level of unemployment in either year.

The miners' strike clearly influenced the behaviour of the economy in 1984 and 1985, and was unanticipated in late 1983. This is an example of a random event influencing forecast error and illustrates how a small error may be misleading as an indicator of model accuracy. The effects of the dispute are likely to be reflected in the models not via different projections of the exogenous variables, but rather via off-model corrections through residual adjustments. We do not attempt to recompute the forecast allowing for the effects of the strike, partly because of the difficulty in assessing appropriate changes in a consistent fashion across the models, and partly because the strike effects themselves appear to be principally those of timing. We indicate some approximate effects on GDP to facilitate comparison of forecast errors for output in individual years, but the main part of our analysis concerns the average of the two years and hence is little affected by the effects of this disruption to economic activity.

Projections of exogenous domestic policy variables were fairly close to the observed outcome, and the main differences of the projections of the exogenous variables from currently known estimates occur for the world economy. The buoyancy of world demand was, in general, underprojected. The unanticipated fall in oil prices led to an overprediction of world inflation, but the timing of the effects suggests that the nature of the relationship between world demand and prices cannot be wholly explained by inappropriate oil price projections.

Rather than reduce forecast errors, the substitution of actual exogenous data for the estimates made by the modelling teams produces the reverse effect. Thus, observed forecast errors cannot be explained by deviations of projections of exogenous variables from their outcomes. Larger forecast errors under the assumption of actual exogenous data suggest some misspecification of the models. In the case of LBS and NIESR, this misspecification appears to lie in the relationship between quantities and prices, although in opposite directions in the two models.

We find that in many cases the role of residual adjustments is to compensate for errors in the model and/or for errors in exogenous variables, and therefore the adjustments reduce the size of forecast errors. The general picture is one of value-added made by forecasters to the accuracy of forecasts, but the corollary is that the models themselves are not particularly good forecasting tools. The main exception to this conclusion is that of NIESR and LBS forecasts of the output measure of GDP, where the mechanical forecast does better than the published forecast incorporating residual intervention. On this basis, the model would appear to be a relatively accurate forecasting tool, with little value-added by the forecaster. However, inspection of growth rate performance together with that of inflation prevents general statements of this type. In addition, the sensitivity of the results can be seen from the superior performance of the LBS expenditure-based forecast over its mechanical counterpart.

It is difficult to do full justice to the role of data revisions. There have been substantial changes to the base-year data. A very simple analysis of the effects of the revisions to the GDP data might revise the level of GDP throughout by the size of the revision. This would improve the ranking of the LPL forecast. A more elaborate analysis involves revising assumptions about residual adjustments in the light of new information regarding the recent database (i.e., 1982 to the first half of 1983). Conducting this type of exercise on both the LBS and NIESR models does not make a great deal of difference to our conclusions, although the influence of data revisions on a forecast error may operate in a far more complex fashion than we have been able to represent.

Another way of judging forecasting accuracy is by comparison with alternative non-structural models. We have estimated a vector autoregressive model against which the structural models can be compared. (This also ignores strike effects.) This model generates larger errors on output and prices than do the structural models, and hence supports our earlier conclusion regarding the importance of forecasting interventions on model accuracy.

Finally, we have attempted to provide an overall measure of forecast accuracy by computing loss functions for the forecasts using mean square errors in the level and growth in GDP, the level of unemployment, and the inflation rate. We find that the LBS (expenditure) forecast can be ranked as superior to that of LPL, which in turn can be ranked higher than the CUBS forecast, one of the first produced by that group. However, neither the NIESR nor LBS (output) forecasts can be ranked in this way since the relative aggregate value of the loss functions incorporating these forecasts depends on the relative weights associated with output, inflation, and unemployment errors. Using equal weights between outcomes would lead to a ranking of the NIESR forecast equally with that of CUBS. The LBS (output) forecast would still rank higher than LPL in terms of forecast accuracy. Ranking of forecasts is dependent on the choice of the endogenous variables included in the loss function, and it is possible to identify alternative variables for inclusion which may radically change the ranking of forecasts. We should also note that the forecast ranking is based on one particular forecast, and even here the conclusions may change as new data become available for 1984 and 1985. This emphasizes the point made earlier in this chapter that there is no absolute or definitive measure of forecast accuracy. Forecast evaluation may depend as much on when the analysis was carried out as on how it was conducted. Nevertheless, the analysis reported here provides a starting-point against which to gauge this sensitivity.

Chapter 5

Econometric Evaluation of Labour Market Models

5.1 Introduction

In many areas of economics, different econometric studies reach conflicting conclusions and, given the available data, there are frequently no effective methods for deciding which conclusion is correct.

Mark Blaug (1980, p. 261)

. . . I consider that a suggested specification should be tested in all possible ways, and only those specifications which survive and correspond to a reasonable economic model should be used.

J. D. Sargan (1975, p. 322)

In this chapter we address the problem identified by Blaug using the approach advocated by Sargan, in the context of the models of the labour market that form part of the seven models of the UK economy with which this book is concerned. Both authors implicitly acknowledge, in different ways, that the process of econometric model-building depicted in many econometrics textbooks does not accurately represent real-world empirical research. In many textbook accounts, the role of econometrics is simply to provide efficient ways of estimating and testing models developed from economic theoretic considerations. It is assumed that economic theory delivers qualitative predictions about the relations among economic variables, and all that remains is their quantification. To this end, methods of estimating the unknown parameters of the model from a sample of economic data are devised, together with methods of testing underlying hypotheses and assumptions, usually in the framework of classical statistical inference. The resulting statistical procedures are themselves assessed by analysing their performance in a 'true' model, or one that departs from the truth in a known way.

In practice the model is not known, and the problem facing the empirical researcher is to discover a model that provides a good representation of the data, is consonant with relevant economic theory, and is adequate for the purpose at hand. Sometimes these requirements appear to conflict. In general, the process of discovery involves a specification search, which continues until a model is found that satisfies a range of statistical diagnostic checks. In such an iterative process, the statistical diagnostics no longer support the formal hypothesis-testing procedures of classical statistical inference; rather, they provide checks of model adequacy or, while the search is in progress, indicators of the direction in which an inadequate model might be improved.

The approach advocated by Sargan has recently been developed and extended in a number of ways, as discussed in the editors' introduction and several chapters of Hendry and Wallis (1984). In particular, systematic comparison of rival models has an important place (Mizon, 1984). Addressing the question of whether a given model accounts for ('encompasses') alternative explanations of the same phenomena allows the progressive improvement of models. Of course, more general models encompass simpler versions of themselves, and so attention concentrates on parsimonious specifications, as usual.

A comprehensive econometric evaluation of the large-scale models is a task of enormous proportions, and so we study one particular sector, nevertheless seeking to go beyond single-equation analysis. The labour market sector has a number of features that facilitate comparative analysis. It is reasonably self-contained, and is concerned with certain key variables, which occur in each of the models. It is broadly the same size across models, and sufficiently small for ease of analysis. Finally, the estimated equations have been subjected to theoretical and econometric scrutiny recently, and so represent up-to-date contributions to labour market research. In addition to improving our understanding of empirical models of the labour market, we also seek to develop methods of econometric comparison through their practical application. For example, what are the practical limitations to the objective of testing 'in all possible ways', and what is a sensible list of procedures to be used in inter-model comparisons?

This chapter is organized as follows. Section 5.2 summarizes the labour market equations of each model. In Section 5.3 we describe how we have replicated the principal labour-market equations, namely, employment and wage equations. In each case we have applied the same estimation method as the model team, ordinary least squares (OLS), or instrumental variables (IV) methods, and have attempted to reach the same results. This material provides our basic point of reference for all subsequent analysis, and is reported in some detail. Equations describing the determination of such variables as hours of work and labour force participation occur in relatively few of the models and are left on one side, given our interest in comparative work. Section 5.4 discusses and reports the single-equation diagnostic tests applied to the estimated equations; these relate to parameter instability and predictive failure, tests of instrument validity, dynamic specification and residual autocorrelation, heteroscedasticity, and non-normality of residuals. Section 5.5 examines comparative issues, which involves a discussion and reporting of non-nested tests and encompassing tests, wherever it has been possible to use these techniques in practice. Section 5.6 contains concluding comments.

5.2 The structure of the labour market models

Our analysis focuses on three key endogenous variables; wages, employment, and unemployment. Of course, these are not determined solely in the labour market sector of the model in general, but are jointly determined endogenous variables of the complete model. In concentrating on such relationships as the labour demand and supply functions and the wage equation, we neglect other interrelationships occuring elsewhere in the model. To fix ideas we partition the complete model, writing the equations of the labour market as the first G_1 equations of the G-equation model; hence in the linear case we have

$$B_{11}y_{1t} + B_{12}y_{2t} + C_1z_t = u_{1t}$$

where B_{11} is $G_1 \times G_1$, B_{12} is $G_1 \times (G - G_1)$, and C_1 is $G_1 \times M$. Identities are specified as equations whose parameter values are known and whose disturbance term is identically zero. The above partitioning distinguishes the elements of y_{1t}, the variables of principal concern — typically, employment, the real wage (or disaggregated measures of each), possibly hours of work, and unemployment — from the elements of y_{2t}, the other endogenous variables in the labour market equations — typically, prices and output. When $B_{12} = 0$ we can speak of the labour market determining the y_{1t} vector, but otherwise there is contemporaneous feedback from the rest of the model. A diagonal normalization of B_{11} is usually employed and so each particular equation can be loosely considered to correspond to a particular endogenous variable, enabling us to speak of the wage equation, and so forth.

In practice, the models are nonlinear in variables, typically containing a mixture of linear and logarithmic equations, but also employing simple ratio variables, such as the unemployment rate. They also differ in respect of the number of equations in the labour market sector, the selection of variables to include, and the precise form of the equations. The specifications rest on considerations of both statistical evidence and economic theory, and the brief accounts that follow emphasize the latter element, summarizing and updating the discussion of our first review, which was not concerned with statistical matters. We consider first the annual models of LPL, CUBS, and CGP, and then the quarterly models, NIESR, LBS, BE, and HMT.

Liverpool (LPL)

The LPL labour market model contains two behavioural equations. The theoretical model that underpins these consists of two sectors, one competitive and the other unionized. In the latter, unions set the wage and firms read off their employment requirements from the competitive demand-for-labour schedule. This is the familiar union monopoly model. In the competitive sector, wages are free to clear the market, except when the level of benefits forms a floor. A weighted average of these two wages provides a specification for a wage equation based on the competitive paradigm, which can be re-interpreted as a re-normalized labour supply equation. The second equation is a standard marginal productivity for labour condition, except that unemployment data replace employment data via an implicit linear relationship between the logarithms of the two variables. We can write the two equations in the following schematic form:

$$\ln (w/p) = f_1 (\ln U, B/p; POP, Z^u) \tag{5.1}$$
$$\ln U = f_2 \{\ln (w/p), y;\} \tag{5.2}$$

Notation is given in the appendix at the end of this chapter. In the list of right-hand-side variables, a semi-colon separates endogenous variables from predetermined variables, and any lagged dependent variables, trends, constants, and dummy variables are neglected for the time being. In recording the elements of the y_1 vector, we note whether a variable is in logarithmic or natural form, so that we can examine whether the block is linear in variables as well as linear in parameters. These two equations determine real wages and unemployment, conditional on the other endogenous variables, namely, real benefits and output. Having determined $\ln U$, the levels of employment and labour supply follow from the standard linear identity

$$U \equiv L - n$$

and the implicit relationship of the form $\ln U = -k \ln n$. The equations are estimated by IV (with different instrument sets) using annual observations, 1956–83.

City University Business School (CUBS)

The CUBS labour market represents a general non-market-clearing model. This consists of a labour demand schedule, a labour supply schedule, and a wage equation. The last of these describes the response of wages to the degree of labour market disequilibrium, the adjustment parameter representing a range of possibilities ranging from perfectly flexible, market-clearing real wages to fixed real wages. In schematic form we have

$$\ln n^m = f_1 \{\ln (w/p), k, q^e/p, q^m/p;\} \tag{5.3}$$
$$\ln L = f_2 \{\ln (w/p); u^r_{-1}, POP\} \tag{5.4}$$
$$\Delta\ln (w/p) = f_3 \{u^r, B/p; \Delta w_{-1}, SC\}. \tag{5.5}$$

When an identity is added to define the unemployment rate, the model is non-linear in four endogenous variables; thus, $G_1 = 4$ and $y'_1 = \{\ln(w/p), \ln n, u^r, \ln L\}$, conditional upon $y'_2 = (q^m/p, q^e/p, k)$. The subscript -1 indicates a lagged variable, and Δ denotes the first-difference operator. The equations were estimated by 3SLS, using annual data, covering the period 1953–82.

Cambridge Growth Project (CGP)

To keep the present exercise to a manageable size, we restrict attention to the labour market equations of the aggregate models, and are unable to contemplate re-estimation of the 39 pairs of employment and hours equations that appear in the CGP model. However, we do consider the model's aggregate wage equation, originally presented by Lawson (1981). The basic paradigm is that of the 'real wage resistance' (RWR) hypothesis, a generic description for all models whose lineage goes back to Sargan (1964). Put simply, nominal wages are determined non-competitively by bargaining between employers and employees, the wage outcome being a dynamic process modelled by partial adjustment towards a target real wage. This may not be attained if other institutional factors, such as incomes policies, come into play, although in the long run homogeneity is usually assumed to prevail. This form of wage equation fits nicely into a standard disequilibrium framework if the target wage is the long-run competitive wage (see CUBS above), having the appearance of a Phillips curve if the speed of adjustment towards the target wage is determined by the tightness or otherwise of the labour market, usually proxied by the actual unemployment rate. Schematically, the CGP wage equation is

$$\ln (w/p) = f_1(\Delta u^r; Z^y, t_2). \tag{5.6}$$

The variable Z^y is a strength-of-incomes-policy index, based in part on estimates, explicit or implicit, of the government's target nominal earnings growth rates. The use of the *change* in the unemployment rate is unusual, and is claimed to be a feature of the data. The equation is estimated from annual observations, 1955–81, by OLS, thus neglecting the endogeneity of unemployment.

All four quarterly models incorporate a disaggregated treatment of employment, and three of them a disaggregated treatment of wages. Before looking at each model individually, we note that the general form of disaggregation into three or four sectors is similar throughout. In particular, we have

NIESR manufacturing, mainly public, other industries (excluding oil and agriculture), and general government
LBS manufacturing, general government, and other
HMT manufacturing, general government, other (excluding oil), and private
BE manufacturing, general government, and other (including public corporations)

It can be seen that the division is not the same across models. Whereas in general one can identify government (g), manufacturing (m), non-manufacturing (n), public (p), and private (pr), only the first two categories are directly comparable across models. Where appropriate, the abbreviations are attached as superscripts to variable symbols, with 'other' being denoted as o.

National Institute of Economic and Social Research (NIESR)

Although there are four sectors identified above, the NIESR model has three estimated employment equations. The exception is public services, where, since output is measured by employment, the latter is calculated as a fixed proportion of the former. The basic form of the estimated equations is the well-known employment function with employment determined by output, which is best interpreted as the firm facing sales constraints with fixed coefficient technology. For manufacturing there is a real-wage term implying some kind of factor substitution (with what is unclear), and so this particular equation may be interpreted as a marginal productivity for labour condition. The NIESR employment equations are presented as a synthesis of three distinct theoretical models, which underpin the behaviour of firms in different market environments, namely, perfect competition, imperfect competition, and disequilibrium. Empirically, however, the general form often reverts to one of the interpretations described above.

Like CGP, the treament of wages is aggregated and follows the RWR hypothesis. Unemployment is determined not by the familiar identity $U = L - n$, but by a dynamic equation depending on employment and demographic labour supply, to allow for the effect of demographic changes and changes in employment (disaggregated) upon the unemployment register. Finally, average hours in manufacturing industry are determined by manufacturing output, the long-run effect being smaller than the short-run.

As noted elsewhere in this volume, the present NIESR model incorporates a significant role for expectations in the employment and wage equations. These issues are discussed in more detail in Section 5.3. For the moment we use an asterisk (*) to indicate that an index of future expected values of a given variable enters the employment equations, and a caret (ˆ) to indicate the single expectation term in the wage equation. The NIESR labour market equations are then given in schematic form as follows:

$$\ln n^m = f_1 \{\ln (wh^m/p^m)^*, y^{m*};\} \tag{5.7}$$
$$\ln n^o = f_2 (y^{o*};) \tag{5.8}$$
$$\ln n^p = f_3 (y^{p*};) \tag{5.9}$$
$$\Delta\ln w - \Delta\ln \hat{p}_{+1} = f_4 \{\Delta\ln h^m; \ln (w\hat{h}^m/p)_{-1}, \Delta^2 u^r_{-1}\} \tag{5.10}$$
$$U = f_5(n^r, n^m; L) \tag{5.11}$$
$$\ln h^m = f(y^m;) \tag{5.12}$$
$$u^r \equiv U/(U+n) \tag{5.13}$$
$$n \equiv n^m + n^o + n^p + \bar{n}. \tag{5.14}$$

This sub-system is more complicated than the previous three in so far as there are more variables owing to disaggregation, a greater degree of nonlinearity, and a large number of expectational variables. Clearly, equations (5.7)–(5.9) together with identity (5.14) determine employment and its three components conditional on all the right-hand-side endogenous variables, of which ln w and ln h^m are also determined within the system if (5.10) and (5.12) are included. Unemployment, U, is determined recursively via equation (5.11) and the unemployment rate via identity (5.13). Taken as a whole, the $G_1 = 8$ equations determine $y_1' = (n^m, n^o, n^p, n, w, h^m, U, u^r)$, conditional on the other endogenous variables $y_2' = (p^m, p, y^m, y^o, y^p)$ and all the forward expectations variables. The presence of such variables, the solution for which in a model-consistent expectations approach requires solution of the complete model, makes it more difficult to isolate the labour market block than would otherwise be the case.

In equation (5.10) the variable $\ln(w\bar{h}^m/p)_{-1}$ is a constructed variable arising from the 'co-integrating' procedure used in estimating the equation, which is examined in Section 5.4. Of the five equations that form part of this study, namely (5.7)–(5.11), four are estimated by IV while the fifth, (5.10), is estimated by OLS, which neglects the endogeneity of hours of work. All are estimated using quarterly data with samples covering the general period 1964–83.

London Business School (LBS)

In the LBS model there is a three-sector disaggregation and so there are three wage equations. As employment in general government is exogenous in the model, however, there are two employment equations; the model also contains a female participation equation. Since our first review the structure of the wage and employment equations has altered considerably, and the labour market paradigm now adopted, described by Smith and Holly (1985) following the treatment of Nickell and Andrews (1983), rests on the observation that a large number of wage settlements is determined by bargaining. Unlike the LPL treatment described above, there is *no* competitive sector, and a different type of bargaining model is incorporated. The LBS model allows for genuine bargaining over wages, whereas the LPL approach assumes that unions are all-powerful. In both models firms retain the right-to-manage, which restricts the solution in real-wage–employment space to the competitive labour demand schedule; but it is easily demonstrated that the LPL solution (the 'union monopoly' model) lies north-west of the LBS solution (the 'right-to-manage' model). Moreover, in the union monopoly version variables that parameterize the position of the firm's labour demand schedule do not appear in the wage equation, whereas in the LBS model both employers' and employees' variables enter the wage equation via a standard comparative statics solution to the (Nash) bargain. This provides a basis of comparison of the two models (see Nickell, 1984a; Minford, 1984), but because the LPL model is

annual and LBS quarterly, a more formal comparison, such as some form
of encompassing test, is difficult. The employment equation is the labour
demand schedule itself. Thus, the behavioural equations with which we are
concerned may be written schematically as

$$\ln n^m = f_1 \{\ln (w^m/p^m), \ln (q/p^m), y^m;\} \tag{5.15}$$
$$\ln n^o = f_2 \{\ln (w^o/p), y^o\} \tag{5.16}$$
$$\ln w^m - \ln \hat{p} = f_3 \{\ln (w^m/p)_{-1}, B/p; u^r_{-1}, t_3\} \tag{5.17}$$
$$\ln w^o - \ln \hat{p} = f_4 \{\ln (w^o/p)_{-1}, \ln (w^m/p)_{-1}, (B/p)_{-1}, u^r_{-1}\} \tag{5.18}$$
$$\ln w^g = f_5 (\ln w^m). \tag{5.19}$$

For this and the remaining models we describe only the equations to be
replicated, neglecting identities and other equations that complete the
labour market specification since, as discussed in Section 5.5, comparative
analysis based on a solution of the whole labour market block is not
possible in the quarterly models.

The form of the two demand schedules is based on Nickell's (1984b)
study, where the firm operates in an industry that faces a downward-
sloping product demand schedule. In this setup the derived demand-for-
labour schedule is conditional upon the level of *aggregate* demand, via cost
minimization, and the price level plays no part. Equation (5.15) is more
easily interpreted, therefore, under the restriction that ensures that
$\ln (w^m/p^m)$ and $\ln (q/p^m)$ can be replaced by $\ln (w^m/q)$. Equation (5.16),
however, can be interpreted as the marginal productivity for labour condition; it suggests that y^o should be treated endogenously in estimation,
which in fact it is not. The dependent variables in the two wage equations
based on the bargaining paradigm are nominal wages deflated by *expected*
prices. This is quite natural in so far as bargains are struck based on the
purchasing power of wages over the next wage round. All the equations are
estimated by OLS, except (5.15), which is estimated by IV. All are
estimated using quarterly data covering the general period 1964–81.

Bank of England (BE)

Of the three sectors identified above, BE estimate employment equations
for manufacturing and other, and wage equations for all three. The specifications predate much recent influential research, following Brechling
(1965) and Ball and St Cyr (1966) for other employment. The manufacturing employment equation is noteworthy, containing only hours and normal
hours; but hours, in turn, are determined by a similar marginal productivity condition, equation (5.20a). When taken as a pair, equations (5.20)
and (5.20a) provide a more standard treatment. The wage equations are
fairly *ad hoc*, corresponding to the wage equations in a typical wage–price
sector. As with almost all wage equations in this study, there is a role for an
unemployment term. The schematic form of the equations of interest is
(including manufacturing hours)

$$\ln n^m = f_1 \ (\ln h^m, \ \ln h_n^m;) \tag{5.20}$$
$$\ln h^m = g \ (\ln y^m, \ \ln W^m; \ \mu) \tag{5.20a}$$
$$\ln n^o = f_2 \ (\ln y^o, \ \ln W^o) \tag{5.21}$$
$$\ln w^m = f_3 \ (\ln U; \ \ln p_{-1}, \ \ln W^p{}_{-1}, \ D, \ t_{2,-1}) \tag{5.22}$$
$$\ln w^p = f_4 \ (\ln p; \ \ln w^m{}_{-1}, \ \ln U_{-1}, \ D) \tag{5.23}$$
$$\ln (w^o/p) = f_5 \ \{\ln (w^m/p), \ \ln U; \ D\}. \tag{5.24}$$

All the equations are estimated by OLS, with samples covering 1964–81.

Her Majesty's Treasury (HMT)

The HMT labour market is the last of the seven to be investigated, and we examine three equations in particular: the two private sector employment equations (manufacturing and non-manufacturing), and the private sector earnings equation.

The two employment equations have been subjected to much empirical scrutiny of late (see Kelly and Owen, 1985), and are substantially different from the ones examined in our first review. They may be written

$$\ln n^m = f_1 \ \{\ln (w^m/q^m), \ \ln (w^m/r^m), \ y^m*;\} \tag{5.25}$$
$$\ln n^n = f_2 \ \{\ln (w^n/r^n), \ y^n;\} \tag{5.26}$$

and are motivated by the work of Nickell (1984b) and Symons (1985). In manufacturing there are three factors of production (labour, capital, and raw materials and fuel), but in non-manufacturing the third is excluded. These are treated as variable inputs in the firm's (short-run) decision problem. Thus the conditional demand for labour depends on two relative factor prices in the manufacturing sector and one in non-manufacturing; in particular, careful construction of data on the price of capital is then required. Both equations are derived from a standard intertemporal cost minimization problem, with adjustment costs, leading to the inclusion of a sequence of expectations terms and lagged dependent variable(s). In the manufacturing sector expectations of output are dealt with explicitly, following Nickell. The basic form of manufacturing employment equations for NIESR, LBS, and HMT is the same — compare equations (5.7), (5.15), and (5.25). The differences relate to the treatment of expectations, which suggests that encompassing tests might be able to separate the models in spite of the similar backgrounds.

While both NIESR and LBS have changed the specification of their wage equations since our first review, the HMT wage equation retains its basic form, namely

$$\ln w^{pr} = f_3(y, \ \Delta p; \ t_1, \ n^g, \ \Delta t_2). \tag{5.27}$$

Equations (5.25) and (5.26) are estimated by OLS, using samples covering the general period 1967–84. Equation (5.27) is not estimated; rather, its coefficients are imposed. This equation is subject to scrutiny below, and is re-estimated to examine whether its coefficients are consistent with the data.

5.3 Statistical estimation

In this section we report our basic estimation results. Our notation is as follows. Without loss of generality, consider the *first* equation of a G_1-equation block, with a sample of T observations, written as

$$y_1 = Y_1\beta_1 + Z_1^a\gamma_1 + u_1 = X_1\delta_1 + u_1 \qquad (5.28)$$

where y_1 and u_1 are $T \times 1$ vectors, Y_1 is a $T \times (g_1 - 1)$ matrix of included right-hand side endogenous variables, and Z_1^a is a $T \times m_1$ matrix of included predetermined variables. Then $X_1 = (Y_1:Z_1^a)$ is a $T \times k_1$ matrix of regressor variables ($k_1 = m_1 + g_1 - 1$) and δ_1 collects the parameters to be estimated. For the block of equations under consideration there are M predetermined variables. These form the set of possible instrumental variables, partitioned as $(Z_1^a:Z_1^b:Z_1^c)$, where Z_1^b is a matrix of $M_1 - m_1$ excluded instruments used in estimating the first equation, and the matrix Z_1^c contains the $M - M_1$ potential but unused instrumental variables. In what follows the subscript 1 is dropped in order to clarify the notation, but subsequently the subscript takes different values to indicate different equations of a given model.

Typically, an equation is estimated by either OLS or IV methods. The estimates, residuals, and predicted values for OLS estimation are denoted by carets (^), whereas IV estimates are denoted by tildes (~). When the equation has been estimated by OLS we report the sample size, T, the sum of squared residuals, $\hat{u}'\hat{u}$, the estimated error variance of the regression, $\hat{\sigma}^2$, computed as $\hat{u}'\hat{u}/(T - k)$, and R^2. As is well-known, tests of r linear restrictions are computed by comparing $\hat{u}'\hat{u}$ between restricted and unrestricted models, and can be based on either the Wald (W), likelihood ratio (LR), or Lagrange multiplier (LM) principle. All three are simple transformations of the standard F-statistic with r and $T - k$ degrees of freedom (d.f.), based on the error variance of the unrestricted model. If the model is estimated by IV, the following information is reported in the tables: sample size, T, the sum of squared residuals, $\tilde{u}'\tilde{u}$, and the error variance of the regression, $\tilde{\sigma}^2$, computed as $\tilde{u}'\tilde{u}/(T - k)$. As there is no known small-sample distribution theory for IV, nor for OLS except in the fixed regressor case, we follow standard practice in appealing to asymptotic theory regarding inference. However, in order to compare estimated error variances between equations estimated by OLS and IV, we use this simple form of degrees of freedom adjustment, which effectively scales the asymptotic quantity by $T/(T - k)$. The IV estimator $\tilde{\delta}$ minimizes

$$S(\delta) = (y - X\delta)'Z(Z'Z)^{-1}Z'(y - X\delta)$$

which generates the minimand $\tilde{u}'Q_Z\tilde{u}$, where $Z = (Z^a:Z^b)$ and $Q_Z = Z(Z'Z)^{-1}Z'$ is the familiar projection matrix. The quantity $\tilde{u}'Q_Z\tilde{u}$ can be computed as the explained sum of squares in the auxiliary regression of $\tilde{u}$ on the set of instrumental variables, $\tilde{u} = Z\hat{\gamma} + \hat{\varepsilon}$, whence $\hat{\varepsilon}'\hat{\varepsilon} = \tilde{u}(I-Q_Z)\tilde{u}$.

Therefore $\bar{u}'Q_Z\bar{u} = \bar{u}'\bar{u} - \hat{\varepsilon}'\hat{\varepsilon}$. The two quantities $\bar{u}'\bar{u}$ and $\bar{u}'Q_Z\bar{u}$ are used in our discussion of tests relating to parameter instability, autocorrelation, and so forth, as well as tests relating to the validity of the IV estimator. In particular, tests of r linear restrictions can be easily computed by taking the difference of $\bar{u}'Q_Z\bar{u}$ for the restricted and unrestricted models, scaled by $\tilde{\sigma}^2$ from the unrestricted model, provided that the same instruments are used for both regressions (Godfrey, 1984). Indeed, it can be demonstrated that this Wald version of the test of such restrictions is again a simple transformation of LM and LR variants (Bowden and Turkington, 1984, p. 28), and so if all three are properly calibrated they define the same test. In keeping with the small-sample F-test above, the Wald version is reported if there is no indication to the contrary, but inference rests, asymptotically, on the chi-square distribution.

Liverpool (LPL)

The estimated versions of equations (5.1) and (5.2) are given in Table 5.1. The estimates obtained are *not* those that form the model code of the current LPL model, reported by Minford *et al.* (1984, Table 2, p. 40). These are derived from 'the quarterly estimates of the long-run coefficients, being the better-determined, except the productivity growth time-trend . . . which comes from the annual unemployment equation' (Minford, 1983, p. 238). These annual estimates also supply the coefficients on the two lagged dependent variables, $\ln W_{-1}$ and $\ln U_{-1}$. In our present exercise statistical evaluation is undertaken on the freely estimated parameters, using annual data. Our estimates are reported in the second column of the table and define our working model. Checking these against the calibrated coefficients reported in the last column gives a chi-square value of 4.6 for the unemployment equation (5 d.f.) and 8.5 for the wage equation (6 d.f.), which implies that the approach adopted by LPL is capturing some salient features of the data. (The wage equation comparison neglects the term in unanticipated inflation in the model equation, for which data were not made available to us.)

City University Business School (CUBS)

Estimates of equations corresponding to (5.3)–(5.5) are presented in Table 5.2. As already noted, the three equations, together with the unemployment identity, form a well-defined block which is linear in parameters and (almost) log-linear in variables. CUBS estimate the three-equation model using 3SLS, treating all the elements in y_{1t} as endogenous. Of the elements in y_{2t} only k (capital stock) is treated as endogenous, and this variable is 'represented by its quasi-reduced form solution $[\hat{k}]$'. We simply take this series as data, noting, however, that it is not the same series that would be generated by projecting k on the instruments used in the 3SLS procedure, because the complete model solution for k is not the same as the sub-block

Table 5.1   *LPL model: unemployment and real-wage equations*
(a) Unemployment equation

Dependent variable: no. of unemployed, $\ln U$ (sample mean 6.56, s.d. 0.689)
Mixed log-linear equation, IV estimates, annual data, 1956–83

Regressor variable	Sample mean	Coefficient estimate	Standard error	Model equation
Real product wage ($\ln W^p$)	−0.0826	1.10	1.08	1.96
Real output ($\ln y$)	11.3	−4.24	0.85	−4.07
...				
No. of unemployed ($\ln U_{-1}$)		0.314	0.123	0.520
Trend (tr)	69.5	0.128	0.040	0.090
Constant		43.7	7.83	43.0

Excluded instruments (Z_1^b): population ($\ln POP$), union density, current and lagged (Z^u, Z^u_{-1}), retail price inflation ($\ln p_{-1} - \ln p_{-2}$), employers tax rate, current and lagged ($t_1, t_{1,-1}$), world trade ($\ln y^w$).
$T = 28, k_1 = 5, g_1 = 3, m_1 = 3, M_1 = 10, \tilde{\sigma} = 0.128, \tilde{u}'\tilde{u} = 0.3752, \tilde{u}'Q\tilde{u} = 0.1837$

(b) Wage equation

Dependent variable: real wage, $\ln W$ (sample mean −0.167, s.d. 0.158)
Mixed log-linear equation, IV estimates, annual data, 1956–83

Regressor variable	Sample mean	Coefficient estimate	Standard error	Model equation
No. of unemployed ($\ln U$)	6.56	−0.0073	0.0206	−0.0200
...				
Real benefits ($\ln B/p$)	−1.37	0.0659	0.0258	0.0960
Real wage ($\ln W_{-1}$)		0.755	0.136	0.800
Population ($\ln POP$)	10.1	−0.472	0.407	−0.014
Union density (Z^u)	0.477	0.749	0.315	0.392
Constant		4.53	4.16	0.186
Unanticipated inflation				−0.65

Excluded instruments (Z_2^b): real weighted benefits, current and lagged, (UB, UB_{-1}), $t_1, t_{1,-1}, tr, y$ (defined above).
$T = 28, k_2 = 6, g_2 = 2, m_2 = 5, M_2 = 11, \tilde{\sigma} = 0.0231, \tilde{u}'\tilde{u} = 0.01171,$
$\tilde{u}'Q\tilde{u} = 0.003829$

Notes to Tables 5.1–5.7:
When an instrumental variables (IV) estimator is employed, a dotted line in the list of regressor variables separates those variables treated as endogenous (above the line) from those treated as predetermined (below the line) at the estimation stage. An equation is described as mixed log-linear when it includes some untransformed variables and some logarithmic variables. Where possible, each equation is re-parameterized to explain the *level* of the dependent variable, whose sample standard deviation is given by 's.d.'

solution. (For further discussion on estimation and model selection methodology, see Beenstock *et al.* 1985, Section III.) This is the only model in
which a systems approach to estimation is used, the model being broken up
into well-defined blocks to each of which 3SLS is applied. However, we find
that IV estimates are similar, and these, presented in the first columns of
Table 5.2, provide the basis for our subsequent single-equation comparative work. The last column contains our 3SLS estimates.

Table 5.2 *CUBS model: labour demand, supply, and wage adjustment
equations*

(a) Labour demand equation

Dependent variable: no. employed in 'marketed' output sector, $\ln n$ (sample mean
9.79, s.d. 0.0434)
Logarithmic equation, IV estimates, annual data, 1953–82

Regressor variable	Sample mean	Coefficient estimate	Standard error	Model equation	3SLS
Real product wage ($\ln W^p$)	−0.292	−0.258	0.123	−0.259	−0.301
Capital stock ($\ln k$)	12.0	0.177	0.084	0.181	0.192
...					
Real price of energy ($\ln(q^e/p)$)	−0.352	−0.181	0.052	−0.211	−0.111
$\ln(q^e/p)_{-1}$		0.134	0.052	0.166	0.058
Real price of raw materials ($\ln(q^m/p)$)	0.00474	0.135	0.047	0.131	0.097
$\ln n_{-1}$		1.326	0.152	1.215	1.195
$\ln n_{-2}$		−0.669	0.202	−0.495	−0.609
Constant		1.135	1.205	0.472	1.630

Excluded instruments (Z_1^b): see notes
$T = 30$, $k_1 = 7$, $g_1 = 4$, $m_1 = 4$, $M = 16$, $\bar{\sigma} = 0.0128$, $\bar{u}'\bar{u} = 0.03622$,
$\bar{u}'Q\bar{u} = 0.002031$

(b) Unemployment equation

Dependent variable: employed plus unemployed, $\ln L$, (sample mean 10.1,
s.d. 0.0415)
Error correction equation, IV estimates, annual data, 1953–82

Regressor variable	Sample mean	Coefficient estimate	Standard error	Model equation	3SLS
Consumption wage ($\ln W^c$)	−0.760	0.0495	0.0287	0.0550	0.032
...					
$\ln W_{-1}$		−0.0610	0.0458	−0.0873	−0.0471
$\ln W_{-2}$		0.0383	0.0279	0.0633	0.0444
Participation ratio		−0.276	0.066	−0.330	−0.315

Table 5.2 *(continued)*

(ln $(L/POP)_{-2}$) Population of working age ($\triangle$ln POP)		1.476	0.322	1.500	1.264
Unemployment rate (u'_{-1})	0.0269	−0.303	0.087	−0.340 −0.300
Constant		−0.0687	0.0194	−0.0820 −0.0795

Excluded instruments (Z_2^b): see notes

$T = 30$, $k_2 = 7$, $g_2 = 2$, $m_2 = 6$, $M = 16$, $\tilde{\sigma} = 0.00531$, $\tilde{u}'\tilde{u} = 0.0006490$, $\tilde{u}'Q\tilde{u} = 0.0003670$

Note:
Sample mean for ln POP is 10.4.

(c) Wage adjustment equation

Dependent variable: rate of growth of pre-tax real wages, $\triangle$ln W (sample mean 0.0190, s.d. 0.0182)
Mixed log-linear equation, IV estimates, annual data, 1953–82

Regressor variable	Sample mean	Coefficient estimate	Standard error	Model equation	3SLS
Unemployment rate (u') ...	0.0307	−0.778	0.218	−0.432	−0.831
Nominal wage growth ($\triangle$ln w_{-1})	0.0907	−0.324	0.081	−0.336	−0.331
$\triangle$ln W_{-2}		−0.225	0.146	−0.225	−0.266
Structural change (SC)	0.0148	1.519	0.402	1.223	1.561
SC_{-1}		−0.277	0.342	−0.477	−0.206
Real benefits (ln (B/p))	−0.137	0.0810	0.0214	0.0559	0.0827
Constant		0.0689	0.0102	0.0660	0.0706

Excluded instruments (Z_3^b): see notes

$T = 30$, $k_3 = 7$, $g_3 = 2$, $m_3 = 6$, $M = 16$, $\tilde{\sigma} = 0.0129$, $\tilde{u}'\tilde{u} = 0.003799$, $\tilde{u}'Q\tilde{u} = 0.001722$

Notes:
1. The same IVs are used for (a), (b), and (c). The complete set is: constant, ln n_{-1}, ln n_{-2}, ln(q^e/p), ln$(q^e/p)_{-1}$, ln(q^m/p), ln $L_{-2}(*)$, ln W^c_{-1}, ln W^c_{-2}, $\triangle$ln POP, $\triangle$ln w_{-1}, $\triangle$ln$(w/p)_{-2}$, SC, $SC_{-1}(*)$, ln(B/p), ln $u'_{-1}(*)$, ln p; (*) indicates lagged variables added by us.
2. The unemployment rate measures differ slightly between (b) and (c); in the former ln $(1 + U/L)$, the latter U/L.

The only change since our first review is that 'the coefficients on [ln n_{-1}] and [ln n_{-2}] have been constrained . . . when they were freely estimated these parameters generated roots that were highly complex . . . we therefore experimented with different coefficients . . . until a plausible lag distribution was estimated which did not significantly increase the standard error of the regression' (Beenstock *et al.*, 1985, p. 38). In Table 5.2 we report unrestricted estimates. The chi-square test statistic of the unrestricted estimates against these constrained values is 0.77 (2 d.f.), and is consistent with the foregoing claims in ensuring that labour demand/employment exhibits monotone adjustment.

Cambridge Growth Project (CGP)

The estimated version of equation (5.6), the CGP wage equation, is presented in Table 5.3. Using the data supplied, the estimated equation corresponds closely to the model code, presented by Barker (1985, p. 34) and in the last column of Table 5.3.

Table 5.3 *CGP model: wage equation*

Dependent variable: real consumption wage, ln W^c (sample mean 7.45, s.d. 0.149)
Mixed log-linear equation, OLS estimates, annual data, 1955–81

Regressor variable	Sample mean	Coefficient estimate	Standard error	Model equation
Unemployment rate ($\triangle \ln u^r$)		−0.0183	0.0999	−0.0172
Real consumption wage (ln W^c_{-1})		0.523	0.077	0.510
Incomes policy dummy (Z^y)	0.783	−0.0173	0.0028	−0.0181
Dummy, 1972 = 1		0.0391	0.0132	0.0380
Trend (tr)	15.0	0.0095	0.0015	0.0098
Constant		3.34	0.55	3.82

$T = 27, k = 6, \hat{\sigma} = 0.0125, \hat{u}'\hat{u} = 0.003272, R^2 = 0.99$

Note:
Sample mean for log unemployment rate is −3.80.

National Institute of Economic and Social Research (NIESR)

Table 5.4 contains estimated labour market equations for the NIESR model, corresponding to the schematic forms given in (5.7)–(5.11). As noted, there is an important role for expectations in the first four of these equations, and so a description of the methodology employed is required. The treatment of expectations, based upon the rational expectations hypothesis, and the background to the four equations is described by Hall and Henry (1985), who also report the wage equation that appears in the model code, given in the last column of Table 5.4(d). Our estimates differ slightly owing to the provision of data of a slightly different vintage, but the differences give no cause for concern.

The basic form for the three employment equations is derived from a standard optimization problem, where the objective function is an infinite future sequence of profits or costs, appropriately discounted, and where adjustment costs are also incurred. The decision rule can be written

$$n_t = \alpha_1 n_{t-1} + \alpha_2 n_{t-2} + \sum_{i=0}^{\infty} \alpha'_{3i} Z^e_{t+i} \qquad (5.29)$$

where Z_{t+i}^e is a sequence of expectations for the vector of forcing variables (in this case real wages, output, and real price of raw materials and fuel). The procedure outined by Hall and Henry is to estimate

$$n_t = \alpha_1 n_{t-1} + \alpha_2 n_{t-2} + \alpha_3' \left(\sum_{i=0}^{4} \lambda_i Z_{t+i}^e \right) \tag{5.30}$$

in two stages. The first obtains estimates of α_{3i}, using the numerical technique described by Hall (1984), which ensures that the forward and backward representations in the underlying Euler condition are treated symmetrically. The impact of the unstable root is the same for all the forcing variables, via the scalars λ_i, $i = 0, \ldots, 4$. The individual impact of each forcing variable is captured in α_3 (a vector), which is estimated in the second stage. This requires the construction of a vector of variables from the expression in brackets, which may be thought of as an index of the future (or permanent) value of output, real wages, etc., denoted by an asterisk in (5.7)–(5.9). Hall and Henry imply that the data used are generated from an auxiliary VAR model, but observed data are in fact used, which invokes a strong form of rationality. Given the presence of these expectational variables, the equations are estimated by IV, an issue

Table 5.4 *NIESR model: disaggregated employment equations; wage and unemployment equations*
(a) Employment in manufacturing

Dependent variable: no. employed in manufacturing, $\ln n^m$ (sample mean 8.93, s.d. 0.124)

Logarithmic equation, IV estimates, quarterly data, adjusted, 1964(1)–1983(4)

Regressor variable	Sample mean	Coefficient estimate	Standard error	Model equation
'Permanent' real product wage (W^p*)	0.0259	−0.103	0.017	−0.1031
'Permanent' future output ($y^{m}*$)	4.62	0.120	0.020	0.122
...				
$\ln n^m_{-1}$		1.194	0.123	1.188
$\ln n^m_{-2}$		−0.275	0.113	−0.267
Constant		0.166	0.049	0.147

Excluded instruments (Z_1^b): $\ln y^m_{-1}$, $\ln y^m_{-2}$, $\ln y^m_{-3}$, $\ln y^m_{4}$, $\ln W^p_{-1}$, $\ln W^p_{-2}$, $\ln W^p_{-3}$, $\ln W^p_{-4}$, tr, world real rate of interest.

$T = 80$, $k_1 = 5$, $g_1 = 3$, $m_1 = 3$, $M_1 = 13$, $\check{\sigma} = 0.00304$, $\check{u}'\check{u} = 0.0006919$, $\check{u}'Q\check{u} = 0.00008086$

Notes:
1. W^p* constructed as $\Sigma_0^4 \lambda_i W_{+i}$; $\lambda_0 = 0.153$, $\lambda_1 = 0.126$, $\lambda_2 = 0.228$, $\lambda_3 = 0.215$, $\lambda_4 = 0.189$, where $W \equiv \ln \{ w(1 + t_1) h^m / p^m \}$
2. $y^{m}*$ constructed $\Sigma_0^4 \lambda_i \ln y_{+i}$; λ_i as above

Table 5.4   *(continued)*
(b) Employment in other industries

Dependent variable: employed in other industries, ln n^o (sample mean 8.79, s.d. 0.0493)
Logarithmic equation, IV estimates, quarterly data, adjusted, 1964(2)–1983(4)

Regressor variable	Sample mean	Coefficient estimate	Standard error	Model equation
'Permanent' output (y^{o*})	0.850	0.0141	0.0055	0.0148
...				
ln n^o_{-1}		1.000	0.041	0.974
Dummy, 1970(4) = 1		−0.00622	0.00850	−0.00535
Dummy, 1971(1) = 1		−0.0335	0.0085	−0.033
Trend (tr)	526.0	−0.000515	0.000262	−0.000400
Constant		−0.645	0.569	−0.450

Excluded instruments (Z^b_2): ln $y^o_{-1}, \ldots,$ ln y^o_{-4}
$T = 79, k_2 = 6, g_2 = 2, m_2 = 5, M_2 = 9, \tilde{\sigma} = 0.00834, \tilde{u}'\tilde{u} = 0.005077,$
$\tilde{u}'Q\tilde{u} = 0.0002447$

Notes:
1. y^{o*} constructed as above, with weights 2.33, 2.157, 1.992, 1.834, and 1.685.
2. The second and fourth columns differ slightly because NIESR formed predictions for y^{o*} using one extra observation, and estimated the structural equation using OLS. We have kept the same sample for the first and second-stage regressions, allowing the use of a standard IV estimator, which gives 'correct' standard errors.

(c) Employment in mainly public industries

Dependent variable: no. employed in mainly public industries, ln n^p (sample mean −0.0969, s.d. 0.0911)
Logarithmic equation, IV estimates, quarterly data, adjusted, 1964(2)–1983(1)

Regressor variable	Sample mean	Coefficient estimate	Standard error	Model equation
'Permanent' output (y^{p*})	4.51	0.0289	0.0126	0.0286
...				
ln n^p_{-1}		1.358	0.110	1.360
ln n^p_{-2}		−0.380	0.108	−0.382
Dummy, first quarter		0.000876	0.00151	0.000863
Dummy, second quarter		0.00355	0.00151	0.00355
Dummy, third quarter		0.00240	0.00149	0.00240
Constant		−0.132	0.058	−0.131

Excluded instruments (Z^b_3): ln $n^p_{-3}, \ldots,$ ln n^p_{-4}, ln $y^p_{-1}, \ldots,$ ln y^p_{-5}, tr
$T = 76, k_3 = 7, g_3 = 2, m_3 = 6, M_3 = 15, \tilde{\sigma} = 0.00459, \tilde{u}'\tilde{u} = 0.001455,$
$\tilde{u}'Q\tilde{u} = 0.0002372$

Note:
y^{p*} constructed as above, with weights 0.252, 0.256, 0.204, 0.160, and 0.128.

Table 5.4   *(continued)*

(d) Wage equation

Dependent variable: $(\ln w - \ln w_{-1}) - (\ln \hat{p}_{+1} - \ln p)$
(sample mean 0.00602, s.d. 0.0183)
Error correction equation, OLS estimates, quarterly data, adjusted, 1963(4)–1983(4)

Regressor variable	Coefficient estimate	Standard error	Model equation
Hours in manufacturing ($\triangle \ln h^m$)	−1.021	0.117	−1.008
Unemployment rate ($\triangle^2 u^r_{-1}$)	−1.102	0.861	−1.201
Co-integrating term	−0.168	0.059	−0.166
Constant	0.00557	0.00147	0.00536

$T = 81, k_4 = 4, \hat{\sigma} = 0.0132, \hat{u}'\hat{u} = 0.01335, R^2 = 0.50$

Note:
Means of manufacturing hours and the unemployment rate are 4.64 and 0.0464, respectively.

(e) Unemployment equation

Dependent variable: no. unemployed, U (sample mean 1224.7, s.d. 906.9)
Mixed log-linear equation, IV estimates, quarterly data, adjusted 1964(2)–1984(4)

Regressor variable	Sample mean	Coefficient estimate	Standard error	Model equation
Manufacturing employment (n^m)	7480	−0.885	0.116	−0.861
Non-manufacturing employment (n^r)	14958	−0.300	0.119	−0.316
...				
U_{-1}		0.907	0.087	0.889
n^m_{-1}		0.788	0.188	0.747
n^r_{-1}		0.282	0.105	0.296
Demographic labour supply (D)	41542	0.227	0.147	0.304
$\bar{D}_{-1}$		−0.224	0.138	−0.295
Constant		994.0	751.0	1003.0

Excluded instruments (Z^b_5): $n^m_{-2}, \ldots, n^m_{-5}, n^r_{-2}, \ldots, n^r_{-5}, \triangle y^m_{-1}, \ldots,$
$\triangle y^m_{-4}, \triangle y^r_{-1}, \ldots, \triangle y^r_{-4}$
$T = 83, k_5 = 8, g_5 = 3, m_5 = 6, M_5 = 22, \hat{\sigma} = 29.7, \bar{u}'\bar{u} = 66355, \bar{u}'Q\bar{u} = 18996.0$

Notes:
1. The demographic labour variable is a four-period moving average, i.e., $(D + D_{-1} + D_{-2} + D_{-3})/4$.
2. The equation has been re-parameterized into levels form.

we discuss in the final part of this section. Discussion of the co-integrating term in the wage equation is deferred to Section 5.4. Although Hall and Henry suggest that an IV estimator should be used, to allow for the endogeneity of the expected price inflation term, the equation is estimated by OLS.

London Business School (LBS)

Corresponding to equations (5.15)–(5.19), we present in Table 5.5 estimated equations based on the data set supplied. In three cases replication of the model equations is extremely accurate, but there are slight differences when the dependent variable in equations (5.17) and (5.18) is a measure of wage deflated by *expected* price, that is $\ln w - \ln \hat{p}$. The latent variable is constructed by taking the fitted values from a third-order autoregression for $\ln p$, which we are unable to replicate exactly (see footnote to Table 5.5(c)).

Table 5.5 *LBS model: disaggregated employment and wage equations*
(a) Employment in manufacturing industry

Dependent variable: no. employed in manufacturing, $\ln n^m$ (sample mean 8.95, s.d. 0.0882)
Logarithmic equation, IV estimates, quarterly data, adjusted, 1965(1)–1981(4)

Regressor variable	Sample mean	Coefficient estimate	Standard error
Real product wage ($\ln W^{pm}$)	−0.073	−0.211	0.054
Real price of raw materials and fuel ($\ln Q^m$)	−0.085	0.0406	0.0217
Output ($\ln y^m$)	4.63	0.0836	0.0197
...			
$\ln n^m_{-1}$		1.184	0.161
$\ln n^m_{-2}$		−0.284	0.147
$\ln W^{pm}_{-1}$		0.138	0.056
$\ln Q^m_{-1}$		−0.0482	0.0192
Constant		0.499	0.149

Excluded instruments (Z^b_1): world GNP, world money stock, world non-oil commodity prices/world consumer prices, current and lagged, general government consumption, world consumer prices, unemployment benefit index, working population (all logarithmic variables)
$T = 68$, $k_1 = 8$, $g_1 = 4$, $m_1 = 5$, $M_1 = 13$, $\hat{\sigma} = 0.00383$, $\bar{u}'\bar{u} = 0.0008808$, $\bar{u}'Q\bar{u} = 0.0000895$

Table 5.5   (continued)

(b) Employment in primary and residual tertiary sectors

Dependent variable: 'other' employment, $\triangle \ln n^o$ (sample mean -0.000412, s.d. 0.00697)

Error correction equation, OLS estimates, quarterly data, adjusted, 1965(1)–1981(4)

Regressor variable	Sample mean	Coefficient estimate	Standard error
$\triangle n^o_{-1}$		0.349	0.106
$\triangle \ln y^o$		0.183	0.054
$\ln n^o_{-2} - \ln y^o_{-1}$		-0.0653	0.0199
Real product wage $(W^{op})_{-2}$	0.133	-0.0709	0.0241
Dummy, 1972(1) = 1		0.0175	0.0051
Dummy, 1972(2) = 1		-0.0114	0.0054
Trend (tr)	74.5	0.000341	0.000134
Constant		0.293	0.093

$T = 68$, $k_2 = 8$, $\hat{o} = 0.00476$, $\hat{u}'\hat{u} = 0.001357$, $R^2 = 0.58$

Notes:
1. Sample means for 'other' employment ($\ln n^o$) and 'other' output ($\ln y^o$) are 9.25 and 4.50, respectively.
2. Solved out autoregressive–distributed lag polynomial is $(1 - 0.349L + 0.414L^2) \ln n^o = (0.183 - 0.118L)\ln y^o + \dots$
3. Model equations in (a) and (b) not reported as replication is exact.

(c) Wages in manufacturing industry

Dependent variable: expected pre-tax real wage in manufacturing, $\ln w^m - \ln \hat{p}$ (sample mean -0.193, s.d. 0.153)

Logarithmic equation, OLS estimates, quarterly data, adjusted, 1965(2)–1981(4)

Regressor variable	Sample mean	Coefficient estimate	Standard error	Model equation
$\ln(w^m/p)_{-1}$		1.084	0.083	1.115
$\ln(w^m/p)_{-2}$		-0.0493	0.1039	-0.0892
$\ln(w^m/p)_{-3}$		-0.216	0.079	-0.223
Unemployment rate ($\ln u^r_{-1}$)	1.101	-0.0543	0.0354	-0.0825
$\ln u^r_{-2}$		0.0801	0.0640	0.137
$\ln u^r_{-3}$		-0.0519	0.0358	-0.081
Real benefits ($\ln(B/p)$)	0.0808	0.0259	0.0284	0.0192
Indirect tax rate ($\ln(1+t_3)$)	0.153	-20.167	0.180	-0.126
Dummies:				
1974(1) = 1, 1974(2) = -1		0.0355	0.0739	0.0310
1972(1) = 1, 1972(2) = -1		0.0325	0.0729	0.0341

Table 5.5 *(c) Wages in manufacturing industry (continued)*

Regressor variable	Sample mean	Coefficient estimate	Standard error	Model equation
Trends:				
t^*		0.00212	0.00072	0.00234
t^{**}		0.00143	0.00037	0.00154
Incomes policy dummy, D		−0.0132	0.0042	−0.0127
Constant		−0.129	0.062	−0.153

$T = 67$, $k_3 = 14$, $\hat{\sigma} = 0.0100$, $\hat{u}'\hat{u} = 0.005315$, $R^2 = 0.997$

Notes:
1. For a brief discussion on the incomes policy dummy, see Smith and Holly (1985).
2. The autoregression for predicting price of private consumption is given in the LBS manual. *Our* estimated coefficients (LBS in parentheses) are 1.66(1.69), −0.60(−0.57), −0.098(−0.126). This clearly explains some of the difference between columns.
3. Unemployment rate is normalized on the working population, rather than labour force.
4. t^* is a trend up to 1973(4) and constant thereafter; t^{**} is zero up to 1973(4), and trended thereafter.

(d) Wages in non-manufacturing industry

Dependent variable: expected pre-tax real wage in non-manufacturing, $\ln w^o - \ln \hat{p}$ (sample mean −0.149, s.d. 0.127)
Logarithmic equation, OLS estimates, quarterly data, adjusted, 1965(2)–1981(4)

Regressor variable	Sample mean	Coefficient estimate	Standard error	Model equation
$\ln(w^o/p)_{-1}$	−0.155	0.374	0.131	0.415
$\ln(w^o/p)_{-2}$		0.322	0.133	0.276
$\ln(w^o/p)_{-3}$		−0.275	0.115	−0.296
$\ln u^r_{-1}$	1.101	−0.159	0.058	−0.146
$\ln u^r_{-2}$		0.295	0.104	0.266
$\ln u^r_{-3}$		−0.190	0.059	−0.169
$\ln(B/P)_{-1}$	0.0818	0.0866	0.0427	0.0978
$\ln(w^m/p)_{-1}$	−0.372	0.135	0.071	0.134
Incomes policy dummy, D		−0.0116	0.0065	−0.0088
t^*		0.00469	0.00135	0.00489
t^{**}		0.00232	0.00067	0.00270
Constant		−0.314	0.111	−0.338

$T = 67$, $k_4 = 12$, $\hat{\sigma} = 0.0168$, $\hat{u}'\hat{u} = 0.01561$, $R^2 = 0.985$

Note:
Predicted values for $\ln \hat{p}$ as in (c) above.

Table 5.5   *(continued)*

(e) Earnings in public administration

Dependent variable: nominal public sector earnings, $\triangle \ln w^g$ (sample mean 0.0286, s.d. 0.0334)

Error correction equation, OLS estimates, quarterly data, adjusted, 1963(4)–1981(4)

Regressor variable	Coefficient estimate	Standard error
$\triangle \ln w^g_{-1}$	0.215	0.097
$\ln w^g_{-1} - \ln w^m_{-3}$	−0.101	0.077
$\triangle \ln w^m$	0.234	0.163
$\triangle \ln w^m_{-1}$	0.936	0.162
$\triangle \ln w^m_{-2}$	0.232	0.207
Dummies:		
1972(1) = −1,1972(2) = 1	−0.0122	0.0138
1975(1) = 1,1975(2) = −1	0.0988	0.0144
'Clegg', 1979(3)−1980(3) = 1	0.0271	0.0105
Constant	−0.00716	0.00585

$T = 73, k_5 = 9, \hat{\sigma} = 0.0194, \hat{u}'\hat{u} = 0.02374, R^2 = 0.70$

Notes:

1. Solved out autoregressive–distributed lag polynomial is $(1 - 1.114L + 0.215L^2) \ln w^p = (0.234 + 0.702L - 0.704L^2 - 0.131L^3)\ln w^m$.
2. Sample means of w^g and w^m are 3.55 and 3.57, respectively.
3. Model equation is not reported as replication is exact.

Bank of England (BE)

Table 5.6 presents the estimated equations corresponding to (5.20)–(5.24). In general, this is our least successful attempt at replicating the model code, particularly for the three wage equations. This is due in part to the unavailability of the unemployment data used in the original empirical work.

Her Majesty's Treasury (HMT)

Corresponding to equations (5.25)–(5.27), we present in Table 5.7 estimated equations using the data set supplied, which for the first two equations is the data set used in the original empirical work (Kelly and Owen, 1985). Small differences in part (b) of the table result from the use of a slightly different sample period. More important, though, is the restriction imposed upon the freely estimated factor price ratio term, $\ln (w^n/r^n)_{-1}$, and the error correction term, $\ln (n^n_{-1}/y^n)$, such that the ratio of their coefficients is 0.11, which measures the long-run effect (i.e., $0.11 = 0.0105/0.095$). This is because, 'though the relative factor cost term was

Table 5.6 *BE model: disaggregated employment and wage equations*
(a) Manufacturing employment

Dependent variable: no. employed in manufacturing, $\ln n^m$ (sample mean 8.95, s.d. 0.0868)

Logarithmic equation, OLS estimates, quarterly data, adjusted, 1965(1)–1981(4)

Regressor variable	Sample mean	Coefficient estimate	Standard error	Model equation
$\ln n^m_{-1}$		0.707	0.041	0.734
Total hours ($\ln h^m$)	12.7	0.457	0.023	0.459
$\ln h^m_{-1}$		−0.172	0.047	−0.193
Normal hours ($\ln h^m_n$)	3.69	0.0165	0.0513	−0.133
Dummies:				
1972(1) = 1		0.00897	0.00198	0.00846
1972(2) = 1		−0.00368	0.00231	−0.00457
1974(1) = 1		0.0275	0.0025	0.0277
1974(2) = 1		−0.0105	0.0034	−0.0117
Trend (tr)		0.000259	0.000042	0.000230
Constant	42.5	−1.061	0.217	−0.523

$T = 68$, $k_1 = 10$, $\hat{\sigma} = 0.000190$, $\hat{u}'\hat{u} = 0.0002083$, $R^2 = 0.9996$

(b) Other employment

Dependent variable: employment in 'other sector, $\ln n^o$ (sample mean 9.29, s.d. 0.0309)

Logarithmic equation, OLS estimates, quarterly data, adjusted, 1965(1)–1981(4)

Regressor variable	Sample mean	Coefficient estimate	Standard error	Model equation
$\ln n^o_{-1}$		1.051	0.114	1.050
$\ln n^o_{-2}$		−0.334	0.098	−0.297
Output ($\ln y^o$)	10.1	0.133	0.040	0.110
$\ln y^o_{-1}$		0.0706	0.0491	0.1372
Wage cost (W^o)	0.0986	−0.000293	0.000774	−0.0229
Denationalization dummy, (D_{-1})	16.7	−0.0133	0.0028	−0.0130
D_{-2}		0.0175	0.0054	0.0172
D_{-3}		−0.00672	0.00279	−0.00677
Split trend (t^*)		−0.000508	0.000381	−0.000460
Constant		0.614	0.256	0.00283

$T = 68$, $k_2 = 10$, $\hat{\sigma} = 0.00356$, $\hat{u}'\hat{u} = 0.0007370$, $R^2 = 0.99$

Notes:
1. Published estimates based on sample including 1964(4), data for which were not available.
2. Denationalization dummy represents planned rundown of manpower in nationalized industries in late 1960s.
3. Split trend is zero up to 1974(4), trended thereafter
4. Wage cost variable is constructed slightly differently to HMT (1985).

Table 5.6   *(continued)*
(c) Wages in manufacturing industry

Dependent variable: nominal earnings in manufacturing, $\ln w^m$ (sample mean 6.09, s.d. 0.539)

Mixed log-linear equation, OLS estimates, quarterly data, adjusted, 1965(3)–1979(4)

Regressor variable	Sample mean	Coefficient estimate	Standard error	Model equation
$\ln w^m_{-1}$		1.098	0.142	0.689
$\ln w^m_{-2}$		−0.364	0.151	−0.3271
No. of unemployed ($\ln U$)	6.54	−0.0222	0.0138	−0.0605
Consumption deflator ($\ln p_{-1}$)	−0.958	0.419	0.149	0.480
$\ln p_{-2}$		−0.297	0.137	−0.227
Incomes policy (D)	0.00972	−0.161	0.140	−0.3677
Public sector earnings ($\ln w^p_{-1}$)	6.01	0.0798	0.0595	0.3578
Tax-term ($t_{2,-1}$)	0.725	−0.182	0.105	−0.1751
$t_{2,-2}$		0.196	0.105	0.100
Trend (tr)	39.5	0.00357	0.00120	0.00594
Constant		1.252	0.6115	2.145

$T = 58$, $k_3 = 11$, $\hat{\sigma} = 0.00965$, $\hat{u}'\hat{u} = 0.004375$, $R^2 = 0.67$

Note:
The unemployment data for (c), (d), and (e) are not as used originally by BE (1985).

(d) Wages in non-trading public sector

Dependent variable: nominal earnings in public sector, $\triangle \ln w^p$ (sample mean 0.02, s.d. 0.0302)

Mixed log-linear equation, OLS estimates, quarterly data, adjusted, 1965(3)–1981(4)

Regressor variable	Coefficient estimate	Standard error	Model equation
$\ln (w^m_{-1}/w^p_{-2})$	0.284	0.096	0.349
$\ln (p/p_{-4})$	−0.0634	−0.3937	0.1997
$\ln (p_{-1}/p_{-4})$	0.0887	0.7245	−0.3488
$\ln (p_{-2}/p_{-4})$	0.332	0.560	0.542
D_{-1}	−0.631	0.322	−0.500
$\ln U_{-4}$	−0.0198	0.0084	−0.0169
Constant	0.125	0.051	0.101

$T = 66$, $k_4 = 7$, $\hat{\sigma} = 0.0256$, $\hat{u}'\hat{u} = 0.03861$, $R^2 = 0.35$

Notes:
1. Sample mean of w^p is 6.17
2. Data for dependent variable not available for pre-1965(3); model equation estimates based on 1964(1)–1981(4).

Table 5.6   *(continued)*
(e) Wages in 'other' sector

Dependent variable: real earnings in 'other' sector, $\triangle\ln(w^o/p)$ (sample mean 0.0060, s.d. 0.0199)
Error correction equation, OLS estimates, quarterly data, adjusted, 1965(2)–1981(4)

Regressor variable	Coefficient estimate	Standard error	Model equation
$\triangle\ln(w^m/p)$	0.473	0.160	0.473
$\ln(w^o/w^m)_{-1}$	−0.398	0.105	−0.579
D	−0.0715	0.210	−0.211
$\ln U$	0.00265	0.00628	−0.0271
$\ln U_{-1}$	−0.00292	0.00646	0.0427
$\ln U_{-2}$	0.00087	0.00609	−0.181
Constant	−0.0103	0.0277	n/a

$T = 67, k_5 = 7, \hat\sigma = 0.0175, \hat u'\hat u = 0.01840, R^2 = 0.29$

Notes:
1. Data for dependent variable not available for pre-1965(2); model equation based on 1964(3)–1981(4).
2. Mean of $\ln(w^o)$ is 6.19.

quite significant, the size of the [long-run] elasticity seemed too small to be consistent with the theory outlined [earlier in the paper]' (Kelly and Owen, 1985, p. 59). We report the freely estimated coefficients, and a test of the nonlinear restriction gives a chi-square statistic (with one d.f.) of 3.70.

The HMT private sector earnings equation has not been estimated in the usual sense, in so far as the model code is not derived from one single regression. Our estimate of the equation is given in Table 5.7(c), using as full a sample as possible. It is quite clear that the model equation and the estimated coefficients have little in common. The chi-square statistic for a test of the 18 restrictions is 82.0, which clearly rejects the null hypothesis, given a 5 per cent critical value of 28.9. This is the only case in the present study in which an equation that has not been directly estimated appears inconsistent with the data.

Generated regressors and expectations variables

In various equations presented above expectations variables occur, either explicitly or implicitly. We now draw together all such occurrences and examine whether the procedures used by the model-builders yield consistent parameter estimates, other things being equal, and 'correct' standard errors. 'By "correct standard errors" we . . . mean that the traditional way of estimating the standard error of the parameter estimators yields a

Table 5.7 *HMT model: employment equations and wage equation*
(a) Manufacturing employment

Dependent variable: manufacturing employment, $\triangle \ln n^m$ (sample mean -0.00619, s.d. 0.00852)
Error correction equation, OLS estimates, quarterly data, adjusted, 1967(4)–1984(3)

Regressor variable	Sample mean	Coefficient estimate	Standard error	Model equation
$\triangle \ln n_{-1}$		0.502	0.068	0.531
$\ln n^m_{-1} - \ln \hat{y}$		-0.0893	0.0118	-0.0848
Output expectations ($\ln \hat{y}_{+1}$ $- \ln \hat{y}$)		0.0493	0.0174	0.0492
$\ln \hat{y}_{+2} - \ln \hat{y}_{+1}$		0.0637	0.0209	0.0580
Factor price ratio ($\ln (w^m/q^m)_{-6}$)	0.349	-0.0245	0.0043	-0.0233
$\triangle \ln (w^m/q^m)_{-6}$		0.0384	0.0082	0.0385
$\ln (w^n/r^m)_{-3}$	2.41	-0.00570	0.00188	-0.00508
Dummy, 1972(2) = 1		0.00521	0.00236	0.00520
Dummy, 1974(2) = 1		0.00819	0.00248	0.00720
Trend (tr)	41.5	-0.000499	0.000069	-0.000475
Constant		0.420	0.056	0.403

$T = 68$, $k_1 = 11$, $\hat{\sigma} = 0.00299$, $\hat{u}'\hat{u} = 0.0002979$, $R^2 = 0.94$

Notes:
1. Solved out autoregressive–distributed lag polynomials are:
$(1 - 1{,}413L + 0.502L^2)\ln n^m = (0.040 - 0.014L^{-1} + 0.0637L^{-2})\ln \hat{y} + \ldots \ldots$
2. *Equations originally estimated with sample starting in 1967(3), but as data for* $\ln (w^m/q^m)$ *for 1965(4) were unavailable, one observation is lost.*
3. Sample means for $\ln \hat{y}_{+1}$ and $\ln \hat{y}_{+2}$ are both 4.64, for $\ln n^m$ is 8.89.

(b) Non-manufacturing employment

Dependent variable: 'full-time equivalents' in non-manufacturing, $\triangle \ln n^n$ (sample mean 0.000661, s.d. 0.00603)
Error correction equation, OLS estimates, quarterly data, adjusted, 1971(4)–1984(3)

Regressor variable	Sample mean	Coefficient estimate	Standard error	Model equation
$\triangle \ln n^n_{-1}$		0.466	0.140	0.527
$\triangle \ln n^n_{-2}$		-0.0838	0.1241	-0.103
$\ln n^n_{-1} - \ln y^n$		-0.138	0.033	-0.095
$\ln (w^n/r^n)_{-1}$	-1.20	-0.00543	0.00373	-0.0105
$\triangle \ln (w^n/r^n)_{-1}$		0.00352	0.00552	0.00820
$\triangle \ln (w^n/r^n)_{-4}$		0.0125	0.00601	0.0158
$\triangle \ln (w^n/r^n)_{-5}$		0.00349	0.00614	0.0070

Table 5.7 *(continued)*

Regressor variable	Sample mean	Coefficient estimate	Standard error	Model equation
Trend (tr)	49.5	-0.000519	0.000125	-0.000385
Constant		-0.0965	0.0229	-0.0398

$T = 52$, $k_2 = 9$, $\hat{\sigma} = 0.00405$, $\hat{u}'\hat{u} = 0.0007043$, $R^2 = 0.62$

Notes:
1. Solved out autoregressive polynomial is $(1 - 1.328L + 0.550L^2 - 0.084L^3)$.
2. Sample mean for $\ln y^n$ is 10.2, for $\ln n^n$ is 9.33.

(c) Private sector earnings

Dependent variable: private earnings per head, $\triangle \ln w^{pr}$ (sample mean 0.0324, s.d. 0.0164)
Mixed log-linear equation, OLS estimates, quarterly data, adjusted, 1972(2)–1983(4)

Regressor variable	Sample mean	Coefficien estimate	Standard error	Model equation
Real activity $(\ln y)$	10.6	0.254	0.181	0.243
$\ln y_{-1}$		-0.295	0.167	-0.243
$\ln y_{-2}$		0.058	0.152	0.081
$\ln y_{-3}$		-0.066	0.119	0.052
$\ln W + (t_1 + t_2)/2$	-0.112	0.329	0.153	-0.133
Public sector employment (n^g)	8.48	0.098	0.165	0.03
$\triangle(\ln p + \ln p^c + t_1)$		0.337	0.085	0.0750
$\triangle(\ln p + \ln p^c + t_1)_{-1}$		0.112	0.098	0.0850
$\triangle(\ln p + \ln p^c + t_1)_{-2}$		-0.058	0.090	0.1038
$\triangle(\ln p + \ln p^c + t_1)_{-3}$		0.066	0.098	0.1231
$\triangle(\ln p + \ln p^c + t_1)_{-4}$		-0.027	0.102	0.1131
$\triangle t_2$		-0.040	0.112	0.0
$\triangle t_{2,-1}$		-0.043	0.106	0.0365
$\triangle t_{2,-2}$		0.157	0.111	0.0165
$\triangle t_{2,-3}$		-0.017	0.144	0.0165
$\triangle t_{2,-4}$		-0.138	0.111	0.0165
Trend (tr)	78.5	-0.000123	0.000781	-0.000029
Constant		-1.547	1.142	-1.0829

$T = 50$, $k_3 = 18$, $\hat{\sigma} = 0.0109$, $\hat{u}'\hat{u} = 0.003823$, $R^2 = 0.71$

Note:
Sample mean for $\ln w^{pr}$ is 6.83; $(\ln p + \ln p^c + t_1)$ is 4.802; t_2 is 0.277.

consistent estimator of the true standard errors' (Pagan, 1984a, fn 1). Pagan addresses general issues related to the the use of constructed regressors, and in what follows we consider all such problems except that of the co-integrating procedure used in the NIESR wage equation, deferred to Section 5.4. The occurrences of expectational variables are as follows:

(i) NIESR employment equations, (5.7)–(5.9), containing indices of permanent output and real factor prices;

(ii) NIESR wage equation, (5.10), containing an expectation of future prices, which deflates nominal wages;

(iii) LBS wage equations, (5.17) and (5.18), same as (ii) above, except that expectations of *current* prices occur;

(iv) LBS employment equations, (5.15) and (5.16), having implicit expectations of future output and real factor prices, substituted out;

(v) HMT manufacturing employment equation, (5.25), containing expectations of output.

These examples cover two main models and different ways of implementing them. First, expectations of variables formed in the previous period may influence contemporaneous behaviour, so that the model is

$$y_t = {}_{t-1}Z_t^e \delta + X_t \gamma + u_t. \tag{5.31}$$

It is then postulated that Z_t depends on explanatory variables W_t, and the unobserved expectation is replaced by the fitted values from an auxiliary regression of Z_t on W_t, giving the generated regressor $\hat{Z}_t$. The estimated equation is then

(A) $$y_t = \hat{Z}_t \delta + X_t \gamma + e_t \tag{5.32}$$

where $\hat{Z}_t = W_t \hat{\alpha}$. This we refer to as case (A), appropriate for (iii) above. (In this particular example the coefficient on Z_t^e is unity, but this does not alter the essence of the analysis, the more general model simply being estimated subject to the restriction $\delta = 1$.)

Second, expectations may be formed in the current period of a variable whose future value is of relevance, giving the model

$$y_t = {}_t Z_{t+1}^e \delta + X_t \gamma + u_t$$

which may be implemented in three different ways. The first follows the auxiliary regression approach as above, except that the fitted values are advanced one period, and so the estimated equation is

(B) $$y_t = \hat{Z}_{t+1} \delta + X_t \gamma + e_t, \tag{5.33}$$

where $\hat{Z}_{t+1} = W_{t+1} \hat{\alpha}$. This case is appropriate for example (v) above, although the actual treatment is more complicated than represented here.

Next, attention may be restricted to purely autoregressive models for the calculation of future expectations. Taking a second-order autoregression, we have ${}_t Z_{t+1}^e = \alpha_1 Z_t + \alpha_2 Z_{t-1}$, which, when substituted into the underlying model, gives the regression equation

(C) $$y_t = Z_t(\delta \alpha_1) + Z_{t-1}(\delta \alpha_2) + X_t \gamma + u_t. \tag{5.34}$$

This is appropriate for analysing example (iv).

Finally, it may be assumed that the unobserved expectation coincides with the conditional expectation of the variable, so that the actual outcome deviates from this only by a random innovation, giving

$$Z_{t+1} = {}_tZ^e_{t+1} + \varepsilon_{t+1}$$

which, when substituted into the underlying model, yields

(D) $$y_t = Z_{t+1}\delta + X_t\gamma + (u_t - \delta\varepsilon_{t+1}).$$ (5.35)

This approach is represented by examples (i) and (ii).

In cases (A) and (B), expectations formation is weakly or partly rational, in so far as W_t is unspecified. The results of Pagan's (1984a) Model 2 apply, namely, that the two-step estimator, applying OLS at the second stage, yields inconsistent estimates if X_t is not contained in W_t, but is consistent otherwise, and that the use of IV at the second stage is consistent, provided that $(W_t : X_t)$ are used as instruments for the expectational variables, and also generates a consistent estimator of the covariance matrix of the structural parameters. Applying this to (iii) and (v) above, consider first the HMT manufacturing employment equation. As this was estimated by OLS, if all the predetermined variables used in Table 5.7(a) appear in the forecasting equation, the estimates are consistent; but the covariance matrix is estimated inconsistently, with standard tests being biased towards a rejection of the null hypothesis. (Kelly and Owen, 1985, para 70–72, are clearly aware of Pagan's analysis.) Now consider the two LBS wage equations, example (iii), whose dependent variable is deflated by expectations of current nominal prices formed in the previous period. These are generated by AR(3) processes, and the equations are estimated by OLS. In the absence of X_t variables in the forecasting scheme, the estimates are inconsistent and inference is invalid.

Case (C) does not represent a generated regressors problem, and consistent estimators of the coefficients of (5.34) are easily available. However, the inability to identify the underlying parameters (δ, α_1, and α_2 in our example) in the absence of the auxiliary (auto)regression is the price that has to be paid. The two LBS employment equations are examples of this approach.

In case (D), the expectational variable is replaced by its observed value, the forecast error moving into the error term. In principle IV estimation can be applied to (5.35) as it stands, as proposed by McCallum (1976). Pagan (1984a) amends a three-stage procedure proposed by Wallis (1980) whereby Z_{t+1} is projected on to $\hat{\Omega}_t$ (the information set), which is previously formed by a projection on to some observed magnitudes. This yields $\hat{Z}_{t+1}$, which, if included in the IV set, yields consistent estimates of δ and γ and correct standard errors. In the NIESR wage equation (with $\delta = 1$ in (5.35) above) the second stage is estimated by OLS, which yields inconsistent estimates. For the NIESR employment equations the variable

Z_{t+1} in (5.35) is a constructed variable, as described following (5.30), and a moving average error process is generated, of the form $u_t - \sum\limits_{i=0}^{4} \delta^i \varepsilon_{t+i}$. As this is not taken into account, even though IV is used, it is possible that the estimates are inconsistent, and whether this is so is discussed in the next section.

5.4   Single-equation diagnostic tests

In this section we report a selection of diagnostic tests for each of the individual equations presented above, relating to a variety of possible departures from the model specification. These are listed as row headings in Table 5.8; in the columns we indicate with a cross cases in which the model-builders themselves present similar information. As noted at the beginning of this chapter, in a specification search diagnostic test statistics represent measures of model (in)adequacy, and the search terminates when the model appears satisfactory according to the various measures considered. A blank cell in Table 5.8 need not imply that the corresponding feature of the model is not scrutinized by the model-builder, but simply that the measure is not reported. It is seen that the type of misspecification on which diagnostic information is given varies considerably across the modelling groups; moreover, we find, not surprisingly, that where there is

Table 5.8   *Diagnostic reporting*

	LPL	CUBS	CGP	NIESR	LBS	HMT	BE
Predictive failure and parameter stability	x	x		x			
Simultaneous equations bias and instrument validity							
Diagonal error covariance matrix							x
Dynamic specification					x		
Autocorrelation							
First-order	x	x	x	x	x		x
First and higher orders		x		x	x	x	
Vector error processes		x					
Functional form							
Heteroscedasticity							
ARCH					x		
Squares of regressors							
Squares and cross-products							
Normality					x		

common ground, for example on testing for autocorrelated error terms, the form of the test and the autocorrelation structure represented in the alternative hypothesis also differ.

Our own choices of diagnostic tests are described below under the various headings. The common characteristics of many of these tests are emphasized by Pagan (1984b), who shows that the test statistics can be computed by the addition of selected variables to the model under consideration, the variables being chosen to elicit a particular form of inadequacy of the model. Different tests result from different choices of added variable, the use of different estimators of the resulting augmented model, and the construction of different statistics from these estimates. Many of the diagnostic tests we consider have been developed for the linear regression model, but these can be generalized to a single equation that is part of a simultaneous equation model, except in the case of tests for heteroscedasticity and non-normality of error terms. As is customary, the tests are applied one at a time, and thus assess a single departure from the specification of the model. The statistical distribution theory that underlies tests for autocorrelation, for example, rests on an assumption of homoscedasticity, and vice versa; and how the outcome of the application of a battery of such unidirectional tests may be interpreted in the framework of classical statistical inference is an open research problem. Accepting one alternative hypothesis following a unidirectional test, may suggest that other tests of the same model have different properties from what is assumed; hence the computed statistics become indices of model performance rather than formal test criteria. However, limited experiments with multidirectional tests on this set of equations suggests that the theoretical problems associated with unidirectional testing (Bera and Jarque, 1982) are not, in practice, important.

Predictive failure

This test examines whether the model, estimated over T observations, adequately predicts the dependent variable over n further observations, conditional on the observed value of the regressors, X_f, where f refers to the n observations in the 'forecast' period. By comparing $\hat{y}_f$ and y_f, the appropriate test follows from examining the first two moments of $\hat{y}_f - y_f$ under the null hypothesis, namely,

$$E(\hat{y}_f - y_f) = 0 \text{ and } \text{cov}(\hat{y}_f - y_f) = \hat{\sigma}^2 I_n + X_f \text{cov}(\hat{\beta}) X_f'.$$

Thus the test is one of n restrictions, based on an unrestricted model with $T - k$ degrees of freedom. The test may be computed by re-running the regression over the extended dataset and introducing n dummy variables, each taking the value of unity for one of the n data points. Salkever (1976) demonstrates that the n estimated coefficients are the forecast errors, $\hat{y}_f - y_f$, and the appropriate sub-block of the coefficient covariance matrix their estimated variances and covariances. This gives rise to the following form of the test:

$$\phi_1 = (\hat{u}^{+\prime}\hat{u}^+ - \hat{u}'\hat{u})/\hat{\sigma}^2 \sim \chi^2(n)$$

where $\hat{u}^+$ is the $T + n$ element residual vector. (In the absence of stochastic regressors, ϕ_1/n has an exact $F(n, T - k)$ distribution.) Generalizing ϕ_1 to IV follows from Salkever's methodology, giving a test of the forecasting performance of the single equation, conditional on the observed values of the right-hand side endogenous variables:

$$\tilde{\phi}_1 = (\bar{u}^{+\prime}Q_z\bar{u}^+ - \bar{u}'Q_z\bar{u})/\hat{\sigma}^2 \sim \chi^2(n).$$

An asymptotic version of the test ($T \to \infty$, n fixed) reduces $\text{cov}(\hat{y}_f - y_f)$ to $\sigma^2 I$ if β has been consistently estimated and so is also applicable to IV, and is written

$$\phi_2 = (\hat{y}_f - y_f)' \, (\hat{y}_f - y_f)/\hat{\sigma}^2 \sim \chi^2(n).$$

The conditions under which ϕ_1 and ϕ_2 are equivalent in finite samples are not easily interpreted, as discussed by Pesaran *et al.* (1985), who also note that ϕ_2 tends to reject a true null hypothesis too frequently.

For comparability, each model is used to predict the same period. Although the sample periods used to estimate the equations vary considerably, as indicated in Table 5.9, we choose 1981–83 as the forecast period. For some of the models this requires the use of additional data to that used in the original specification. For others the original estimation period goes beyond 1983, in which case the test loses its forecast interpretation, but is none the less valid as a test of parameter stability. In this case the test is weaker, since the specifications for these equations were chosen over a period that included 1981–83.

Four of the six models have difficulty in passing the predictive failure tests for employment, but the wage equations perform relatively better. The NIESR and LBS models do particularly well overall, having possibly used this test statistic in their model selection procedures. It is noticeable that HMT and BE have particular difficulty in forecasting employment.

As discussed in more detail in the next section, comparisons across the models are possible only in certain areas. Forecasts from the annual models' wage equations may be compared as they all have the same dependent variable. The forecast errors (standard errors in parentheses) of the logarithm of real wages are as follows:

	1981	1982	1983
LPL	−0.0024 (0.0300)	0.0022 (0.0320)	0.0464 (0.0339)
CUBS	0.0662 (0.0246)	0.0389 (0.0192)	
CGP	−0.0018 (0.0144)	−0.0085 (0.0142)	−0.0035 (0.0148)

We see that CGP are able to stay well on track throughout the period, whereas the CUBS forecast error exceeds twice its standard error in both years of the forecast period, with LPL occupying an intermediate position.

Table 5.9 *Tests of predictive failure and parameter stability*

	Sample period	Data to end 1983	Estima- tion method	ϕ_2	ϕ_1 or $\bar{\phi}_1$	ϕ_3 or $\bar{\phi}_3$
LPL						
Unemployment	1956–83		IV	1.9 (3)	0.4 (3)	
Real wage	1956–83		IV	7.7* (3)	2.5 (3)	
CUBS						
Employment	1953–82	N	IV	23.3**(2)	11.3**(2)	
Labour supply	1953–82	N	IV	10.3**(2)	4.1 (2)	
Real wage	1953–82	N	IV	35.9**(2)	7.4**(2)	
CGP						
Real wage	1955–81	Y	OLS	0.5 (3)	0.5 (3)	
NIESR						
Mfg empl't	1964(1)–83(4)		IV	44.4**(12)	16.8 (12)	4.0 (10)
Other empl't	1964(2)–83(4)		IV	5.7 (12)	4.6 (12)	n/a
Public empl't	1964(2)–83(1)	N	IV	2.4 (9)	11.3 (9)	37.8**(14)
Wage	1953(4)–83(4)		OLS	7.6 (12)	7.1 (12)	2.8 (4)
Unemployment	1964(2)–83(4)		IV	10.9 (12)	7.8 (12)	34.7**(7)
LBS						
Mfg empl't	1965(1)–81(4)	Y	IV	17.6 (12)	5.1 (12)	18.8**(8)
Other empl't	1965(1)–81(4)	Y	OLS	16.7 (12)	9.7 (12)	15.1**(6)
Mfg wages	1965(2)–81(4)	Y	OLS	n/a	n/a	15.6 (12)
Non-mfg wages	1965(2)–81(4)	Y	OLS	n/a	n/a	28.4**(11)
Public wages	1963(4)–81(4)	Y	OLS	11.4 (12)	11.4 (12)	11.2* (6)
HMT						
Mfg empl't	1967(4)–84(3)		OLS	34.4**(12)	31.8**(12)	11.8 (9)
Non-mfg empl't	1971(4)–84(3)		OLS	38.0**(12)	12.1 (9)	14.9 (9)
Wages	1972(2)–83(4)		OLS	28.8**(12)	9.2 (12)	37.9**(18)
BE						
Mfg empl't	1965(1)–81(4)	Y	OLS	808.0**(12)	48.7**(12)	15.0**(6)
Other empl't	1965(1)–81(4)	Y	OLS	1054.1**(12)	15.6 (12)	13.4**(6)
Mfg wages	1965(3)–79(4)	Y	OLS	18.7 (12)	4.3 (12)	14.6 (11)
Public wages	1965(3)–81(4)	Y	OLS	15.0 (12)	8.9 (12)	2.2 (7)
Other wages	1965(2)–81(4)	Y	OLS	161.2**(12)	7.3 (12)	14.3**(7)

Notes to Tables 5.9–5.17:

*   denotes test is significant at the 10% level
**   denotes test is significant at the 5% level
n/a denotes that a test is not applicable in the particular circumstance
–   denotes that a test cannot be calculated, usually due to lack of degrees of freedom, or singularity.
Degrees of freedom are given in parentheses, except stated otherwise.

On comparing the manufacturing employment equations of the four quarterly models in a similar manner, all except LBS do badly, as indicated by the test results. In general, the models are unable to capture the large employment shakeout of the period 1981–83, typically all overpredicting throughout the 12 observations, despite the explicit modelling of expectations in the NIESR and HMT equations. The value of the BE test statistics are noteworthy, and are caused by overfitting, leading to particularly small estimates of the error variance. Also, the main explanatory variable in the manufacturing equation — hours worked — in fact recovered slightly over the forecast period. It could be argued that, since hours is a potentially endogenous variable in this equation, conditioning predictive failure tests on this variable is inappropriate. Accordingly, we also calculate appropriate generalizations of ϕ_1 and ϕ_2 taking the hours and employment equations as a two-equation system, obtaining values of 54.70 and 1906, respectively, both distributed as chi-square with 24 d.f. In fact, because the hours and employment equation errors are uncorrelated, and the hours equation itself shows signs of overfitting, the calculated value of the appropriate generalization of ϕ_2 is very similar to the sum of the two single-equation statistics.

Parameter constancy

The familiar test for parameter constancy, conditional on variance equality, is calculated by splitting the sample at some arbitrary point and re-estimating the equations over the two sub-periods. The test can also be calculated through variable addition. Gujarati (1970) demonstrates that the test can be based on one regression for the entire sample, including additional multiplicative dummy variables for each regressor in the relationship. This yields two further sums of squared residuals, $\hat{u}_1'\hat{u}_1$ and $\hat{u}_2'\hat{u}_2$, say (redefining u_1), and the test statistic is

$$\phi_3 = \frac{(\hat{u}'\hat{u} - \hat{u}_1'\hat{u}_1 - \hat{u}_2'\hat{u}_2)}{(\hat{u}_1'\hat{u}_1 + \hat{u}_2'\hat{u}_2)/(T - 2k)} \sim \chi^2(k).$$

Under the null hypothesis it is clear that splitting the sample leaves the estimated residuals unaffected, so that $\hat{u}' = (\hat{u}_1':\hat{u}_2')$ and $\hat{u}_1'\hat{u}_1 + \hat{u}_2'\hat{u}_2 = \hat{u}'\hat{u}$. A generalization to IV is suggested by Lo and Newey (1985), who state that the 'appropriate test statistic has the same form as the standard linear regression case except the residuals here are first projected on the instruments' (p. 352), so that the test statistic becomes

$$\tilde{\phi}_3 = \frac{(\tilde{u}'Q\tilde{u} - \tilde{u}_1'Q_1\tilde{u}_1 - \tilde{u}_2'Q_2\tilde{u}_2)}{(u_1'Q_1\tilde{u}_1 + \tilde{u}_2'Q_2\tilde{u}_2)/(T - 2k)} \sim \chi^2(k).$$

Since all the annual models except CGP are estimated by IV, and the Lo–Newey test is valid only asymptotically, it is inappropriate to calculate tests of parameter constancy when the numbers of degrees of freedom in each sub-sample ($T/2 - k$) is so small. For the quarterly models we choose to split the samples at a particularly turbulent point in history: the first quarter of 1974. The HMT wage equation is an exception: as its estimation period begins only in 1972(2), we split the sample at 1977(4). To avoid the problem caused by the inclusion of certain variables in only one sub-sample, such as dummy variables for the three-day week, the tests of parameter constancy are carried out on a sub-set of the parameter vector excluding these variables. If there is one such variable, then we have a test of $2(k - 1)$ restrictions with $T - 2k + 1$ degrees of freedom. The tests use estimates based upon the original sample period, not necessarily including 1981–83, and the results are given in the final column of Table 5.9. Many of the tests reject the null hypothesis, or give a test statistic with a relatively high value, so that we cannot readily accept that the parameters of these equations are constant. In general, the wage equations do better than the employment equations, which is not surprising given the relatively smooth evolution of real wages.

Simultaneous equation bias

If an equation includes potentially endogenous variables among the regressors, we calculate the Wu–Hausman test for the orthogonality of these regressors and the equation's residual. This involves testing the significance of the reduced-form prediction error for the endogenous right-hand-side variable(s) when included in the equation in question (see Hausman, 1978).

In Table 5.10 we report the Wu-Hausman tests. Where an equation is estimated by instrumental variables, the test is based on the chosen instruments. The exceptions to this are the LPL wage equation and the CUBS employment and real-wage equations, which are estimated with instruments used for only a subset of the potentially endogenous regressors. We present two results for these equations: the first using the endogenous/exogenous classification originally specified and the second, treating all current-dated or generated regressors as endogenous. Where an equation is estimated by OLS, the question of the choice of an appropriate IV set arises, and whenever possible we adopt the standard of using a fourth-order vector autoregressive equation for all the variables in the equation in question to approximate the unrestricted reduced form that generates predictions of the potentially endogenous regressors. Where degrees of freedom considerations prevent the estimation of these equations, we use the longest lag-length that the data permit. Where the test is a composite hypothesis concerning a number of regressors, in the final column of Table 5.10 we indicate which regressors must be treated as endogenous, and report a Wald test (adjusted for degrees of freedom) for the significance of the reduced-form prediction error for that particular variable.

In all three annual models, the hypothesis of regressor-disturbance independence cannot be rejected. LPL and CUBS use simultaneous equation estimation methods, but the tests show that the use of an IV estimator does not significantly alter the parameters of their equations. This may reflect overfitting of the reduced form. In this case, potentially endogenous variables are subject to only a small reduced-form residual error, and the actual values of the regressor and its reduced-form predictions are highly correlated.

In the quarterly equations, the use by NIESR and LBS of an IV estimator for manufacturing employment is justified, although in the LBS equation only the wage term (W^{pm}) is significantly affected by the use of IV. The large difference in the calculated value of the Wu–Hausman test

Table 5.10   *Wu–Hausman tests*

	Original estimation method	Wu–Hausman test	Significant reduced-form errors (Wald test)
LPL			
Unemployment	IV	0.30 (2)	—
Real wage	IV	(a) 0.51 (1)	—
		(b) 0.50 (2)	—
CUBS			
Employment	IV	(a) 1.35 (2)	—
		(b) 2.23 (4)	—
Labour supply	IV	0.06 (1)	—
Real wage	IV	(a) 1.03 (1)	—
		(b) 0.31 (2)	—
CGP			
Real wage	OLS	0.47 (1)	—
NIESR			
Mfg employment	IV	7.80**(2)	$w^p*(8.4)**$, $y^m*(3.1)*$
Other employment	IV	0.87 (1)	—
Public employment	IV	0.00 (1)	—
Wage	OLS	1.04 (2)	—
Unemployment	IV	5.78* (2)	n^m (4.0)**
LBS			
Mfg employment	IV	33.92**(3)	$w^{pm}(19.0)**$
Non-mfg employment	OLS	1.79 (1)	—
Mfg wages	OLS	12.40**(2)	$\ln(1+t_3)$ (6.0)**
			$\ln(B/p)$ (4.0)**
Non-mfg wages	OLS	n/a	n/a
Public wages	OLS	0.40 (1)	—
HMT			
Mfg employment	OLS	1.40 (3)	—
Non-mfg employment	OLS	5.54**(1)	$\ln n^n_{-1} - \ln y^n$ (5.54)**
Wages	—	n/a	n/a
BE			
Mfg employment	OLS	0.07 (1)	—
Other employment	OLS	5.16* (2)	$w^o(4.0)**$
Mfg wages	OLS	8.46**(1)	$\ln U$ (8.46)**
Public wages	OLS	2.23 (1)	—
Other wages	OLS	17.98**(2)	—

and the Wald test on the significance of the reduced-form error for W^{pm} is due to the presence of autocorrelation in the equation residuals, the lagged dependent variables in the equation being highly significant in the auxiliary regression used to calculate the test statistics. A similar case is the BE 'other wages' equation. The calculated value of the test is greater than the 5 per cent critical value, owing to the significance of the lagged dependent variable rather than the reduced-form prediction errors for the current-dated regressors.

The parameters of the other two NIESR employment equations are unaffected by the use of an IV estimator. Both the LBS and BE equations for wages in manufacturing show signs of simultaneous equation bias, as does the HMT employment in non-manufacturing equation and the BE 'other employment' relationship.

Tests of instrument validity

We consider the Sargan (1958) test for instrument validity, which may also be interpreted as a test of the overidentifying restrictions. This test is only appropriate, of course, for equations estimated by IV and so can be applied to less than one-half of the equations under consideration. In Table 5.11 we present the asymptotic version of the test,

$$\phi_4 = \bar{u}' Q_Z \bar{u}/\tilde{\sigma}^2 \sim \chi^2(M - k)$$

which may also be calculated as $T - k$ times the R^2 of the auxiliary regression of $\bar{u}$ on Z. All the information used in constructing the test may be found in Tables 5.1–5.7, but is repeated for convenience.

Table 5.11 *Sargan tests*

	$\bar{u}'\bar{u}$	$\bar{u}'Q\bar{u}$	R^2	$M-k$	$T-k$	ϕ_4
LPL						
Unemployment	0.3752	0.1837	0.49	5	23	11.3**
Real wage	0.01171	0.00383	0.33	5	22	7.2
CUBS						
Demand	0.003622	0.002031	0.56	9	23	12.9
Supply	0.0006490	0.0003670	0.57	9	23	13.0
Real wage	0.003799	0.001722	0.45	9	23	10.4
NIESR						
Mfg employment	0.0006919	0.0000809	0.12	8	67	7.8
Other employment	0.005077	0.000245	0.05	3	73	3.5
Public employment	0.001455	0.000237	0.16	8	67	10.9
Unemployment	66354.6	18996.4	0.29	14	75	21.5*
LBS						
Mfg employment	0.0008808	0.0000895	0.10	5	55	5.6

Note:
$R^2 = \bar{u}'Q\bar{u}/\bar{u}'\bar{u}$, $\phi_4 = (T-k) R^2$

In the case of the LPL unemployment equation, we reject the hypothesis that the excluded instruments are independent of the disturbance term and therefore regard the equation as misspecified, and the parameter estimates as inconsistent. The NIESR unemployment equation is also estimated with inappropriate instruments, although the test statistic is only just significant at the 10 per cent level. (Both equations are rejected on the basis of the tests of dynamic specification reported below.)

Diagonal covariance matrix for the disturbances of different equations

If the error terms in different equations are contemporaneously correlated, more efficient estimation methods than OLS or IV are available, such as FIML, even if the equations show no sign of simultaneous equation bias. We therefore test the hypothesis that the residuals from each of the

Table 5.12   *Tests of diagonal error covariance structure*

LPL		
Unemployment	0.25	(1)
Real wage	0.86	(1)
CUBS		
Employment	7.79**	(2)
Labour supply	5.32*	(2)
Real wage	0.31	(2)
CGP		
Real wage	n/a	
NIESR		
Mfg employment	7.97	(5)
Other employment	12.77**	(5)
Public employment	1.18	(5)
Wage	11.85**	(5)
Unemployment	17.87**	(5)
LBS		
Mfg employment	16.60**	(5)
Other employment	3.95	(5)
Mfg wages	13.15**	(5)
Non-mfg wages	4.77	(5)
Public wages	4.73	(5)
HMT		
Mfg employment	1.40	(2)
Other employment	5.54*	(2)
Wages	n/a	
BE		
Mfg employment	6.45	(5)
Other employment	5.05	(5)
Mfg wages	11.34**	(5)
Public wages	12.93**	(5)
Other wages	8.32	(5)

equations are contemporaneously uncorrelated with the other equations in the labour market. The test, proposed by Engle (1984) and Harvey and Phillips (1982), augments an equation with the residuals of other equations in that particular block, estimated by IV methods where appropriate. The test is calculated over the largest data set common to all equations under consideration in each model. In three cases — LBS, NIESR, and BE — the models are augmented by equations which, although part of the labour market specification of these models, are not our main focus: these equations relate to female participation (in the LBS model) and to hours worked in manufacturing (NIESR and BE). Where the Wu–Hausman test indicates that the appropriate estimation procedure is IV rather than OLS, we also compute the test based on IV residuals for that particular equation; these results are not significantly different from those obtained using OLS, however, and are not reported,

The results are shown in Table 5.12. These show significant contemporaneous correlations between the equations in the various quarterly models which the investigators do not exploit in the estimation of these equations. For example, the LBS could achieve more efficient estimates by considering the manufacturing wage and employment pair as a system.

In the annual models, the LPL real-wage and unemployment relationships are statistically independent. The results for CUBS suggest that employment and labour supply form a system of equations, but the real-wage relationship could be estimated independently by OLS. We also compute joint tests of regressor-disturbance orthogonality and the independence of the disturbances for the CUBS labour market model, giving $\chi^2(4) = 13.06$, $\chi^2(3) = 9.58$, and $\chi^2(3) = 1.12$, respectively. The results are qualitatively the same, although regressor-disturbance independence is now rejected for the employment equation. A Wald test on the significance of the change in the coefficient on the real wage gives $\chi^2(1) = 8.91$. All of the parameters in the employment equation are significantly different from those obtained through IV estimation, which suggests that the equation is misspecified.

Dynamic specification

Each equation is tested against a more general model which includes an extended lag distribution for all the variables in the equation. As the alternative hypothesis, we specify a general fourth-order distributed lag in the case of the quarterly models, and a second-order distributed lag for the annual models. Since HMT include lag lengths greater than four in their equations, the unrestricted form is taken as the longest lag on each variable in the equations in question. In a number of cases estimation of the most general model is not possible owing to a lack of degrees of freedom, or of data to enable each variable to be lagged a sufficient number of times. In these cases we estimate the most general model that our data set permits.

Table 5.13   *Tests of dynamic misspecification and autocorrelation*

	Dynamic misspeci-fication	Auto-correlation	Significant autoregressive parameters (Wald test)
LPL			
Unemployment	11.34**(5)	8.96**(2)	AR1 1.70**(7.8)
Real wage	7.32 (9)	7.87**(2)	AR1 −0.91**(4.4)
CUBS			
Employment	9.23* (5)	4.16 (2)	AR2 −0.72* (2.9)
Labour supply	7.90 (5)	5.92* (2)	AR2 −1.10**(7.3)
Real wage	13.48**(5)	5.21* (2)	—
CGP			
Real wage	1.53 (3)	0.53 (2)	—
NIESR			
Mfg employment	16.53* (9)	7.59 (4)	
Other employment	6.87 (7)	10.14**(4)	AR1 −0.49* (2.9) AR2 0.42* (2.8)
Public employment	7.24 (6)	7.40 (4)	AR4 0.25* (3.6)
Wage	23.32**(12)	8.86**(4)	AR2 0.28**(4.8) AR4 −0.28**(4.8)
Unemployment	19.10 (9)	10.92**(4)	AR2 0.29* (3.3) AR4 0.22* (3.5)
LBS			
Mfg employment	17.13 (12)	9.16* (4)	AR1 0.30* (2.9)
Other employment	10.67 (9)	6.90 (4)	AR1 −0.59**(4.4) AR2 0.29* (2.9)
Mfg wages	14.30**(7)	4.92 (4)	—
Non-mfg wages	10.88 (8)	5.36 (4)	AR2 −0.44**(4.0) AR4 −0.34**(4.8)
Public wages	7.56 (4)	0.31 (4)	—
HMT			
Mfg employment	24.41 (32)	3.23 (4)	—
Other employment	10.16 (12)	7.59 (4)	AR3 −0.27* (3.1)
Wages	13.77 (16)	6.42 (4)	
BE			
Mfg employment	11.18* (6)	15.43**(4)	AR1 0.39**(6.3) AR3 0.34**(5.3)
Other employment	0.94 (5)	4.98 (4)	AR2 −0.33**(2.9)
Mfg wages	26.45**(12)	6.59* (4)	AR3 −0.42**(3.8)
Public wages	22.52**(12)	14.13**(4)	AR1 −0.54**(14.4)
Other wages	10.55 (11)	10.52 (4)	AR4 −0.33**(6.2)

   The results in Table 5.13 indicate that over a quarter of the equations show signs of dynamic misspecification. With the exception of HMT (and CGP), at least one equation in each model is rejected against the more general formulation. The form taken by the misspecification varies between equations. In some equations lagged dependent variables are invalidly excluded, while in others dynamics in variables other than the dependent variable are inappropriately omitted. Dynamic misspecification tends to occur less frequently in equations from those groups that adopt a general-to-specific dynamic modelling methodology for the selection of their equations, but inappropriate specifications are nevertheless observed, suggesting that the methodology is sometimes inappropriately implemented.

A somewhat different dynamic modelling methodology is used by NIESR in the estimation of the wage equation (Hall, 1985), which in view of its novelty is considered in greater detail. For this relationship a two-step approach is used, in which the dynamic form of the model is derived conditional on an estimate of the long-run relationship given by the co-integrating procedure developed by Granger and Engle (1985). Variables are said to be co-integrated if they are integrated or difference-stationary processes but there exists a linear combination of them that is a stationary process. The variables then tend to exhibit common trends, and this idea provides a statistical interpretation of the notion of the long run. A correspondence with the error correction model also exists, the dynamic relationship among the variables being modelled in this manner, with the deviation from the long-run linear combination of variables representing the error that causes short-run adjustment.

In the first step of the NIESR procedure a levels regression is performed which allows the hypothesis of co-integration to be tested and, if accepted, provides an estimate of the long-run relationship. If the variables are not co-integrated there is little point in pursuing a full-scale modelling exercise to determine the dynamic form of the relationship. In the second step the dynamic specification is considered, with the lagged value of the residuals from the co-integrating regression appearing among the regressors. Thus, questions of the appropriate specification of the dynamic elements of the model are handled independently of the specification of the long-run position. Since the co-integrating regression provides consistent estimates of the long-run parameters, imposing these prior coefficients in the second step leaves fewer coefficients to be estimated in the dynamic model, resulting in a gain in efficiency. On the other hand, the standard errors of the parameter estimates from the co-integrating regression are biased. Inference on the form of the long run is therefore difficult, and a generated regressor problem may arise in the dynamic regression. Finally, we note that many of the empirical examples available to date consider two or three variables at a time (Granger and Engle, 1985), whereas the NIESR co-integrating regression contains four variables in all: earnings, hours, unemployment, and a time trend (*sic*). Little is yet known about the impact of alternative normalizations of this regression.

In the first column of Table 5.14 we report the two-step estimator, where the co-integrating regression is normalized on earnings. The first four elements of this column refer to the estimates of the long-run parameters obtained in this co-integrating regression. We do not report standard errors on the long-run parameters, since the high degree of autocorrelation in the equation error process means that they are biased. The coefficients and standard errors for the remaining three variables are calculated in the

Table 5.14   *A comparison of alternative estimators of the NIESR wage equation*

	Two-step ECM	OLS
Constant	3.890	4.680
		(2.604)
Time	0.0063	0.0061
		(0.0009)
u^r	−1.200	−1.400
		(0.579)
$\ln h^m$	−0.830	−0.990
		(0.564)
$\triangle^2 u^r_{-1}$	−1.102	−1.259
	(0.860)	(0.912)
$\triangle \ln h^m$	−1.021	−1.029
	(0.117)	(0.132)
Co-integration parameter	−0.168	−0.173
	(0.059)	(0.060)
$\hat{u}'\hat{u}$	0.01335	0.01322

second step of the procedure, when the parameter on the lagged residual from the co-integrating regression is estimated together with other terms reflecting the dynamics of the relationship. The reported constant combines the effects of the constant terms included at each step of the procedure. The parameter associated with the residual from the co-integrating regression is denoted the co-integration parameter. In the second column we report the corresponding equation where the long-run parameters are jointly estimated with the dynamic components of the relationship in a single OLS regression. The first four elements of the second column refer to the freely estimated implied long-run coefficients from this regression, with asymptotic standard errors in parentheses; the final three parameters are the direct estimates of the dynamic form of the equation.

Both sets of parameters are very similar. A Wald test on the differences in the two sets of parameters gives $\chi^2(4) = 5.23$, so we cannot reject the null hypothesis of parameter equality; imposing the long-run parameters through the co-integrating regression does not worsen the fit of the equation. A likelihood ratio test of the restrictions implied by the two-step approach gives $\chi^2(4) = 0.72$. Note that the standard errors of the last three coefficients increase on moving from the first to the second column, suggesting that they are underestimated in the two-step procedure.

These tests support the view that the long-run form of the equation is appropriately specified. However, in Table 5.13 we see that the equation is dynamically misspecified and has autocorrelated residuals, suggesting that in the second step the dynamic form of the equation is inappropriately specified. This proposition is tested by including additional lags of the residual from the co-integrating regression in the dynamic form, and testing their significance, so enabling the steady-state relationship to remain unaltered while allowing the dynamics of the equation to change. On adding two further lagged values of the error correction term we find that, while they are not jointly significant, individual Wald tests give $\chi^2(1)$ = 2.9 for the two-period lag and $\chi^2(1) = 4.4$ for the three-period lag. The significant coefficient on the third lag of this constructed variable indicates that the equation is dynamically misspecified.

Autocorrelation

In the quarterly models we test for autocorrelation of up to fourth order, and in the annual models up to second order, augmenting each equation with the appropriate number of lags in the equation residual (see Godfrey, 1978). The results are shown in Table 5.13.

Very few of the equations have serially uncorrelated residuals. In the auxiliary regression used to calculate the LM test, at least one of the coefficients on the lagged residuals is significantly different from zero in the majority of equations. Since the alternative hypothesis is rather general, the portmanteau form of the test has low power against specific auto-regressive structures, and in the last column of Table 5.13 we report the individual autoregressive coefficients that appear significant in the port-manteau form of the test, with their associated t-statistics (which have a Wald test interpretation).

When the equations are estimated subject to the particular order of autocorrelation correction suggested by the LM tests, the coefficients on the systematic components of the equations tend to change very little. Tests of dynamic specification are presented above, and in general we are not able to proceed further, for example, to test common factor restrictions on the distributed lag coefficients. The truncation of initial observations and the large number of coefficients in the unrestricted transformed equation typically exhaust available degrees of freedom. On testing for serial correlation among the residuals of the various equations in each model, we find no sign of significant cross-equation residual serial correlation.

Functional form

A simple test of correct functional form is provided by Ramsey's (1969) RESET test. It is constructed as a test of the significance of the predicted values from the equation raised to the second and third powers in the regression of $\hat{u}_1$ on X_1 and these variables. We choose second and third powers, although any number could be entertained given sufficient degrees of freedom. For an equation estimated by instrumental variable methods we use powers of reduced-form predictions, following the suggestion of Pagan (1984b). The results are shown in Table 5.15.

The calculated value of the test tends to be relatively high when the equation shows signs of residual autocorrelation, an inappropriate dynamic form, or predictive failure, as detected in the preceding tests.

Heteroscedasticity

Heteroscedasticity implies a misspecification of the conditional variance of the model, departing from the standard assumption of the regression model that the conditional variance of the disturbances is constant. We

Table 5.15 *Tests of functional form, heteroscedasticity, and normality*

	RESET	ARCH	Squares of regressors	Squares and cross-products	Normality
LPL					
Unemployment	—	0.03 (1)	6.30 (7)	5.98 (9)	1.91 (2)
Real wage	4.48* (2)	0.02 (1)	7.69 (7)	7.38 (14)	100.22**(2)
CUBS					
Employment	—	0.19 (1)	5.54 (11)	1.71 (24)	0.01 (2)
Labour supply	3.06 (2)	1.91 (1)	2.74 (12)	3.81 (22)	0.62 (2)
Real wage	0.68 (2)	0.12 (1)	10.97 (12)	1.42 (21)	0.17 (2)
CGP					
Real wage	4.13**(1)	1.30 (1)	6.70 (9)	6.05 (11)	1.61 (2)
NIESR					
Mfg employment	10.64**(2)	n/a	n/a	n/a	n/a
Other employment	—	0.04 (1)	11.46 (7)	11.95 (9)	0.72 (2)
Public employment	15.74**(2)	1.00 (1)	10.36 (9)	8.51 (9)	18.02**(2)
Wage	9.74**(2)	0.16 (1)	6.78 (6)	3.84 (6)	12.62**(2)
Unemployment	11.74**(2)	n/a	n/a	n/a	n/a
LBS					
Mfg employment	—	n/a	n/a	n/a	n/a
Other employment	0.70 (2)	0.15 (1)	4.70 (11)	4.70 (11)	1.18 (2)
Mfg wages	1.97 (2)	0.66 (1)	16.13 (24)	—	0.41 (2)
Non-mfg wages	5.41* (2)	0.01 (1)	8.80 (22)	—	1.27 (2)
Public wages	5.33* (2)	0.42 (1)	9.91 (13)	15.22 (18)	0.36 (2)
HMT					
Mfg employment	0.84 (2)	1.77 (1)	10.05 (18)	15.69 (38)	1.09 (2)
Non-mfg employment	2.98 (2)	1.18 (1)	16.59 (16)	12.83 (36)	6.46**(2)
Wages	1.46 (2)	0.01 (1)	—	—	0.01 (2)
BE					
Mfg employment	4.93**(1)	0.99 (1)	18.37 (10)	17.99 (12)	0.43 (2)
Other employment	—	0.03 (1)	9.26 (14)	12.04 (22)	0.01 (2)
Mfg wages	3.97 (2)	2.93* (1)	18.69 (20)	—	0.01 (2)
Public wages	7.27**(2)	15.68**(1)	37.37**(11)	35.20**(21)	29.89**(2)
Other wages	0.20 (2)	0.24 (1)	5.29 (21)	15.01 (21)	150.02**(2)

report three tests that reflect different assumptions on the form of the heteroscedasticity. The first is Engle's (1982) ARCH test, in which the model is augmented by the lagged value of the squared residual. We also report two variants of White's (1980) test for heteroscedasticity. The first augments the model with squares of the regressors (Hendry, 1986), and the second introduces in addition all the non-singular cross-products of the regressors. These tests are not applicable if an equation is estimated by IV methods. For completeness, we report the statistic based upon OLS estimates for all cases where an equation, although estimated by IV, shows no sign of simultaneous equation bias on a Wu–Hausman test. (If these OLS estimates are significantly different from the IV estimates, then we proceed no further.) The results are given in Table 5.15.

Only two of the equations show signs of an ARCH process in the residuals. Like the RESET test, the ARCH test tends to reject those equations that show signs of autocorrelation, particularly if the first-order autocorrelation coefficient is significantly different from zero. Since the test is formed as a regression on the lagged value of the squared residual, the test may well be contaminated by the presence of first-order serial correlation. On extending the ARCH tests, to a fourth-order process in the quarterly equations and a second-order process in the annual equations, no higher-order effects are detected, except for a significant third-order ARCH effect in the BE manufacturing employment equation.

Only the BE public sector wage equation is rejected by the two tests for heteroscedasticity proposed by White (1980). In this case, the complete battery of test statistics is recomputed using a heteroscedastic-consistent estimate of the covariance matrix, since inference on the basis of the estimated covariance matrix is inappropriate. This equation is rejected by all the other tests we report except the Wu–Hausman test for regressor-disturbance independence and the parameter stability test, irrespective of whether conventional or heteroscedastic-consistent standard errors are used as the basis of the test statistics.

Normality

Specification tests can be based on higher moments of the residual distribution, although attention in the literature focuses on tests for the appropriate specification of the mean and variance. We compute Jarque and Bera's (1980) test for normality, based on the third and fourth moments of the residual distribution. As with tests for heteroscedasticity, this test is valid only under the assumption that all the regressors are weakly exogenous, and so we report the results of tests for normality for equations estimated by OLS; where an IV estimator is used and no significant differences between OLS and IV methods are indicated, we report the test based on OLS residuals. The results are shown in the final column of Table 5.15.

In small samples the normality assumption is often violated owing to the presence of outliers. The normality test can therefore be interpreted as a goodness-of-fit test, and when the assumption of normality is rejected it is interesting to examine the residuals to identify particular events in history which the equation fails to predict accurately. If such periods are detected by the investigator, they might be dealt with by introducing a zero-one dummy variable for that particular period, which changes a bad residual to one that is identically zero. While for some periods of history this procedure might have merit, as a general modelling procedure it has little to recommend it.

Six equations are rejected on the normality test, four of these being wage equations. The NIESR wage equation and the BE wage equations for the public and other sectors all have positive residuals in 1975(1) which exceed two and a half times the standard error of the equation. This probably reflects a failure to capture the rapid increase in wage settlements following the introduction of the Labour Government's social contract in December 1974. The BE equation for wages in other sectors also has difficulty in predicting the catch-up in wage settlements after the 1966 freeze. The NIESR equation overpredicts earnings during the three-day week, when shorter hours reduced take-home pay although wage rates were unaffected. The LPL wage equation overpredicts during 1977, a period of strict and successful incomes policy, when the residual is nearly four times the standard error of the equation. Omitting this period from the LPL wage equation considerably sharpens the estimates of the coefficients in the equation and improves the fit by a factor of two.

Non-manufacturing employment in the HMT model has a large positive residual in 1972(1) and a large negative residual in 1975(1), possibly reflecting the shedding of labour in response to the first OPEC shock. Public sector employment in the NIESR model is underpredicted in 1979(3) at the time of the Clegg awards. This equation also has large and offsetting negative and positive residuals in 1967(3)/(4), for which we can find no obvious explanation.

Concluding comment

As a percentage of the total number of tests for each labour market equation, the rejection frequency for each model is as follows:

	%
Liverpool (LPL)	26
City University Business School (CUBS)	17
Cambridge Growth Project (CGP)	11
National Institute for Economic and Social Research (NIESR)	30
London Business School (LBS)	14
Bank of England (BE)	38
Her Majesty's Treasury (HMT)	22

The rejection rate is relatively high, suggesting a degree of misspecification in all the models, although no allowance is made for the different number of equations in each model or the estimation procedures used, and, moreover, the tests are not necessarily independent; for example, dynamic misspecification may be reflected in the tests of autocorrelation, parameter stability, and functional form. Each test is weighted equally, while in practice an investigator may wish to place more emphasis on tests of dynamic specification and predictive failure as indicators of model misspecification.

The LBS modellers report a wider range of diagnostic tests than the other groups and it seems reasonable to presume that the choice of equation to include in the model is influenced by its performance in the various tests. HMT researchers also emphasize the selection of an equation with an appropriate dynamic form. The NIESR rejection frequency reflects the unsuccessful use of the co-integrating regression procedure for the wage equation, and the incorporation of proxy variables for rational expectations in a number of relationships at the expense of dynamic specification.

In the case of the annual models, both LPL and CUBS use an IV estimator, but on the basis of the instrument sets used this does not cause the coefficients of the equations to change significantly from the OLS estimates. Both models also suffer from dynamic misspecification. The detection of significant autocorrelation is more of a surprise in the case of the CUBS model, since they explicitly adopt general-to-specific modelling techniques to identify appropriate dynamic forms (Beenstock *et al.*, 1985, p. 31). LPL place more emphasis on the specification of the long-run equilibrium solution of the model than the adjustment path by which this equilibrium is achieved. Our results for the CGP model are based on a single equation, and we do not include any of the disaggregate wage or employment equations in this study.

Turning to the tests themselves, the rejection frequencies of the various tests, classified into the broad categories of misspecification are as follows:

	%
Predictive failure and parameter stability	38
Simultaneous equations bias, instrument validity, and covariance information	22
Dynamic misspecification and autocorrelation	27
Functional form	36
Heteroscedasticity	7
Normality	29

The tests of predictive failure and parameter stability have the highest rejection frequency. These tests are particularly powerful when conducted over turbulent periods of history, as in the present exercise. They are not

very powerful when data correlations are unchanged between the estimation period and the forecast period, since poor equations may then continue to predict badly but the in-sample and forecast period variances are
broadly comparable, leading to an insignificant test statistic.

The RESET test is also a useful device for detecting misspecification. None
of the investigators includes this test in the diagnostics they present, so the
test is likely to have more power since it was not part of the decision
calculus used in the selection of the various equations.

As noted above, the annual models show little sign of simultaneous
equation bias, suggesting that the labour market can be treated separately
from other areas of the models for the purpose of inference. In the
quarterly models, however, other macroeconomic variables in the y_2 vector, such as output, are found to be contemporaneously correlated with the
equation disturbance terms. In these models labour market behaviour is
not recursive to the rest of the model, and inference on the basis of OLS
estimates is likely to be invalid. None of the quarterly models exploits the
significant cross-correlations that exist between the residuals of the various
equations to provide more efficient parameter estimates. On the other
hand, the use of a limited information estimation procedure such as OLS
or IV prevents the transmission of misspecification in one equation to other
equations in the model.

The high number of significant autocorrelations in some of the equation
residuals is unexpected, given the emphasis on dynamic modelling procedures in recent literature. Portmanteau test statistics for the significance
of a large number of autocorrelations have low power, and the degree of
autocorrelation in the models may be reduced if these are supplemented
with closer scrutiny of the individual autocorrelation coefficients.

Inspection of the significant outliers from the various equations suggests
that a number of equations fail to model the impact of various incomes
policies on wage behaviour. This is particularly so in the case of the wage
explosion following the introduction of the Social Contract in December
1974.

5.5   Comparative issues and non-nested tests

In this section we turn from the econometric performance of individual
equations to inter-model comparisons. Since no single model is a special
case of another model, such analysis necessarily involves the use of non-
nested tests, which is related to the notion of encompassing. For a number
of reasons it is not possible to carry out a comprehensive exercise across
the seven models. In what follows we first discuss and identify areas where
non-nested tests may applied, and then report the results of some single-
equation comparisons.

It is often suggested that encompassing tests should be used as a further diagnostic check on the (in)adequacy of a particular model. An investigator, satisfied with the results of exercises such as those discussed in the previous section, now wishes to discover whether the resulting model, denoted M_1, can explain the features of a rival model, M_2. It is a further kind of predictive test of M_1, in which the new information is the competing model, M_2. In such applications there is always a preferred model, M_1, treated as the null hypothesis, and the alternative model, M_2. In our own application, however, we treat all the competing models on an equal footing in the model comparison exercise, and so take each model in turn as the null hypothesis. This distinction has practical implications. For the investigator testing a preferred model, characteristics such as the sample period, data series for the dependent variable, choice of instruments, estimation method, and so forth are part of the specification of M_1 and need not be changed when M_2 is confronted. In a model comparison exercise, however, these characteristics change as the null model changes, and for comparative purposes it is necessary to re-estimate the equations in a common framework. Once this is done, there is no longer an exact correspondence to the models deposited at the Bureau by the modelling teams; rather, the comparison is based on stylized versions of the models. None the less, such re-estimation may be useful in itself, because it can help to identify whether a particular model is too finely tuned to the data. In certain areas this can be checked using formal tests; for example, if re-estimation involves only a change in the sample period, then a test of parameter stability or predictive failure can be calculated as above. An obvious feature that hinders investigation, however, is that formal procedures can be applied only across the quarterly models, or the annual models, and cannot be used to compare a quarterly model with an annual model.

From the evidence adduced in the previous section, none of the labour market models represents an adequate characterization of the data and consequently none provides a good basis for (conditional) inference. Thus it might be argued that further tests, such as non-nested comparisons, are unnecessary. However, the present exercise has two additional objectives. First, applications of inter-model comparisons are rare (relative to intra-model comparisons), and the degree to which practical constraints hinder analysis merits investigation. Second, the comparisons may suggest modifications to existing models and so provide useful information, although such a procedure might not be advocated as a coherent strategy by proponents of general-to-specific modelling.

We now turn to the single-equation tests, surveyed by Godfrey (1984), for example, who also discusses their extensions to IV estimation where possible. All the tests have a natural added-regressor interpretation, as with those employed in Section 5.4. Our original estimating equation,

(5.28), is denoted M_1, and in addition, for the same dependent variables, we have competing models M_2, M_3, . . ., thus:

$$M_i : y = X_i\delta_i + u_i, i = 1, 2, \ldots$$

The available tests fall conveniently into two groups: variance-encompassing or one degree of freedom tests, and parameter-encompassing or k degrees of freedom tests. The former are derived from Cox (1961, 1962) and compare M_1 and M_2, say, on the basis of their maximized log-likelihoods, from which are obtained (using Godfrey's acronyms) the Cox/Pesaran N-test, the Davidson/MacKinnon J-test, and the Fisher/McAleer/Atkinson JA-test. If M_1 is the null hypothesis, the J-test is based on the t-ratio of the coefficient of the fitted values from M_2, denoted $\hat{y}_2$, when added to M_1:

$$y = X_1\delta_1 + \alpha\hat{y}_2 + u_1.$$

The JA-test takes account of the stochastic nature of $\hat{y}_2$ by using its expectation under M_1, which can be estimated by regressing $X_1\hat{\delta}_1$ on X_2; the resulting fitted values replace $\hat{y}_2$ in the above regression equation. In the absence of stochastic regressors this yields an exact t-test, in contrast to the J-test, which rests on asymptotic distribution theory.

The parameter-encompassing test (F-test) requires construction of the composite alternative hypothesis:

$$M_C : y = X_1\delta_1 + X_2\delta_2 + u.$$

A test of the validity of M_1 (resp. M_2) is the appropriate test of the hypothesis that $\delta_2 = 0$ (resp. $\delta_1 = 0$), with proper allowance for the presence of common variables, such as the constant and lagged dependent variables. The test is of k_2 (resp. k_1) parameter restrictions, giving rise to its inappropriate acronym, since the chi-square distribution is typically used. Two extensions are used in our work. First, if M_1 and M_2 are estimated by IV, the test is generalized by re-estimating M_1 and M_2 so that all three models have the same IV set. There is little benefit in extending the tests to non-common IV sets, which is feasible but not practicable. Second, this test is used for testing M_1 against more than one alternative by forming

$$M_C : y = X_1\delta_1 + X_2\delta_2 = X_3\delta_3 + \ldots + u.$$

A test of M_1 is given by a joint test of $\delta_2 = \delta_3 = \ldots = 0$.

The J, JA, and F-tests can all be derived using the encompassing principle (Mizon and Richard, 1986). Little is known, however, about the small sample distributions of the three tests. Monte Carlo results reported by Davidson and MacKinnon (1982) and Godfrey and Pesaran (1983) suggest that the J-test tends to reject the true model too frequently, often with a marginal significance level that is relatively large, making an appeal to asymptotically valid critical values untenable.

Single-equation analysis: annual wage equations

We first note the similarity of the wage equations of the three annual models:

LPL	$\ln(w/p) = g_1(\ln U,\ B/p;\ POP,\ Z^u)$	(IV)	(5.1)
CUBS	$\Delta\ln(w/p) = g_2(u^r,\ B/p;\ \Delta w_{-1},\ SC)$	(IV)	(5.5)
CGP	$\ln\{(w-t_2)/p\} = g_3(\Delta u^r; Z^y)$	(OLS)	(5.6)

Although their theoretical underpinnings are quite distinct, there is a common channel through which the rest of the model influences wages: namely, unemployment and real benefits. Given that these are endogenous variables, two equations have been estimated by IV; so the extension of non-nested tests to this case is required, although results in Section 5.4 suggest that the use of OLS is not inappropriate in any event.

In order that re-estimation with common sample periods, *y*-series, and instrument sets does not alter the original specifications more than is necessary, the three wage equations are examined pairwise. The second requirement gives the most difficulty, for, whereas each model is concerned with the determination of the same latent variable — aggregate real wages — each modeller has chosen a different measure. Nominal wages is measured either (i) by taking aggregate nominal earnings and dividing by employment, or (ii) by taking an index of basic weekly wage rates for males in manufacturing. Similarly, the price series is either (a) the GDP deflator at factor cost or (b) the consumer expenditure deflator. Of the four possible combinations to give a real-wage measure, LPL take (i) with (a), CGP (i) with (b), and CUBS (ii) with (b). Thus a judicious choice of measure is necessary in pairwise comparisons, and its impact can be assessed by comparing the re-estimated equations with Tables 5.1(b), 5.2(c), and 5.3.

For reasons cited above, we give primary consideration to the parameter-encompassing test, although the *J* and *JA*-tests are also reported. All three exercises are based on IV versions of the test in the first instance. For CUBS and LPL this requires the construction of a composite IV set which in principle should be the union of the two individual ones: in practice, there are upper and lower bounds to its size. A small set may render the composite regression underidentified, whereas too large a set, containing say 20 instruments, renders IV equivalent to OLS given the sample size. For the two exercises involving the CGP model this problem does not arise as the second IV set is null. Indeed, the use of OLS does not alter the results to any appreciable degree, because unemployment and real benefits are weakly exogenous, as adduced above, and OLS estimates are reported. Using tests of restrictions on a composite model also accommodates the uncomfortable fact that the dependent variable in the models is expressed differently, namely, as the rate of growth of pre-tax real wages for CUBS, its level for LPL, and the real consumption wage for CGP.

Writing

$$\ln W_t = \Pi_1 \ln (1 - t_2)_t + \Pi_2 \ln W_{t-1} + \Pi_3 \ln (1 - t_2)_{t-1} + \ldots,$$

the CUBS specification requires $\Pi_1 = \Pi_3 = 0$ and $\Pi_2 = 1$, the CGP specification requires $\Pi_1 = -1$ and $\Pi_2 = \Pi_3$, and the LPL, $\Pi_1 = \Pi_3 = 0$. Tests are based on differences in the sum of squared residuals, relative to the number of implicit restrictions.

Turning to the results, and taking CUBS and LPL together first of all, the first two columns of Table 5.16 report the coefficients and standard errors of the composite model, then follow the coefficient estimates of the two separate models, treated in turn as the null hypothesis. Examining the change in coefficients between the null hypotheses and the composite alternative, it is clear that the CUBS equation changes less when LPL variables are added, compared with adding CUBS variables to the LPL model. More important is the observation that all but two of the regressors in the composite model are significant, suggesting that the parameter-encompassing F-tests reject both null hypotheses. The formal chi-square statistic for the four LPL variables, together with $\Pi_2 = 1$, is 12.5, which accepts the CUBS null hypothesis at the 2.5 per cent level. A test of the six alien CUBS variables in the LPL model gives 24.6, which implies rejection of the LPL null by the CUBS specification. Note that different unemployment measures are employed, and so both appear in the composite regression. However, the LPL measure ($\ln U$) does better than the CUBS measure (u^r), being significant in the composite model, with no change of sign from the null model. (The sample correlation between the two variables is 0.94.) As already noted, the exercise is little different using IV estimates, the only difference being that neither u^r nor $\ln U$ are significant in the composite regression, and so rejection of the LPL null in favour of CUBS is more emphatic, while CUBS now easily passes. The statistics corresponding to those above are $\chi^2(5) = 5.4$ and $\chi^2(6) = 21.4$.

The tentative conclusion that LPL is rejected against CUBS is not surprising, and is consistent with other evidence that rejects aggregate market-clearing. This is because the CUBS labour market is a standard disequilibrium model, which in principle generalizes the LPL structure. Considering the CUBS wage adjustment equation on its own, the null hypothesis in question is that the reciprocal of the coefficient on unemployment should be zero. As can be seen by examining equation (5.5), this gives the interpretation that u^r is at its 'natural' rate. Using the evidence supplied in Table 5.2(c), a chi-square statistic of 12.7 (1 d.f.) confirms the result of Andrews and Nickell (1986), who compute a similar test, but with different specifications. A further test of this hypothesis is provided by the non-nested test reported here. However, a more complete analysis of this issue should consider the labour market as a whole.

Turning to a comparison of CUBS with CGP, we find that both equa-

Table 5.16 *Annual wage equations : initial and composite models*

Sample period: Dependent variable:	CUBS/LPL 1956–82 Pre-tax real wages, CUBS measure				CUBS/CGP 1957–82 Pre-tax real wages, CGP measure				LPL/CGP 1956–83 Pre-tax real wages, CGP measure			
	Composite		CUBS	LPL	Composite		CUBS	CGP	Composite		LPL	CGP
	Coeff.	S.E.			Coeff.	S.E.			Coeff.	S.E.		
Constant	3.53	2.80	0.0688	3.70	4.19	1.75	0.08	3.51	7.36	4.47	5.68	3.48
$\ln W_{-1}$	1.04	0.15	1.0*	0.759	0.411	0.245	1.0*	0.510*	0.500	0.120	0.808	0.515*
u^r	0.256	0.492	−0.724		−0.0117	0.0064	−0.0027					
$\Delta \ln w_{-1}$	−0.377	0.106	−0.347		−0.301	0.113	−0.398					
$\Delta \ln W_{-2}$	−0.181	0.144	−0.171		−0.166	0.163	−0.175					
SC	1.54	0.40	1.52		1.818	0.450	1.85					
SC_{-1}	−0.859	0.427	−0.314		0.302	0.864	−1.55					
$\ln (B/p)$	0.115	0.078	0.093		−0.0337	0.0606	0.0738					
$\ln U$	−0.582	0.0216		−0.017					−0.0100	0.0248	0.0100	
$\ln (B/p)$	0.010	0.045		0.121					−0.0288	0.0471	0.0872	
$\ln POP$	−0.316	0.266		−0.362					−0.361	0.405	−0.424	
Z^u	0.252	0.218		0.475					−0.307	0.235	0.345	
Δu^r					0.00114	0.0177		−0.0200	0.0093	0.0168		−0.0202
Z^y					−0.0141	0.0030		−0.0175	−0.0175	0.0048		−0.0174
Dummy, 1972=1					0.0312	0.0206		0.0395	0.0316	0.0166		0.0395
tr					0.0143	0.0070		0.0098	0.0144	0.0055		0.0098
$\ln (1-t_2)$					−1.073	0.395		−1.00*	−0.753	0.340		−1.00*
$\ln (1-t_2)_{-1}$					0.416	0.345		0.510*	−0.220	0.303		0.515*
Sum of squared residuals	0.001649		0.003028	0.004359	0.001075		0.005518	0.003135	0.002507		0.010738	0.003216
Standard error	0.0105		0.0123	0.0144	0.0094		0.0170	0.0125	0.0125		0.0221	0.0121

* denotes constrained coefficients

tions maintain their general form when alien regressors are added, leading to a rejection of both null hypotheses. The F-test for the CUBS null hypothesis is $\chi^2(8) = 49.6$ and for the CGP null hypothesis, $\chi^2(7) = 23.0$. Some particular coefficients change considerably, however, in the presence of alien regressors; CUBS impose a unit coefficient on the first lag of the dependent variable when the freely estimated parameter is 0.4 (contrast the CUBS/LPL comparison), while CGP have by far the worst of the unemployment measures, using the first difference in this variable, with a t-ratio in M_C of 0.06, rather than its level. It can be argued that CGP falls down because it has ignored the powerful structural change variable of CUBS. On the other hand, it is not surprising to find the CUBS model rejected against a specification using CGP regressors when one considers that an important explanation of disequilibrium is incomes policy, the t-ratio of 4.7 on the incomes policy variable in the composite model telling its own story.

The final pairing of this trilogy is CGP and LPL. Here the LPL null hypothesis is clearly rejected (chi-square statistic of 52.5 on six restrictions), whereas the test of the CGP null hypothesis is easily accepted (chi-square of 4.5, again on six restrictions). The only improvement suggested on the CGP specification by the addition of LPL variables is that the union density variable might be included, although comparing its t-ratio of 1.3 with that of the incomes policy variable (3.7) does perhaps provide evidence in favour of ameliorating real-wage increases by incomes policy rather than by restricting the influence of unions. Notice that neither unemployment measure is significant.

The results for the variance-encompassing and parameter-encompassing tests are summarized in Table 5.17. The J-tests tend to confirm the general conclusions discussed above. However, the JA-tests tell a quite different story, with only one rejection. This reflects the finding of Monte Carlo studies (Godfrey and Pesaran, 1983) that the JA-test has lower power.

Table 5.17 *Annual wage equations: non-nested test statistics*

		Alternative hypothesis (M_2)		
		CUBS	LPL	CGP
(a) Variance-encompassing J, JA-tests (1 d.f.) based on OLS estimates				
Null	CUBS		0.1, 0.6	3.0*, 0.2
hypothesis	LPL	20.3**, 0.3		59.6**, 10.3**
(M_1)	CGP	10.2**, 0.1	0.0, 0.2	
(b) Parameter-encompassing F-tests (k d.f.) based on OLS estimates				
Null	CUBS		12.5**(5)	49.6**(8)
hypothesis	LPL	24.6**(6)		52.5**(6)
(M_1)	CGP	23.0**(7)	4.5 (6)	

Our conclusions on the wage equation comparisons are that (i) LPL is rejected against both CUBS and CGP, but (ii) CUBS and CGP reject each other, with CGP doing the better of the two. This suggests that some alternative specification is a better approximation to the data generation process. The composite model reported cannot be considered seriously in this regard as part of a coherent modelling strategy, but it does suggest which of the pre-tax or consumption real wage is the more appropriate; whether structural change, incomes policy, and union density variables might enter; whether the dynamics of wage equations exhibit a unit root; whether labour market slackness should be in level or derivative form; and so forth.

Single-equation analysis: quarterly manufacturing employment

Although the sectoral disaggregation of the quarterly models differs in general, we note that all four models have a manufacturing employment equation:

NIESR	$\ln n^m = g_4\{\ln (wh^m/p^m)^*, y^{m*};\}$	(IV)	(5.7)
LBS	$\ln n^m = g_5\{\ln (w^m/p^m), \ln (q/p^m), y^m;\}$	(IV)	(5.15)
BE	$\ln n^m = g_6(\ln h^m, \ln h^m_n;)$	(OLS)	(5.20)
HMT	$\ln n^m = g_7\{\ln (w^m/q^m), \ln (w^m/r^m), y^{m*};\}$	(OLS)	(5.25)

All are based on the firm's demand-for-labour schedule; indeed, for three models — NIESR, LBS, and HMT — the similarities are quite striking in so far as they all condition on a given level of (expected) output, with differences relating to the modelling of price effects and the treatment of expectations. The BE equation is of a similar form once the explanation of hours of work, equation (5.20a), is incorporated.

Unlike the real-wage variable, for manufacturing employment the data series used by the four teams are almost identical, and we use the HMT series in what follows. The test we consider is a generalization of the parameter-encompassing test, discussed above, whereby the composite model is constructed from four separate models, each considered in turn as the null hypothesis. This is then estimated by IV methods, following the LBS and NIESR treatment. The parameter-encompassing test is a test of the joint significance of those regressors of the other three models that do not appear in the null hypothesis under investigation. It is possible that the original specification of each individual model is not exactly replicated, because a common IV set is used, but in practice there are no differences worthy of attention.

The common data set is from 1967(3) to 1981(4). The four chi-square test statistics (d.f.) are: for NIESR, 642.2 (19); for LBS, 601.6 (16); for HMT, 271.7 (13); and for BE, 266.0 (14). The results reject each null hypothesis in turn, convincingly, against the composite alternative. This is because each null hypothesis contributes a little towards the overall regression model (not reported). The following variables have t-ratios greater than one: $\ln n^m_{-1}$, $\ln n^m_{-2}$ (common); y^{m*} (NIESR); $\ln W^m$ (LBS); $\hat{y}_{+1}$, $\hat{y}_{+2}$ (HMT); $\ln h^m$, $\ln h^m_{-1}$ (BE); and dummies for 1972(1) and 1974(1). The dominant role of output and its expectations suggests that Nickell's (1984b) non-competitive approach is closer to the mark than the more competitive contributions of Symons (see, for example, Symons, 1985), which emphasize the role of substitution in the firm's demand for labour, signalled by real and relative prices of other factor inputs. Indeed, $\ln W^m$ above has the wrong (i.e. positive) sign.

5.6　Summary and conclusions

The abundance of tests for a variety of forms of model inadequacy now available to the applied researcher goes some way to countering Blaug's pessimistic critique cited at the beginning of this chapter. Given sufficient information on the statistical performance of a single equation or a simultaneous equation model, then, according to the approach advocated by Sargan, the investigator is able to evaluate the plausibility of its econometric specification, and also to judge the validity of inference based thereon.

One of the intentions of this chapter has been to improve the general understanding of empirical models of the aggregate labour market through the application of a consistent and comprehensive range of diagnostic tests. These fall into two broad categories, based on intra- and inter-model checks for misspecification. The first, based on nested hypothesis testing, evaluates the models against simple extensions of the assumed (classical) statistical framework, considering in turn autocorrelation, simultaneous equation bias, parameter variation, heteroscedasticity, and so forth. Rejection on the basis of these tests is usually unconstructive, and although a deficiency in the model is indicated, the alternative hypothesis may not be of interest in itself, nor indicate how the original model is to be appropriately respecified. On the other hand, the second class of tests, based on non-nested hypotheses, suggests that improvements in the models can be obtained by addressing the question of whether a particular model encompasses competing explanations of the same phenomena. For example, in our first review we remarked on the relatively simplistic treatment of incomes policy. A recurring theme in the present exercise is that the effect of incomes policy on real wages cannot be ignored, and this emerges both from our non-nested testing exercises and from the tests of specification.

The second aim of this chapter has been to develop methods of comparison through the practical application of the various test statistics. In some cases these are novel to the applied literature, such as tests of blockrecursiveness. Indeed, testing the validity of a particular conditioning of the potential endogenous variables in the labour market structure has an impact on the way in which model selection and inference proceeds. In particular, the parameter-encompassing tests are based on OLS estimates, although the models are originally estimated by IV methods, because unemployment is typically weakly exogenous for real wages. Furthermore, our results also indicate that a number of models fail to exploit information contained in the covariance structure of the equations.

Turning to some specific results, we find that tests against particular alternatives, such as individual orders of autocorrelation, have more power than portmanteau forms of the test statistic. The NIESR use a two-step co-integration regression technique to estimate the parameters of the wage equation. Our results suggest that little advantage is gained from using these procedures in preference to conventional methods, which estimate parameters associated with the long-run or equilibrium relationship simul-taneously with the parameters of the short-run dynamics. At the same time, the theoretical work that underpins the use of these techniques concentrates on the bivariate case. Clearly, further theoretical work is necessary to extend these results to the multivariate case, in particular to analyse the impact of different normalizations of the co-integrating regres-sion and to offer guidance on this question.

In common with most applied work, the tests employed are uni-directional, assessing only a single departure from the model specification. Little is known about the small-sample behaviour and power of such unidirectional tests in the face of multiple alternatives. Limited experi-ments with multidirectional tests, in which the implicit alternative hypo-thesis, representing a variety of departures from classical assumptions, can be estimated by introducing jointly the appropriate added regressors, were undertaken. These suggest that the results are very similar to those obtained from unidirectional tests.

The formal apparatus of classical statistical inference is strictly inapplic-able during the conventional specification search, in which the investigator is seeking a model that adequately characterizes a sample of non-experi-mental data. Rather, the tests are design criteria, and the search terminates when a model has been designed that 'passes' the various tests. In our work we have taken the models as given, and evaluated them in a variety of ways, without seeking improved specifications when a model is found wanting. Nevertheless, the results suggest that in the majority of cases the modellers' specification search terminated too soon.

Given an adequately designed model, the encompassing principle sug-gests that the investigator should test it against competing models. If it is itself encompassed by existing specifications, then it cannot be said to represent a contribution to knowledge. On the other hand, its ability to encompass rival specifications provides further evidence in its favour.

More generally, the use of the encompassing principle helps to ensure that the continuing process of model modification is progressive rather than degenerate. We present applications of the relevant procedures in our model comparison exercise, and illustrate some of the practical difficulties that arise. Although no single equation under scrutiny adequately characterizes the data and hence provides a sound foundation for non-nested tests, we find that the preferred parameter-encompassing tests themselves suggest possible model improvements. Attention is restricted to single-equation comparisons, and similar techniques for the comparison of small systems of nonlinear equations are not as yet available: their development is a pressing research problem.

Appendix: notation

w	nominal wage
p	price level
W	real wage
U	number of unemployed
B	nominal benefits
POP	population of working age
L	labour force/supply
Z^u	proportion of workforce unionized
y	real output
n	employment
k	capital stock
q^e	nominal price of energy
q^m	nominal price of raw materials
u^r	unemployment rate
SC	structural change (CUBS)
Z^y	incomes policy variable (CGP)
t_2	income tax rate
h	hours (h^n, normal hours)
t_3	indirect tax rate
t_1	employer's tax rate
μ	'proxy for net income gearing of non-North Sea ICCS' (BE)
D	incomes policy dummy (contrast Z^y)
r	price of capital

General

*	permanent
~	co-integrating term
^	expectation of a current dated variable

References

Andrews, M. J. and Nickell, S. J. (1986). A disaggregated disequilibrium model of the labour market. *Oxford Economic Papers*, **38**.

Ash, J. C. K. and Smyth, D. J. (1973). *Forecasting the UK Economy*. Lexington, Massachusetts: Lexington Books.

Ball, R. J. and St Cyr, E. B. A. (1966). Short-term employment functions in British manufacturing industry. *Review of Economic Studies*, **33**, 179–197.

Barker, T. S. (1985). The Cambridge multisectoral dynamic model version 6. Cambridge Growth Project Manual, no.5.

Beenstock, M., Warburton, P., Lewington, P., and Dalziel, A. (1985). A medium-term macroeconometric model of the UK 1953–1982. City University Business School Working Paper.

Bera, A. K. and Jarque, C. M. (1982). Model specification tests: a simultaneous approach. *Journal of Econometrics*, **20**, 59–82.

Blaug, M. (1980). *The Methodology of Economics*. Cambridge: Cambridge University Press.

Bowden, R. J. and Turkington, D. A. (1984). *Instrumental Variables*. Cambridge: Cambridge University Press.

Brechling, F. (1965). The relationship between output and employment in British manufacturing industries. *Review of Economic Studies*, **32**, 187–216.

Chong, Y. Y. and Hendry, D. F. (1986). Econometric evaluation of linear macro-economic models. *Review of Economic Studies*, **53**, 671–690.

Cox, D. R. (1961). Tests of separate families of hypotheses. *Proceedings of the Fourth Berkeley Symposium on Mathematical Statistics and Probability*, Vol. 1, 105–123.

Cox, D. R. (1962). Further results on tests of separate families of hypotheses. *Journal of the Royal Statistical Society* B, **24**, 406–424.

Davidson, R. and MacKinnon, J. G. (1982). Some non-nested hypothesis tests and the relations among them. *Review of Economic Studies*, **49**, 551–565.

Engle, R. F. (1982). Autoregressive conditional heteroscedasticity with estimates of the variance of UK inflation. *Econometrica*, **50**, 987–1007.

Engle, R. F. (1984). Wald, likelihood ratio and lagrange multiplier tests in econometrics. In *Handbook of Econometrics*, Vol.2 (Z. Griliches and M. D. Intriligator, eds), pp. 776–826. Amsterdam: North-Holland.

Godfrey, L. G. (1978). Testing against general autoregressive and moving average error models when the regressors include lagged dependent variables. *Econometrica*, **46**, 1293–1302.

Godfrey, L. G. (1984). On the use of misspecification checks and tests of non-nested hypotheses in empirical econometrics. *Economic Journal*, **94** (supplement), 69–81.

Godfrey, L. G. and Pesaran, M. H. (1983). Tests of non-nested regression models: small sample adjustments and Monte Carlo evidence. *Journal of Econometrics*, **21**, 133–154.

Granger, C. W. J. and Engle, R. F. (1985). Dynamic model specification with equilibrium constraints; co-integration and error correction. Discussion paper 85–18, University of California, San Diego.

Granger, C. W. J. and Newbold, P. (1977). *Forecasting Economic Time Series.* London: Academic Press.

Gujarati, D. (1970). Use of dummy variables in testing for equality between sets of coefficients in two linear regressions: a note. *The American Statistician*, **24**, 50–52.

Hall, S. G. (1984). On the solution of high order symmetric difference equations. *Oxford Bulletin of Economics and Statistics*, **4**, 85–88.

Hall, S. G. (1985). An application of the Granger and Engle two-step estimation procedure to UK aggregate wage data. National Institute of Economic and Social Research, Discussion Paper no.109.

Hall, S. G. and Henry, S. G. B. (1985). Rational expectations in an econometric model: NIESR model 8. *National Institute Economic Review*, **114**, 58–68.

Harvey, A. C. and Phillips, G. D. A. (1982). Testing for contemporaneous correlation of disturbances in systems of regression equations. *Bulletin of Economic Research*, **34**, 79–91.

Hausman, J. A. (1978). Specification tests in econometrics. *Econometrica*, **46**, 1251–1272.

Hendry, D. F. (1986). Using PC–GIVE in econometrics teaching. *Oxford Bulletin of Economics and Statistics*, **48**, 87–98.

Hendry, D. F. and Wallis, K. F. (eds) (1984). *Econometrics and Quantitative Economics.* Oxford: Basil Blackwell.

Holden, K. and Peel, D. A. (1983). Forecasts and expectations: some evidence for the UK. *Journal of Forecasting*, **2**, 51–58.

Holden, K. and Peel, D. A. (1985). An evaluation of quarterly National Institute forecasts. *Journal of Forecasting*, **4**, 227–234.

Holden, K., Peel, D. A., and Thompson, J. L. (1985). *Expectations: Theory and Evidence.* London: Macmillan.

Jarque, C. M. and Bera, A. K. (1980). Efficient tests for normality, heteroscedasticity and serial independence in regression residuals. *Economics Letters*, **6**, 255–259.

Kelly, C. and Owen, D. (1985). Factor prices in the Treasury model. Government Economic Service Working Paper, no.83.

Kenny, P. B. (1985). Revisions to quarterly estimates of gross domestic product. *Economic Trends*, **381**, 97–112.

Kiviet, J. F. (1986). On the rigour of some misspecification tests for modelling dynamic relationships. *Review of Economic Studies*, **53**, 241–262.

Lawson, T. (1981). Incomes policy and the real wage resistance hypothesis: econometric evidence for the UK, 1955–79. Cambridge Growth Project Paper no. 509.

Litterman, R. B. (1986). Forecasting with Bayesian vector autoregressions — five years of experience. *Journal of Business and Economic Statistics*, **4**, 29–36.

Lo, A. W. and Newey, W. K. (1985). A large sample Chow test for the linear simultaneous equation. *Economics Letters*, **18**, 351–353.

Matthews, K., Minford, A. P. L., and Riley, J. (1985). The forecast performance of the Liverpool Group: the record straightened. *Quarterly Economic Bulletin*, **6**, 25–31.

McCallum, B. T. (1976). Rational expectations and the estimation of econometric models: an alternative procedure. *International Economic Review,* **17**, 484–490.

McNees, S. K. (1981). The methodology of macroeconometric model comparisons. In *Large Scale Macroeconometric Models* (J. Kmenta and J. B. Ramsey, eds), pp. 397–422. Amsterdam: North-Holland.

Minford, A. P. L (1983). Labour market equilibrium in an open economy. *Oxford Economic Papers,* **35** (supplement), 207–244.

Minford, A. P. L. (1984). Response to Nickell. *Economic Journal,* **94**, 954–959.

Minford, A. P. L., Marwaha, S., Matthews, K., and Sprague, A. (1984). The Liverpool macroeconomic model of the United Kingdom. *Economic Modelling,* **1**, 24–62.

Minford, A. P. L. and Peel, D. A. (1983). *Rational Expectations and the New Macroeconomics.* Oxford: Martin Robertson.

Mizon, G. E. (1984). The encompassing approach in econometrics. In *Econometrics and Quantitative Economics* (D. F. Hendry and K. F. Wallis, eds), pp. 135–172. Oxford: Basil Blackwell.

Mizon, G. E. and Richard, J. F. (1986). The encompassing principle and its application to testing non-nested hypotheses. *Econometrica,* **54**, 657–678.

Nelson, C. R. (1972). The prediction performance of the FRB–MIT–PENN model of the US economy. *American Economic Review,* **62**, 902–917.

Nickell, S. J. (1984a). A review of *Unemployment: Cause and Cure* by Patrick Minford, with David Davies, Michael Peel and Alison Sprague. *Economic Journal,* **94**, 946–953.

Nickell, S. J. (1984b). An investigation of the determinants of manufacturing employment in the UK. *Review of Economic Studies,* **51**, 529–557.

Nickell, S. J. and Andrews, M. J. (1983). Unions, real wages and employment in Britain, 1951–1979. *Oxford Economic Papers,* **35** (supplement), 183–206.

Osborn, D. R. and Teal, F. (1979). An assessment and comparison of two NIESR econometric model forecasts. *National Institute Economic Review,* **88**, 50–62.

Pagan, A. R. (1984a). Econometric issues in the analysis of regressions with generated regressors. *International Economic Review,* **25**, 221–247.

Pagan, A. R. (1984b). Model evaluation by variable addition. In *Econometrics and Quantitative Economics* (D. F. Hendry and K. F. Wallis, eds), pp. 103–134. Oxford: Basil Blackwell.

Pesaran, M. H. (1974). On the general problem of model selection. *Review of Economic Studies,* **41**, 153–171.

Pesaran, M. H. and Deaton, A. S. (1978). Testing non-nested nonlinear regression models. *Econometrica,* **46**, 677–694.

Pesaran, M. H., Smith, R. P., and Yeo, J. S. (1985). Testing for structural stability and predictive failure: a review. *The Manchester School,* **53**, 280–295.

Ramsey, J. B. (1969). Tests for specification errors in classical linear least squares regression analysis. *Journal of the Royal Statistical Society* B, **31**, 350–371.

Salkever, D. S. (1976). The use of dummy variables to compute predictions, prediction errors and confidence intervals. *Journal of Econometrics,* **4**, 393–397.

Salmon, M. H. and Wallis, K. F. (1982). Model validation and forecast comparisons: theoretical and practical considerations. In *Evaluating the Reliability of Macroeconomic Models* (G. Chow and P. Corsi, eds), pp. 219–249. Chichester: John Wiley.

Sargan, J. D. (1958). The estimation of economic relationships using instrumental variables. *Econometrica*, **26**, 393–415.

Sargan, J. D. (1964). Wages and prices in the United Kingdom: a study in econometric methodology. In *Econometric Analysis for National Economic Planning* (P. G. Hart, G. Mills, and J. K. Whitaker, eds), pp. 22–54. London: Butterworth. Reprinted in *Econometrics and Quantitative Economics* (D. F. Hendry and K. F. Wallis, eds), pp. 275–314. Oxford: Basil Blackwell.

Sargan, J. D. (1975). Discussion on misspecification. In *Modelling the Economy* (G. A. Renton, ed.), pp. 321–2. London: Heinemann.

Smith, P. and Holly, S. (1985). Wage and employment determination in the UK. Centre for Economic Forecasting, Discussion Paper no.137. London Business School.

Symons, J. S. V. (1985). Relative prices and the demand for labour in British manufacturing. *Economica*, **52**, 37–49.

Wallis, K. F. (1980). Econometric implications of the rational expectations hypothesis. *Econometrica*, **48**, 49–73.

Wallis, K. F. (1986). Forecasting with an econometric model: the 'ragged edge' problem. *Journal of Forecasting*, **5**, 1–14.

Wallis, K. F. (ed.), Andrews, M. J., Bell, D. N. F., Fisher, P. G., and Whitley, J. D. (1985) *Models of the UK Economy: A Second Review by the ESRC Macroeconomic Modelling Bureau*. Oxford: Oxford University Press.

Wallis, K. F. (ed.), Andrews, M. J., Bell, D. N. F., Fisher, P. G., and Whitley, J. D. (1985). *Models of the UK Economy: A Second Review by the ESRC Macroeconomic Modelling Bureau*. Oxford: Oxford University Press.

White, H. (1980). A heteroscedasticity consistent covariance matrix estimator and a direct test for heteroscedasticity. *Econometrica*, **48**, 817–883.